VERANDAH

James Pope-Hennessy's grandfather was Sir John Pope-Hennessy an Irishman who died in 1891; he was a Colonial Governor in the days of the British Empire and said to be the model for Trollope's Phineas Finn. His humanitarianism and unconventional style of administration made him popular with the natives of colonies from Hong Kong to Sierra Leone—where they used to honour him by celebrating 'Pope Hennessy's day'.

John Pope-Hennessy was born in 1834 in Cork into a commercial middle class family who styled themselves 'Hennessy of Bally-hennessy' and claimed descent from the Irish landed gentry. After training in Cork as a man of medicine, he longed for the wider stage of London and in 1855 he arrived there to take up an Indian medical commission and determined 'not to lose time' and 'to push on'. Always with an eye to 'success', he read for a law degree in his spare time, and by the time he was twenty-three he had become a Member of Parliament at the invitation of his hero Benjamin Disraeli. 1867 saw him leave to take up the governorship of Labuan—never a successful colonial acquisition—but it was to be Governor Pope-Hennessy's personal challenge, though he was only thirty-three.

In *Verandah* James Pope-Hennessy follows his grandfather's career as governor of six different colonial outposts—Barbados, Hong Kong, Mauritius, The Bahamas, Sierra Leone and Labuan (off Borneo)—throwing a spotlight on Britain's imperial heyday. The result allows us to view the sepia-tinted past as vivid and immediate, and to raise the ghosts of Empire.

VERANDAH

SOME EPISODES
IN THE CROWN COLONIES
1867-1889

JAMES POPE-HENNESSY

CENTURY PUBLISHING
LONDON

Reprinted in Great Britain by
Richard Clay (The Chaucer Press) Ltd,
Bungay, Suffolk

TO MRS W.

The British Empire at the time of Sir John Pope Hennessy's Governorships

CONTENTS

———————

BOOK VII: MAURITIUS 1883–1889

AUTHOR'S NOTE

Apart from the private papers of my grandfather, Sir John Pope Hennessy, which are in my own possession, the chief sources on which this study of life in some of the Victorian Colonies is based are the relevant Colonial Office documents of the period, preserved in the Public Record Office in Chancery Lane, and those of the Mauritian Government Archives in William Newton Street, Port Louis, Mauritius. Although I have decided against filling the text with reference notes for each quotation made, these quotations are, of course, verbatim. Unpublished Crown Copyright material in the Public Record Office is reproduced by permission of the Controller of Her Majesty's Stationery Office.

During the three years occupied in working on this book I have followed my grandfather's footsteps to many parts of the tropical world. In all these places I have received much help and hospitality. In Labuan I was lucky enough to be shown round the island by Mr Daniel Chong Fui Kong. In Malaya I was the guest of Mr and Mrs John Parkinson, then of the Bukit Kajang Estate near Malacca, and of Mr Donald Davies of Kuala Lumpur. In Hong Kong I was shown Government House by Sir Robert and Lady Black, and the city of Victoria by Mr Derek Adkins and Mr Don Clark. In Ghana I stayed as the guest of the Kwame Nkrumah University of Science and Technology at Kumasi and of its distinguished Vice-Chancellor, Dr Robert Baffour; and I also received much aid from the Keeper of the National Monuments of Ghana, Mr William Obuibisa of Fort San Iago, Elmina. In Mauritius Dr Auguste Toussaint, the Government Archivist, placed his Archives and his unrivalled knowledge of Mauritian history at my disposal. Sir Colville Montgomery-Delville, then Governor of the Colony, and his wife made me welcome at Le Réduit. The Bishop of Port Louis gave me access to the archives in the Bishop's Palace, Port Louis, while others who kindly helped me with letters and documents include the Misses S. and Y. Leclézio, of Eureka, Moka; Mr Jean-Louis Lincoln of Curepipe and his cousin Mr René Lincoln; and Mr Chapuiset le Merle of Le Vallon, Vieux Grand Port. Mr Léon Daruty de Grandpré generously gave me a medal struck in memory of my grandfather in 1889. Finally, I wish

to thank Mr and Mrs Philippe de la Hogue Rey, without whose
guidance and friendship I should not have seen the beautiful island
of Mauritius as thoroughly as I did in the winter months of 1961 to
1962.

I must also record my gratitude to friends who have most kindly
allowed me to write large sections of this book in their houses in the
country, most especially Mrs A. E. Pleydell-Bouverie, of Julians, and
Mr and Mrs Anthony Marreco, of Port Hall, co. Donegal.

For secretarial and other assistance I would like to thank Mrs. Joan
Saunders and her assistants, of the Writer's and Speaker's Research,
Mr Len Adams, Mr Rudolf Kandaouroff and Mr Bryan Leembruggen.
During his short visit to Mauritius in 1963 Mr Cecil Beaton found time
to photograph for me the statue of my grandfather in the Place
d'Armes, Port Louis. Mr John Murphy has done careful work on the
other photographs which illustrate the text.

JAMES POPE-HENNESSY

Schönberg-im-Taunus
Park Hotel, Curepipe
Albergo Piànone, Bergamo
Port Hall, co. Donegal
Julians, Hertfordshire
9 Ladbroke Grove, London, W.11

PROLOGUE

When I was born, in London in 1916, my father, a regular soldier, was serving in what was then called Somaliland, and my mother, engaged in work connected with British Prisoners of War, was living in a Crescent in South Kensington. Surviving letters between my parents show that, when the Zeppelin raids became 'bad', my brother and myself were sent off with our nurse and nursery-maid to Devonshire, to stay with my paternal grandmother who had a house in the sea-side town of Teignmouth. I do not think that I remember these early wartime visits, but I do clearly recollect weeks spent at Teignmouth between the Armistice of 1918 and the death of my grandmother, which occurred in 1923 when I was almost six years old. The widow of an impetuous and unconventional Colonial Governor, who was as frequently hated by his subordinates and colleagues as he was loved by the peoples whom he ruled, my grandmother had married again in 1894, this time selecting a man very much younger than herself. It was with this couple, my grandmother and her second husband, that my brother and I would go to stay.

The house at Teignmouth was called Riverside, because its walled garden overlooked an estuary, along which seaweed and marbled pebbles would lie shining at low tide. Whenever I smell wallflowers I can see this narrow garden clearly in my mind's eye, just as the musty smell of the common geranium leaf brings back to me the sight of the little glassed-in conservatories which sheltered the front and side doors of the house from winter gales. Yet it was not until a recent, and first, voyage to the East that I encountered a certain scent—a trifle like that of good Turkish cigarettes, but more elusive—which at once called up for me the strange atmosphere inside the house itself. As I smelt it, the crowded Hong Kong street in which I was standing seemed to vanish from my view. Instead I saw again the pale L-shaped drawing-room at Teignmouth, dominated by a long, low, six-folded Japanese screen on which, against a gleaming golden background, oriental persons were portrayed seated beneath small temple porticoes, or taking part in a bullock procession which wound uphill from fold to fold. I saw again the great banner of embroidered Chinese silk which covered part of one wall; the boxes of eastern lacquer, scarlet-

and-gold or black-and-gold; the glass cabinets filled with silver boxes
and also with animals in silver. These animals my grandmother, who
spoiled us, would allow me to play with in my bath.

At the time at which I can remember her, my grandmother was in
her seventies. Her clothes, like her toques, were made of grey satin.
Her hair was white. Her eyes, which were piercing and so bright that
they seemed designed to brave a fiercer sun than that of Devonshire,
were of a startling light grey. Around her neck and wrists she wore a
multitude of silver chains and ornaments, which tinkled as she moved.
I was fond of her, no doubt because she spoiled me; but she instilled
into us, with an almost wanton diligence, a whole litany of supersti-
tious fears. As bedtime approached she would regale us with stories of
ghosts and evil spirits, and sometimes show us books of coloured
Japanese woodcuts, which I seem to remember one read from back to
front, and which displayed scenes of tortures and decapitations, and
pictures of grinning, ill-intentioned Eastern gods. She would warn us
that if we woke up in the night we might expect to see a coffin surrounded by corpse-candles standing in the middle of the room.
Looking back now, I realise that she was, in many ways, an unusual
grandmother; and she was made all the more mysterious by the fact
that, when she had died and we were growing up, my parents hardly
ever spoke to us about her. What little we did learn aroused my
curiosity, for she seemed to have brought us a strange heritage.

We gleaned, haphazardly, that my grandmother had not been an
ideal parent, for she had cosseted my father when he was a small child,
and utterly ignored him as an adolescent; she even left him to learn of
her second marriage, when he was at Sandhurst, from an announcement in *The Times*. It seemed, too, that she had not entirely liked her
first husband, my grandfather Sir John Pope Hennessy, that she was
wrong to have married as her second husband a man twenty years her
junior, that she was impossibly extravagant about money, and that,
although a practising Roman Catholic, she had allowed her life to be
largely governed by spirit messages which reached her through a
ouija-board. Amongst a great variety of directives, this board had
instructed her to sell and otherwise disperse my grandfather's books
and collections in Ireland, and to destroy most of his private papers.
I do not suppose that she required its urgings to borrow money on
the Irish property, Rostellan Castle, a cumbrous place situated on
Queenstown Harbour which Sir John, aspiring to a peerage, had
purchased not long before his death. By the destruction of my grand-

father's records, and the dispersal of his library and other possessions, she did not notably benefit her grandchildren, but by mortgaging Rostellan so that it could not be kept in the family there is no question that she did. It is easy to see that her vagaries led my grandmother to be judged harshly by her immediate connections, but reflecting on it now I cannot help wondering whether more allowance should not have been made for those elements of superstition and of *dolce far niente* which seem innate in those who have Eurasian blood.

After my grandmother's death, a quantity of oriental objects from Teignmouth invaded our London house. The best of them—including the sixteenth-century Japanese screen, some lacquer boxes and the remnants of my grandfather's collection of blue-and-white hawthorn pattern porcelain—fitted in well with my parents' own collection of early Chinese jades. The others, comprising Malayan krieses, African staves of office crowned by sinister birds' heads with jewelled eyes, and a mass of pentagonal silver boxes (which I now recognise as having come from Kelantan, up on the Siamese border) were put out of sight. By the time that in our turn, my brother and I inherited these unfriendly weapons and small alien silver objects—works of craftmanship but not of art—I was more interested in them; for by then I had learned that the life I had seen my grandmother leading on the coast of Devon was but the tail end of one that had begun seven decades earlier on the small and swampy island of Labuan set close against the shores of Borneo, and within sound of the lolling waves of the turquoise-shaded China Sea.

This interest led me to investigate the lives of my paternal grand-parents more closely, and even to embark on a number of journeys to see the places in which they had been passed. Combined with research into the relevant documents, the sight of these far-away places conjured up for me the arduous and erratic existences of many dead and long-forgotten persons whose days were spent in hot, unhealthy climates, operating (or in many cases impeding) the slow machinery of British Imperialism in Queen Victoria's reign. Obsessed by these ghosts of Empire, I wish to try to evoke them in this book. Some, like my grandfather himself, remain vivid characters. Others seem as faded as their beige-tinted photographs in my grandmother's albums. Others, again, faceless and featureless, have drifted away over the tropical horizon beyond hope of recall.

Lives of the obscure, these may well seem to be lives of the objec-tionable as well; in mitigation one can only plead—as they themselves

scarcely ever did—the harsh effects of the climate and of their circumstances, remembering too that these imperial outposts did not then
offer desirable careers, and tended to attract civilian counterparts of
Kipling's Gentlemen Troopers rather than the finer flower of Queen
Victoria's island race.

BOOK I

THE CONSOLATION PRIZE

CHAPTER ONE

O N A WINDSWEPT HILLTOP high above Cork City
lies an old cemetery surrounded by a wall. Between the gravel
paths the grass grows rank, pressing against the crowded
memorials to the dead. Most of these monuments are as elaborate as
you would expect to find them in a Southern Irish Catholic graveyard
of the last century. There are throngs of mourning angels in stone, of
iron or marble crucifixes, of crocketed mortuary chapels sheltering
their altars from the rain. Here and there, however, you may stumble
on a headstone of modest dimensions and of simple form. One such,
now tilted at a lurching angle in the soft earth, is ornamented merely
with a runic cross. Blotched by discs of yellow lichen, its sole inscrip-
tion reads: '*Burial place of John Hennessy and family. R.I.P.*'

Few persons choose to linger over gravestones. Having glanced at
this one we may now forget it, remarking only that it seems to symbo-
lise the quiet and restricted circumstances of a small merchant family
in Cork one hundred years ago. Upon another hill, St Patrick's,
beyond the river Lea and the Mall, centre of Cork City, stands the
little house—one of a set of narrow, three-storey terrace buildings—in
which John Hennessy, who dealt in hides from an office on Pope's
Quay, and his wife Elizabeth, the daughter of a member of the butter
trade, brought up their five sons and three daughters in the love of
God and in hatred of the English soldiers and administrators of the
'Famine Queen'.

The genteel, penurious existence of this family at Number 4, Mount
Verdon Terrace, formed the antithesis of the exotic. Yet from these
unpromising and cramped surroundings there sprang the enigmatic
and emotional figure of my grandfather Sir John Pope Hennessy—in
youth allegedly the prototype for Trollope's character of Phineas
Finn, and subsequently a Colonial Governor whose humanitarian
beliefs, volatile judgements and autocratic behaviour had made
tropical verandahs echo with resentful protests from North Borneo to
Barbados, from the Gold Coast to Hong Kong.

In October 1891 Sir John Pope Hennessy had died at Rostellan

Castle, a large house, now reduced to rubble, on the shores of Queenstown Harbour, and which he had purchased a few years before his death. Dying of tropical anaemia at the fairly early age of fifty-seven, he was buried in his father's grave in Cork cemetery, with no separate headstone or private monument. In a lengthy obituary notice *The Times* newspaper (from which Sir John had recently won twenty thousand pounds in a successful suit for libel) wished that he had been 'differently, or less brilliantly gifted', declaring that his colonial career 'says very little for the intelligence or discretion with which the Colonial Office exercises its patronage. He ought never to have been placed in charge of such colonies as Hongkong or the Mauritius, where the pretensions of the natives threatened to make trouble. The sympathiser with the down-trodden Catholics of West Ireland was an enthusiast with regard to the equal rights of men.' No epitaph would have gratified its subject more.

The *Dictionary of National Biography*, while admitting his 'humane and sympathetic but impulsive temperament', condemns Pope Hennessy for his partisanship and his want of judgement, for 'irritating where he might conciliate', for never acquiring 'the habit of making a definite and accurate statement' and for tortuousness of mind. 'As to Sir J. P. Hennessy' [we read in a great history of Hong Kong written by one of Sir John's discarded protégés] 'the less said the better. . . . His acts speak powerfully enough. The centre of his world was he himself. But with all the crowd of dark and bright powers that were wrestling within him, he could not help doing some good and the Colony emerged from the ordeal of his administration practically unscathed.'

Against these severe judgements we may set such facts as that of the spontaneous celebration, for many years, of 'Pope Hennessy's Day' by the natives of Sierra Leone; that he is still remembered with affection by the negroes of Barbados and the Chinese of Hong Kong; and that his statue stands in the Place d'Armes, Port Louis, Mauritius, erected by public subscription twenty years after he had left the island for good. The natives of these colonies believed that here, at last, was a Governor who put their welfare and their interests before those of British commerce. Moreover, Pope Hennessy possessed to a singular degree the dangerous gift of charm, with which, in a personal interview, he could hypnotise even the most exasperated Secretary of State for the Colonies, only too well aware of Hennessy's habit of disobeying explicit but unwelcome instructions, and of ignoring distasteful Colonial Office despatches by mislaying them or by locking them away, unanswered, in some drawer. His warm heart and winning manner brought him many devoted friends, just as his talent for intrigue and his determination never to be thwarted earned him many enemies. 'The most lively of Irish companions' the Imperialist poet Alfred Austin wrote ten years after John Pope Hennessy's death: 'I suppose that he is now pretty nigh forgotten, but he was an exceedingly interesting man.'

Forgotten assuredly he is, and so he might be left, resting in Cork graveyard in a peace which, alive, he never knew. That such oblivion would be much against his wishes forms in itself no valid reason for trying to resurrect him in a book. It is, rather, that his vitality and his convictions, his role of catalyst and his modernity of outlook on Colonial matters make him worth remembering today, when that haphazard institution, the old Victorian Empire, is defunct.

During his official career Pope Hennessy administered six Colonial territories—the islet of Labuan, off Borneo; the West African Settlements; the Bahamas; Barbados; Hong Kong; Mauritius. By concentrating upon selected episodes from each of these administrations we may peer, as through a telescope, at some very curious fragments of our dead imperial past. Spectators, we should be so with detachment, content to watch but not necessarily to judge. This may not be as easy as it sounds, for Governor Hennessy was essentially a man who produced the most violent reactions in all those with whom he came in contact. He was thirty-three when he was appointed Governor of Labuan, and though his character gathered power as he grew older, it was, like that of most men, already formed by his heritage and the experiences of his earlier years. Before focusing upon Government House, Labuan, in the late eighteen-sixties, we must therefore swivel the telescope back to John Pope Hennessy's birthplace—the warm, wet, seedy little city of Cork.

II

John Pope Hennessy was born in Cork on 8 August 1834. He was the third of the five sons of John Hennessy, the hide merchant of Pope's Quay, whose father and father-in-law had both been in the butter trade, for which Cork was at that period the chief centre in Ireland. In an earlier generation a direct forebear, James Bryan Hennessy of Killavullen, County Cork, had married into the family of Pope 'of

Riverdale and Causeway, county Kerry'. To commemorate what they evidently regarded as an advantageous connection, the Cork Hennessys would always insert 'Pope' between the Christian name and surname of each of their progeny. It was not then secured to 'Hennessy' by a hyphen, and in the case of several of my grandfather's brothers seems to have come altogether adrift or been let lapse.

Like many of their native Irish contemporaries engaged in some form of trade, the Cork Hennessys firmly believed themselves to be of aristocratic origin. They styled themselves 'Hennessy of Ballyhennessy', a derelict estate in County Kerry near the prettily-named hamlet of Ballybunion, perched on a windy cliff top at the mouth of the Shannon. The family's tradition was that a younger son of an ancestor had, in the long ago, abjured Roman Catholicism, thus acquiring possession of Ballyhennessy and turning out the rightful heir. Other members of the clan had left Ireland in the eighteenth century and, joining the Irish Regiment of Louis XV known as the 'Wild Geese', had ended up by making a brandy fortune in the Charentais town of Cognac. When my grandfather, as a fashionable young Member of Parliament, had achieved success in life, he would go to stay at Cognac with the head of the French branch of the Hennessys, who used to address him in letters as *'mon cousin'*; James Hennessy of Ballymacmoy House, a connection who had in some way managed to retain his status as a country gentleman, used also to call my grandfather 'cousin' when he met him strolling in the streets of Cork.

Whether the Cork Hennessys had indeed 'sunk', as they themselves would surely have termed it, down into the commercial middle-class, or whether they had risen up into it from some yet obscurer sphere it is no longer possible to ascertain. In itself the point is neither of importance nor of interest; but the fact that the Cork Hennessys believed it to be true, clinging to what may well have been a legend as fervidly as to some major article of faith, coloured their lives. It gave them at once a grievance and consolation. Cooped up in Mount Verdon Terrace in the rain, the Hennessy children—Bryan and Henry and John and Willy and Cha, Mary and Annie and Liz—could all eight of them recollect, in moments of despondency, that they were born for broader acres and formed for better things. The conviction that he descended from the indigenous Irish landed gentry, evicted from their estates in the seventeenth and eighteenth centuries to make room for English Protestant landlords bound body and soul to maintain the English connection had, in particular, a vivid and profound effect upon my grandfather's ambitions and on his subsequent career. He was brought up to feel that he was deprived of his birthright, and that he was living in a country under the armed occupation of a foreign, and Protestant, power. He was told how, in 1796, his grandfather Bryan Pope Hennessy had shouldered his pack and trudged, like many another Irishman, to Bantry Bay to welcome Hoche and the French Army of Liberation; but this army never landed. From eye-witnesses the boy learned of the wholesale hangings of patriots, which followed the unsuccessful rising of that fated year, and of the savagery with which the soldiers of the English Yeomanry Regiments revenged themselves, plundering and raping and burning throughout the South and West. At the age of twelve, John Pope Hennessy had himself seen the effects of the Irish famine of 1846, when the corpses of the men, women and children who had died of starvation in the Cork streets during the night would be collected each morning by a municipal cart. In later years he had watched volunteer after volunteer for the South Cork Infantry Regiment rejected by the recruiting officers for being under-sized from malnutrition.

Irish memories are long. Reared on anecdotes of oppression, and on tales of centuries-old 'misgovernment and ignorance', John Pope Hennessy was inevitably conditioned by this environment. Towards the very end of his life, at a moment in which the grant of Home Rule to Ireland seemed to him and to some other Irish optimists to be imminent, he wrote to his eldest son: 'How happy ought we to be in reflecting that we actually have the chance—if we live a little longer the certainty—of seeing the persecutions & struggles of 700 years ended. Recall to your mind how many Irishmen during that long time prayed & hoped & died to secure the result we may soon witness.' As a child he was given a square of paper signed in Clonmel Gaol by John Mitchel, the Irish Nationalist solicitor transported for sedition in 1848; this signature, together with those of earlier Irish 'rebels', he treasured as another boy might treasure a rare stamp. Hatred, which has never been an English characteristic, smouldered everywhere beneath the surface of Southern Irish life. Young John Pope Hennessy was gay and high-spirited, persuasive and an excellent talker; but at the same time he learned to look on quarrelling as a natural activity and to assume that those who were not his friends must be his enemies. When, aged twenty-one, he wrote to his parents that he was determined on 'fighting his way in the world' this was no mere figure of speech. Throughout his life he remained desperately partisan.

A Public School training might possibly have helped to calm the restlessness of John Pope Hennessy's character, as well as giving him a more balanced outlook. In the Ireland of his youth, however, no such schools for Catholic boys existed. In any case he was in childhood a semi-invalid from chronic bronchitis, 'a delicate-looking little fellow', who was sent in wintertime to the Hydropathic Establishment at Blarney, and whose lessons were taught him by an unexacting private tutor. His education was completed during five years at the Queen's College, Cork, where he won a reputation for brilliance and hard work. There Hennessy achieved first-class honours in surgery and in medicine, the latter the profession which his family, in their poverty, had decided it would be safest for him to pursue.

The cultivated world of mid-Victorian Cork, though infinitely small, was erudite. There were literary, artistic and musical clubs, public lectures on historical or topical subjects, and a debating society for the students, in which John Pope Hennessy, a leading light, would propose such a motion as: 'Does the advance of Science diminish the domain of the Poet?' A glimpse of my grandfather in his youth is given in the *Reminiscences* of his closest Cork friend, Justin McCarthy: 'Hennessy and I', writes McCarthy, 'were boys together in the city of Cork. He was four years younger than I, but we were friends and comrades, and grew up together. We spoke in the local debating societies; we were members of the Temperance Institute founded by Father Mathew; we were often oarsmen together in the same boat on the River Lee and in Queenstown Harbour; we were constant visitors at each others' houses, and were comrades in many a youthful adventure. John Hennessy was a singularly clever boy, full of courage and self-confidence, and inspired by an evident desire to distinguish himself in the world.' In another volume of recollections, McCarthy also tells how he and John Pope Hennessy would wander together in the beautiful woods of the mysterious demesne of Rostellan, a property on Queenstown Harbour owned by an absentee landlord. McCarthy relates that Hennessy contracted a boyish passion for Rostellan, swearing an oath that it would one day be his home. In this passion, at least, as in that for the freedom of Ireland, my grandfather was supremely consistent. When he heard, in the late 'eighties, that Rostellan was up for sale, he bought the property. Although he only lived to enjoy possession of it for a few years, it was at Rostellan that he died.

III

It requires a minimum of imagination to realise that mid-nineteenth century Cork offered no scope to a youth of John Pope Hennessy's gifts and determination. A surviving diary kept by my grandfather for the year 1855 (when he was twenty) suggests the monotonous activities and the mild amusements which that city could provide. He read each morning in the Queen's College Library, where the students talked so much that concentration became impossible: 'a whisper' he noted 'is as bad as a shout'. He attended College lectures and surgical demonstrations assiduously; he would rise to work at dawn, and he was still working late at night. Recreations consisted in playing backgammon or billiards, in 'coffee and cigar' parties in the rooms of his contemporaries, in reading classics such as *Tristram Shandy* and in a fevered study of the political news from London in the columns of *The Times* and of a leading Dublin newspaper. A typical diary entry runs: 'Dined in my room with Sam. Then we went to the Athenaeum with the girls & my mother. Great crowd. Everybody. Sophia B., looking very pretty, sang. Drove to Elm Park 9 o'c at night.' There are one or two references to a frustrated emotion: 'Met X— for the first time for this year and the last for many, many years to come' he noted in January 1855: 'On the whole I have acted properly, but I was too cold. I should not have affected so much indifference.' Sometimes he would go to stay with a country doctor, the father of a friend, at Rathcormac. At others he would go boating on the river, or to ride, shoot or fish in the desolate Rostellan demesne. His interest in politics was already highly developed and, like many Irish Catholics at that moment, angered by the Liberals' attitude over the Queen's Colleges and the Ecclesiastical Titles Bill, he was a violent Tory. Cabinet crises fascinated him even more than the progress of the Crimean War. His heart set on London and on the great world beyond, he chafed at the restrictions and above all at the boredom of Cork life. 'Grey told me all about Paris and Naples, the fortunate man', he wrote of a friend who had been lucky enough to escape, if only briefly, from Cork City. Another intimate friend, by name O'Brien, had migrated to London where he was living in the Chambers of Serjeant Murphy and whence he would write John Pope Hennessy exciting letters about London life: 'how I should like to be with him in the midst of literary and political lions' my grandfather wistfully noted. Suddenly, in April 1855, his chance came.

In the previous year, 1854, the Director General of the British Army Medical Department had for the first time placed a recommendation for an Indian Medical Commission at the disposal of the Queen's College, Cork. The Faculty decided to recommend young Pope Hennessy. In May 1855, he set off for London, armed with a certificate from the Queen's College Faculty and with a personal letter from the head of the Medical School, Dr Fleming, who had known him for eight years. Dr Fleming described young Hennessy's career at Queen's College as 'eminently distinguished', his intellect as 'acute and vigorous', his powers of observation as 'excellent' and his knowledge 'of general and medical science' as extensive. 'He is a gentleman in manner, temper and feeling', added Dr Fleming, 'and of excellent moral and general character.' Besides these testimonials, young Hennessy had other assets which neither the Faculty of Queen's College nor the good Dr Fleming would necessarily have regarded in this light. Although diminutive in stature, he was distinctly handsome, with luxuriant curling hair of a light brown colour, a mouth which was constantly smiling, deep-set blue eyes and a somewhat Roman nose. His charm, as we have earlier noticed, was considerable; he was seductive, witty and a good *raconteur*. There hung about him a bright air of vigour and of youth which he retained well into his middle age. Thus equipped for life John Pope Hennessy set out, on the morning of 18 May 1855, to seek his fortune in London, the capital and centre of the nation which he felt had ruined his country, dispossessed his family, and deprived him of his rights. 'Up at 4½' he noted in his diary: 'Bid goodbye to my father & kissed my mother, Mary & Lizzie at 5½ & was steaming down the river at 6 o'clock. It was so rough that the steamer (the Shamrock) was tossed between the ports, & pitched so much that I was sea sick a little beyond the lighthouse about 9 o'c. I did not leave my berth till next morning. It was the most disagreeable day & night I ever spent.' Next morning all was well again. 'Eat an enormous breakfast going up the Bristol Channel.' His first sight of the English countryside impressed him: 'Had a compartment of a 1st c. carriage to myself & enjoyed the beautiful scenery very much. Trees and hedges are the distinguishing feature of the English country. Drove to Serjeant's Inn.'

Thus ended the first, and only placid, phase of my grandfather's career.

I N SERJEANT'S INN, where for some weeks he shared his friend O'Brien's chambers, John Pope Hennessy settled down to a life as studious and, at first, as uneventful as that which he had been leading in Cork. Early each weekday morning an old laundress tidied the rooms, lit the fire, and laid the breakfast table. The young men made their own breakfast, hungrily consuming the ham, tongue, country butter and raspberry vinegar, which, with other wholesome Irish fare, John Hennessy's mother sent over at regular intervals from Cork. In the 'exquisitely furnished' sitting-room they then worked at their books at separate tables for three or four hours, after which Hennessy would go on foot to Charing Cross Hospital to attend lectures, courses in midwifery and in medical jurisprudence, and walking home again, reach Serjeant's Inn in time for more work before their six o'clock supper. After this meal he read *The Times* with diligence, did another spell of work, and went to bed at eleven o'clock. Supper was prepared by Serjeant Murphy's old servant, an excellent cook who had been the model for a famous domestic in one of Thackeray's novels.

Occasional visitors—Irish legal or medical students, and often enough Serjeant Murphy himself—would drop in of an evening, and then the conversation might be kept up till one or two o'clock in the morning; for talking was already John Pope Hennessy's favourite form of relaxation. Later in life he made a reputation for his 'rare gift for story telling . . . and if it were possible', wrote an admirer, 'for him to tell a dull story—a possibility I could not admit—he would most assuredly have made it seem bright by his manner of recounting it'. This run of anecdote was never the result of stimulants, for all through his life my grandfather was a man of strangely abstemious habits. His early membership of Father Mathew's Temperance Association in Cork had left its mark: his 'favourite idea of a midnight revel seemed to be represented by a glass of milk'. He was fond of good food, and had a real passion for eating fruit, but although he learned about wines, and, as a Colonial Governor, kept as good vintages in his cellars as was feasible in a tropical climate, 'wine was to him rather a conventional ornament of the feast than a delight or stimulant to the palate . . . [he] only tasted it now and then as a ceremonial, and then forgot all about it'. In these early London days he was austere to the verge of priggishness: 'They are all going to the theatre tonight', he wrote during his first month in London, 'but I shall not go with them, as I have determined not to lose time.'

This determination 'not to lose time' was synonymous with the determination to 'fight his way' in life. It influenced his whole approach to the exterior world: 'The few acquaintances I have in London are all men who can be of assistance in pushing me on', he wrote to his father after the first five months in London: 'I am determined not to make any other sort of acquaintance.' These are not sentences which chime sympathetically in a grandson's ear, for while they are at any rate perfectly frank, this merit seems offset by their writer's evident assumption that cold-blooded calculation is a virtue. We should not, on the other hand, forget the magnitude of the task which this twenty-one-year-old provincial boy from Cork had secretly set himself in mid-Victorian London. This was no less than to reach, and then to join, the circles of political power in the metropolis. From long and earnest study of newspapers, as well as from a multitude of political books and pamphlets of the day, he had gained some insight into the machinery of this glittering world of power. He had gained, too, a strong impression that once an intelligent and single-minded young man got a toe-hold in that world, he might go far. It is significant that the hero of his life was Benjamin Disraeli, whom he once described as a man 'belonging to a different race, who by sheer ability and indomitable courage, has carried himself into his present high position. In an age of considerable mediocrity he does stand high as a great man—original, powerful and successful.' It is said that you can judge a man's character and ideals by the epithets most frequently upon his lips; to my grandfather words such as 'original', 'powerful' and 'successful' came readily as terms of praise, together with phrases such as 'high position' and 'in the best style'.

As we have seen, John Pope Hennessy was brought up in a lowly position and in a cramped style. His aim was not only to make his own fortune, but (as he saw it) to restore that lost to the family of Hennessy of Ballyhennessy, and to show his gratitude to parents of whom he was fond. He wished, too, to help his dowerless sisters to satisfactory marriages: 'I quite agree with you', he wrote in 1859 to his sister Annie, 'that three Miss H.'s on the *tapis* are much better off in Dublin, & have a better chance of *going off* too, than the same young ladies in the beautiful city. When I am, to some extent, settled in the World I intend devoting all my energy to looking out amongst my legal & other friends for desirable matches for Mary, Liz & yourself.— This is a profound secret.' He was only too aware of the drabness of Cork life. Writing in 1858 to another of his sisters, Lizzie, he asked her how they had all enjoyed their Easter: 'I suppose like myself your enjoyment was not very intense,—as far as parties are concerned. However, *our* parties will all come in good time.'

Meanwhile John Pope Hennessy watched and waited, closely examining as much as he could of the London world, and drawing therefrom conclusions favourable to himself. He had no money, and no influential relations, patrons or friends. He had had a good, but lopsided, education. His real assets, as we have seen, were several and important: he had youth, intelligence, industry, audacity and charm. More than all these he held within himself the mysterious and magnetic secret of success, which is perhaps nothing more than the absolute conviction that you will succeed. He had no intention whatever of ending up as an assistant surgeon at a London hospital, still less as a medical officer in some fly-blown Indian cantonment. It never once crossed his mind that he could fail to make his name.

It is clear that for my grandfather the medical profession held no allure. He viewed his recommendation for the Indian Army Medical Service as little more than a convenient escape-hatch from Cork. Writing to one of his sisters a few weeks after his arrival in London he declared that he looked 'upon it as a matter of certainty that I will be beaten at the Indian examinations', which for him was tantamount to saying that he had decided to be beaten. In October 1855, after less than five months in London, he wrote to his father in some excitement:

At length I have something of importance to tell you. I have just this moment returned from Downing Street where I had an interview with Lord Granville's Secretary who informed me that his lordship has placed my name upon his list for a supplemental clerkship in the Privy Council Office. . . . The candidates whose names are on the list will have to undergo two examinations. . . . These examinations are quite elementary. . . . I feel pretty certain that if I held such an office & that Disraeli's party got into power, I would be pushed up.

Young John Pope Hennessy did not explain to his bemused family on what he based this certainty. He would have been hard put to it to do so: the only basis for it was his own native conviction that so delightful, promising and talented an Irish Tory lad could not long be overlooked by the great leaders of the Conservative Party.

This clerkship in the Privy Council Office, a post which, since it brought in the minute salary of eighty pounds a year, naturally fussed his father, Pope Hennessy had obtained entirely on his own initiative. He had simply sat down one evening in the furnished bed-sitting-room he was then temporarily occupying in South Molton Street, and had written a long letter to Lord Granville, currently Lord President of the Council in a Whig administration, and whom, of course, he did not know. This document was all about himself, his history and his aspirations. It must have been well expressed, for it caught the Lord President's languid eye. Writing to Pope Hennessy fifteen years afterward when he was himself Secretary of State for the Colonies and my grandfather was Governor of Labuan, Lord Granville wrote: 'Some years ago it was owing to what appeared to me to be a very good letter, that I put your name on the list of candidates for employment in the Council Office. I have now to acknowledge another good one from a gentleman, whose name is no longer unknown to me.' John Pope Hennessy told his father that he had sent Lord Granville 'a full account of my collegiate position, the College recommendation & Kane's letters . . . I heard nothing about my application until last night, when I received a communication "On Her Majesty's Service" requesting me to call at Downing Street at ½ past 1 today . . . I will say more in my next as to what changes this will make in my arrangements about the medical & arts degrees &c'.

What he said in his next letter about changes in his arrangements for the medical and arts degrees was that these arrangements had undergone the pretty final alteration of being entirely shelved. He said that he would prefer 'such a junior appointment in a Government office to a thousand a year as a medical practitioner' and used the age-old excuse of all children bent on thwarting their parents' plans— should his own choice of career not prove successful, he could always revert to that which he had jettisoned. He believed, as such sons always have believed, that his own decision offered 'a certainty of ultimate success', whereas in his father's schemes for him 'everything' was 'uncertain':

'The state', he wrote, 'of the Civil Service & of political parties here at present is such, that any man who has got his foot into Downing Street,

& who is determined to work hard & avoid every sort of dissipation, is certain of gaining a high position. What I have got is but the first step on the ladder. The most junior clerks in the Downing street offices belong to the first circles of London's society. Whatever the salary may be at first, these appointments confer, as far as social standing is concerned, a very high position. I was never easy in mind at the prospects before me until now.'

The first week of December 1855 thus found John Pope Hennessy comfortably ensconced in the Privy Council Office in 'one of the rooms of the large building at the Horse Guards side of Whitehall. . . . The same building contains the Treasury, the Foreign Office & the Board of Trade. The entrance to my department is at the south corner, in Downing Street.' The room was warm, carpeted in a thick Turkey carpet, and wainscoted to the ceiling. In the centre stood a large square desk, at which Hennessy and three other clerks worked, each at one side of the table. 'Our principal business appears to be the regulating of correspondence. On every letter that is received, a short abstract of its contents is written by a clerk. Lord Granville, or one of the principal secretaries then writes the headings of a reply, or in important cases, the whole reply, which is then copied by a clerk for his signature. The letters are then sent up to us again to be folded, sealed and directed.'

Pope Hennessy worked assiduously at this clerical drudgery and could soon report that he had been complimented by his superiors on his 'great zeal and ability'. It was not an exciting beginning: but the Irish youth who had seemed, twelve months earlier, to have no chance of ever leaving Ireland or seeing the world could now reflect that he was working in a building which housed not only the Lord President of the Council, but the Secretary of State for Foreign Affairs, the Lords of the Treasury and the President of the Board of Trade as well. He could make friends with those enviable colleagues who belonged to 'the first circles of London society'. In 1857 he was able to write home that his name had been published in 'the last edition of the Royal Red Book for *the first time*, this year'. 'I enclose you', he added in a letter to his dazzled mother in Mount Verdon Terrace, 'the printed form which the compilers of this Book (which so many Londoners are dying to appear in) have just sent me.'

Since he realised that promotion to a post with a respectable salary might take even him some years to achieve, John Pope Hennessy determined to spend his evenings reading for a law degree. He moved into rooms of his own in Tanfield Court in the Middle Temple, which he told his sister Mary was 'one of the best parts of the Temple. Several MPs & QCs live here. . . . Going up to the top of the staircase, you come to a door painted, like all the others, black, with a small brass knocker, & a bell handle at the side. Across the top of the door is painted in white letters "Mr Hennessy". . . . The bed-room is about six yards long by five yards broad & has two windows with a fire place. The windows look to the west across Tanfield Court. The sitting room . . . looks to the East, across the gardens & open space of King's Bench Walk. Being very close to the sky, the ceilings are rather low, but as the rent is also very low I am not at all annoyed at that. The whole place has been newly painted for me; & new locks, fireplaces, &c have been put in. To-day I settled, after a hard fight, about the papering. . . .'

II

In the year 1857, some months after my grandfather's installation in his attic chambers in Tanfield Court, the rooms on the floor immediately below his were taken by a young Roman Catholic of his own age, who had just been called to the Bar and had joined the Northern Circuit. This was Alfred Austin, who, later abandoning law for a poetic career, died Poet Laureate and is chiefly remembered as the author of many volumes of unconsciously humorous epic verse. The two young men quickly found that they had much in common— religion, strong Tory convictions, and the study of law amongst them —and they became fast friends. It was probably Austin who introduced Pope Hennessy into the ultramontane Roman Catholic Conservative circle, the headquarters of which was the Stafford Club.

Austin observed that Pope Hennessy's 'mode of life', like his own, 'was modest and frugal'. A physically delicate youth who had inherited a small private fortune, Alfred Austin was by nature prudent. Since he knew that his neighbour had nothing whatever to live upon beyond his salary—by then £120 per annum—he was greatly perturbed by an incident which occurred in his rooms at Tanfield Court, one day in the spring of 1859. Lord Derby, the Tory Prime Minister, had announced that a General Election would be held immediately. This announcement was naturally of vivid interest to Alfred Austin and to his equally politically-minded Irish friend. But Austin was astonished when Hennessy came bounding down the stairs of Tanfield Court, thrusting upon him a sealed letter he was carrying in his hand. 'I am going to Ireland to stand as an Irish Nationalist Conservative', he explained, 'and, on receiving a telegram from me, will you go at once and hand this letter to the Head of the Education Department? It contains my resignation, without which I cannot stand for Parliament.' Apart from the fact that no one had hitherto heard of an 'Irish Nationalist Conservative', which anyway sounded like a contradiction in terms, Austin was appalled at the gambling spirit displayed by a man who could thus wantonly throw up his only means of livelihood, and his only chance of a career, for an obvious fantasy. How could an unknown Irish youth with not a penny to his name aspire to become a Member of Parliament—a position which, at that time, still implied a certain financial stability? 'My dear fellow', said Austin, 'you will die in a ditch.'

This prophecy was not fulfilled. Far from dying in a ditch Hennessy was returned at the head of the poll for King's County in June 1859. A week or two later as Alfred Austin was wandering through Tanfield Court, he was stopped by a messenger who urgently asked him for Mr Hennessy's address since he had a letter to deliver to him. Austin undertook to deliver the letter and was amazed to find that it was an invitation to dinner from Mr Disraeli. It was thus that, at the age of twenty-three, with no money, little backing and no powerful patrons, the former medical student from Queen's College, Cork, became a Member of Parliament. 'It is no wrong to him', is Austin's comment on this episode, 'to say that he was endowed with the spirit of the adventurer.'

In Cork City, the Hennessy family were as bewildered by this whirlwind decision and its immediate success as was that of Phineas Finn in Trollope's novel. 'My dearest Eliza,' wrote John Pope Hennessy's mother to one of her daughters, then in Dublin: 'I opened the enclosed letter written at 2 o'c—to send *You* a Letter I recd. from our Dear Child—at 5 o'c—*that you and all our family* in Dublin may participate in that great pleasure I have felt on reading it. May the Almighty in his infinite Mercy, preserve and Direct our Dear Child—John Pope—as He has hitherto been to him so Merciful, directing his Steps—I hope to the Greater Honour & Glory of God.' The only person not surprised by the turn of events was the 'Dear Child' himself, who had written from Tullamore on nomination day that he had 'every reason to be confident of success'. He was one of those who, having everything to lose, do not admit the possibility of failure.

Since this book in no sense aims at being a biography of my grandfather, there would be neither object nor interest in going into the details of his first election to Parliament, nor of his subsequent career there which, beginning with great promise, came to an abrupt end in 1865, chiefly through lack of money to pay his debts and his election expenses. We may, however, remark that his luck in the 1859 election confirmed Hennessy in a dangerous belief that for himself the impossible did not exist. It confirmed, too, his latent lack of judgement in practical matters, and his distaste for weighing the pros and cons of any given step or situation.

Although my grandfather's decision over the 1859 election was certainly impulsive and seemed to his friends and family to be almost mad, he had in fact been laying the basis for it for some time. He had assiduously practised the art of debate at the Westminster Debating Society, which met in an old-fashioned room in the Westminster Tavern near Westminster Bridge, had several young barristers and journalists amongst its members and closely imitated the forms of the House of Commons. Hennessy had also joined the Stafford Club, had courted Cardinal Wiseman and other Roman Catholic leaders, and had published a pamphlet attacking the Whig educational policy in Ireland. He had studied *Hansard*, he had attended House of Commons debates; and he had at length perceived how he might himself achieve a seat in the House.

Until 1859 every Roman Catholic Member of Parliament had been Liberal. The Whigs had passed the Catholic Emancipation Act; the Tories, as chief supporters of the Established Church, were rated anti-Catholic. But, for a variety of reasons which included the Ecclesiastical Titles Act, a section of leading English Catholics were becoming restive under their Whig allegiance. In Ireland the question of the Queen's Colleges and of Mixed Education had led many young men of Pope Hennessy's generation to suspect that their country's progress might be safest in Conservative hands, even though the Tories were 'inextricably bound up with the Orange Party in Ireland'. Aware of this atmosphere of discontent, and always alert for the possibility of making a dramatic effect, John Pope Hennessy foresaw that a brand-new role lay awaiting a sufficiently bold young man: that of an Irish Catholic Nationalist Member of Parliament who was at the same time a die-hard Tory. Such a man might rally important sections of Irish and English Catholic opinion to Derby and Disraeli, obtaining in return valuable concessions over certain Irish issues like Education and the Land Act. Moreover, active and unique, such an Irish Catholic Conservative Member might, if he played his cards properly, make himself so indispensable that he would soon achieve junior Cabinet rank. Today this particular scheme—born of a mixture of opportunism and idealism not uncommon in politics—may not sound either thrilling or novel. In 1859 it was sensational and almost revolutionary.

The scheme worked like a charm. 'John Pope Hennessy', wrote a fellow-member in the House: 'created a new character in politics—the character of an ardent young Irish Catholic and Nationalist who was also a devoted member of the Conservative Party. The new Character took immensely. . . . He had graceful manners, a clear voice, and a presence which suggested aristocratic birth and training. . . . There was something quite new to the House in the presence of a young Nationalist Irishman who made no pretence at floridity of eloquence and talked as if talking were a practical business and not a declamatory art. . . . He had an audacity which nothing could possibly dismay or even discourage, while at the same time he never seemed intrusive or overbearing. He would argue with Lord Palmerston on a question of foreign policy, or with Gladstone on the details of a financial scheme.' Pope Hennessy himself had absolutely no doubts as to his Parliamentary popularity: 'Everybody here says I am the most successful new member in this Parliament', he told his parents in Cork. 'I have got the ear of the House, and no Irish member is heard with such marked attention.'

Verbal wit and the gift for repartee are of their very essence ephemeral. Neither amongst my grandfather's surviving papers, nor in the double-columned pages of *Hansard*, does one find much evidence of the sparkling sallies with which for six long years he is reported to have enlivened the House of Commons. A good part of these performances would seem to have consisted in baiting the Whig leaders. He could coolly enrage Lord Palmerston, put Mr Gladstone 'into a white heat of passion' and irritate the burly and radical Sir Robert Peel until 'he sometimes roared like a bull'. He indulged freely in the very Irish pastime of turning general issues of principle into personal feuds; and although he cherished burning convictions about the freedom of Ireland and of Poland, or about the importance of throwing open the Civil Service to public competition, much of his time was spent in sending Disraeli little notes of backstairs gossip, and in generally pursuing his own ambitious schemes. Throughout his life Pope Hennessy succeeded in surrounding many fine conceptions with a fog of private prejudice and a cobweb of intrigue. Some of his colleagues in the House, such as Bernal Osborne, whom he did not like, openly accused the Member for King's County of prevarication. He certainly had little gift for plain statement, possibly because he did not always have a firm grasp of plain facts.

By and large, however, Pope Hennessy quickly gained in the House of Commons a reputation not merely for audacity and wit, but for hard work as well. He carried out to the letter a piece of advice given him soon after his election by Disraeli; if he wanted to succeed, Disraeli told him, 'When the House is sitting, be in your place. When it is not sitting, read *Hansard*.' With his vivacity and charm Hennessy soon made life-long friends amongst some of the younger Members of the House of Commons, although, being virtually teetotal, he did not frequent the smoking-room but usually repaired to the tea-room instead. Here, at half-past nine each evening, he would find Lord Palmerston, who was also drinking tea. He recalled how loudly Lord Palmerston's false teeth clattered in his head, how exquisite were the old man's manners to the waitresses whom some members treated in an offhand way, and how he would ask: 'How is the Pope, Mr Hennessy? How is he in health? Do you think he will live out the year?' To which the young Irish member would adroitly reply that so far as he knew the Pope was well, but that he did not suppose that His Holiness would outlive Lord Palmerston.

At this period of the nineteenth century membership of the House of Commons entailed considerable personal and social prestige. During the eighteenth century, and indeed up until the passage of the 1832 Reform Bill, MPs were even less sought after than they are at the present day. But in the 'sixties and 'seventies of the last century, membership of the House opened many otherwise closed doors in the world of London Society, especially if the Member were young, personable, original and a lively conversationalist. Pope Hennessy soon found himself asked to dine at the Duchess of Richmond's, to shoot at Longleat, or to pass a week with the Carnarvons at Highclere. Gone were the days when, an obscure clerk in a Government office, he had been surprised to receive a card for a ball at a Mrs Fordati's three whole weeks before the ball took place. Gone, too, were the days when he would have an overcoat with a cape made up from a length of Irish frieze which his mother had sent over in the food hamper from Cork City. He now became something of a dandy, went to the best tailors and bootmakers and began to keep a brougham—most of this on credit. 'I have got several invitations for the Autumn. My mind is not yet made up where I shall spend the two or three months between the close of the Session and Christmas. . . . If possible I will, however, run over to see you & my father in the first instance', he would now write to his proud mother in Cork.

John Pope Hennessy was in fact undergoing the metamorphosis which so fascinated Trollope and which partly inspired him to write *Phineas Finn*. He was now becoming a man of the world—or, at any rate, a man of a certain world. As concessionaire in a British project for building railways in France, he could pay free visits to Paris. In the winter of 1860 he toured Italy as the guest of a friend whose name we do not know: 'The luxury of travelling on the invitation & at the expense of a rich friend gives an additional zest to the tour', he wrote with considerable candour from Siena in December 1860: 'We stay at the best Hotels, my friend spares no money, & as he said in his letter asking me to accompany him, the trip will not cost me one penny from the time I left London till I return.' In Paris he made friends with Montalembert and an impression upon Baron James de Rothschild, the original of Disraeli's 'Sidonia', who would lend him his box at the Opera. 'I confess', Hennessy recalled many years later: 'I often felt, when seated in the box in that magnificent opera house, that I was there under false pretences, and when I saw all the lorgnettes in the house directed towards me, I imagined the spectators saying, "Look at that young man! He is rolling in wealth! What a lucky fellow he is!" ' Himself the centre of his own world, it may not have occurred to him that the lorgnettes could have been directed at someone in the box next door.

The French Hennessys welcomed the young Irishman as a cousin at the Château de Batignolles near Cognac, giving a family dinner-party in his honour and commenting on the fact that he also had the battle-axe (which they were already using as their brandy trade-mark) as his crest. Here he was interested to find that the two younger sons of his host, Auguste Hennessy, were as physically diminutive as himself.

On none of these journeys did he waste his time. Whether hob-nobbing with Lord Cowley in the British Embassy in Paris, discussing high finance with Rothschild or the wine trade with Auguste Hennessy, he was collecting data likely to be of use to him in the House of Commons. During his Italian tour, he told his father, he had 'accumu-lated a mass of facts & most valuable information . . . about the con-dition of Italy & the state of public opinion. . . . The Italian question', he wrote, 'will be the great one for some time to come.' In 1860 he had already decided that, apart from Ireland, he would specialise on 'the Italian question' in the House of Commons; then in 1863 he took up the cause of Poland. '*Déjà, malgré son extrême jeunesse*', Montalembert wrote of Hennessy in April 1863: '*l'un des orateurs les plus écoutés de la Chambre des Communes. Il s'est signalé par le courage et l'intelligence de ses attaques contre la politique anglaise en Italie, non moins que par son zèle pour la Catholique Pologne. Il est lui même Catholique et irlandais, mais au lieu de s'enrégimenter comme ses collègues de la même origine sous le drapeau de Lord Palmerston, il s'est fait l'allié de Lord Derby et du parti conservateur.*' The role of the young Irish Catholic Conservative was as novel and as acceptable to right-wing intellectuals on the Continent as it had proved amongst the Tories of London.

III

The Insurrection of the Polish Provinces of Russia in 1863 and its brutal crushing by Czarist troops with Prussian connivance aroused a storm of popular sympathy in England and in France. It was a nation-wide reaction far transcending mere party politics. 'There were almost as many Conservatives as Radicals who were ready to favour the idea of some effort being made on [Poland's] behalf', wrote a contemporary historian. 'Lord Ellenborough spoke up for Poland in the House of Lords with poetic and impassioned eloquence. Lord Shaftesbury from the opposite benches denounced the conduct of Russia. The Irish Catholic was as ardent for Polish liberty as the London artisan. Among its most conspicuous and energetic advocates in England were Mr Pope Hennessy, a Catholic and Irish Member of Parliament, and Mr Edmond Beales, the leader of a great Radical organisation in London. The question was raised in Parliament by Mr Hennessy, and aroused much sympathy there. Great public meetings were held, at which Russia was denounced and Poland advocated, not merely by popular orators, but by men of high rank and grave responsibility.'

Although an actual declaration of war upon Russia was not called for by the majority of the British partisans of Poland, Lord Palmerston's Ministry was urged on every side to combine with France in a protest to the Russian Government, and to invoke the clause of the Treaty of Vienna which still guaranteed the rights—such as they were —of the Poles in Russia. It was along these lines that Pope Hennessy, in a long and earnest speech, moved an Address to the Crown. Nothing came of this move, nor of further attempts by Pope Hennessy and his supporters in the House to goad the Government into action.

The leading part played by my grandfather in the Polish intervention movement brought him great, if transitory, popularity in this country and a temporary European fame. In the spring of 1863 he was invited by the grateful Poles to visit Cracow. He set off thither in April, stopping in Paris for an audience with Napoleon III, and in Vienna for an audience with the Emperor Francis Joseph, who wished to have the foreign policy of Disraeli and the Conservative Opposition clarified for him.

The Emperor Napoleon, whom he found 'like any ordinary mortal', received young Hennessy with affability. 'Take a chair, Mr Hennessy. We will have no ceremony. I want to have a business conversation', he remarked in his study at the Tuileries, after dismissing the British Ambassador, Lord Cowley, who had introduced the Irish MP. The business conversation covered Poland, Italy and 'other subjects of political interest'; but the notes which my grandfather took of this interview have not survived. From the Hotel Meurice, that evening, Pope Hennessy wrote a private letter to Disraeli, to say that the Emperor had given him a number of messages for the Conservative leader, which were of too secret a nature to be committed to paper. Hennessy's copious pencilled jottings of his conversation—or rather of his argument—with the Emperor Francis Joseph do, on the other hand, exist. The Emperor, who courteously welcomed him as 'a Member of Parliament, and a great Catholic and an Irishman' began by drawing a parallel between his own Polish province of Galicia and Ireland. 'What would be said in England, Mr Hennessy, if you proposed to give up Ireland from Great Britain?' This was not a happy opening for a talk with an Irish Nationalist and Home Ruler; but, never at a loss, my grandfather explained to the Austrian Emperor that it was quite improbable that he could conceivably retain Galicia within his Empire forever, and that he should seek compensation 'elsewhere'. He also pointed out that fifteen million Catholic Poles now under Russian domination were subject to persecution on religious grounds. The remainder of the conversation is of merely academic interest; but the whole incident serves to show that the audacious young man from Cork City remained quite unabashed when confronted with personages of international position and imperial power. In Paris he had also talked to Prince Napoleon, who discussed Poland with him for an hour, and in Vienna he paid his respects to the Archduchess Sophia, to whose Chamberlain Montalembert had written to say that he was certain that *'cette auguste Princesse éprouverait peut être quelque satis-faction à voir un homme politique d'un aussi grand avenir et qui porte à la Maison d'Autriche un dévoûment aussi sincère qu'éclairé'*.

In Cracow John Pope Hennessy was received as a popular hero:

'I have been here since yesterday', he wrote to his father from Cracow on 17 April 1863: 'in the midst of all my friends. I am staying at the house of Count Potocki, the principal person in the province; and to give you an idea of the gratitude of the Poles, for the last two hours over two hundred & fifty visiting cards have been left for me. My arrival in Poland was announced in the Czas, the Crown Journal, this morning, and since twelve o'clock the hall porter is constantly employed taking in the cards of those who are calling on me.

'A deputation has just now waited on me to invite me to a public dinner of the citizens of Cracow on Sunday next. . . .'

When he left Cracow for Vienna he was presented with many souvenirs, including a mother-of-pearl album containing cartes-de-visites photographs of all those whom he had met during his stay in the Polish capital, and a framed fire-screen of mammoth proportions embroidered by the ladies of Poland in gold thread.

It is not surprising that, already in his fourth year in the House of Commons, Hennessy's confidence increased. 'No man had higher hopes or brighter prospects for the future', wrote a friend and com-patriot. 'He had risen rapidly; he was a man of ideas not phrases. He was popular with the party; appreciated by Disraeli. In due time promotion would have come to him.' He had already done work of solid value in the House—obtaining the amendment of the Irish poor law; opposing the Government system of Irish education as being 'anti-national'; promoting the passage through Parliament of the Prison Ministers Act of 1863; and forcing through amendments in the Mines Regulations Acts, for which he had been publicly thanked by the miners of Great Britain. It was also due to his exertions that the Select Committee which recommended the system of open competition for admission to the public service had been appointed, and it was authoritatively rumoured that when the Conservatives should return to office Lord Derby intended to allot to Hennessy a junior position in the Government. His career was developing exactly as he had intended that it should. Everything was going his way.

On 6 July 1865 Parliament was dissolved, having sat for just over six years. The Liberals were once more returned, and in triumph, for they had increased their majority from thirteen seats to between sixty and seventy. But when Parliament reassembled to hear the Queen's Speech, John Pope Hennessy was not among the Conservative members of the Lower House listening at the Bar. He had lost his seat by seven votes.

IV

'I have learnt, with the greatest concern, the strange and unexpected conclusion of the contest for King's County', Disraeli wrote to John Pope Hennessy from Hughenden on 28 July 1865. 'By your powers of debate, great information, indefatigable industry & fidelity of conduct, during the six years you were in the House of Commons, you established a parliamentary name—and obtained the confidence of all who acted with you. It will be a reflection on the sense and spirit of your countrymen, if they do not soon restore you to a position for which by talents & character you are eminently fitted.' This letter was despatched from High Wycombe a few days after the declaration of the poll. It is warmer in tone that the conventional missive sent by a party leader to a henchman who has lost his seat in a General Election; many years later Disraeli's private secretary Montagu Corry bore witness to Disraeli's 'appreciation' of John Hennessy, and to Hennessy's awareness of it. From his boyhood in Cork onwards, John Pope Hennessy had admired Disraeli passionately. There is evidence that, when he got to know the young Irishman, Disraeli liked him in return, finding him useful and subtle in the House, and recognising in him a determination to succeed as great as that he had himself shown as an obscure young Jew entering British politics. At any rate, so long as Disraeli lived, he fostered his protégé's subsequent colonial career.

To Disraeli, and to Hennessy's friends and contemporaries in the House of Commons, the defeat in King's County seemed nothing more than a tiresome, if startling, set-back. He had only, they would have argued, to wait for an Irish by-election—or if the worst came to the worst for a new General Election—to gain a seat. To John Pope Hennessy it spelt total disaster, for he well knew that he could not afford to wait. It is likely that, while in the House, he had been helped by party funds; he had also benefited by a Member of Parliament's immunity to arrest for debt, and by the long-term credit which in those halcyon days London tailors and shopkeepers were anxious to extend to young gentlemen with a future before them in public life. Once out of Parliament he could immediately be prosecuted, and sent to a debtors' prison. Although he had taken silk in 1861 and had begun a modest practice at the Bar, Hennessy was not yet well known enough in the legal world to be able to make a living as a barrister. Nor can one suppose—since he had absolutely no gift for finance— that his dabbling in French railway shares had been especially productive. He simply could not sit back and wait for another chance to enter the House.

My grandfather thereupon took up a line in which most probably— given his capacity for self-deception—he himself honestly believed. He declared, and so wrote to Disraeli and to his parents, that he had not been defeated at all. He was still the Member for King's County: by an oversight or else a deliberate plot of the Sheriff's assessors the votes had been miscounted. 'Though I was at the very last moment put in a minority by some very wrong decision of the Sheriff's assessors, I assure you the result has not in the slightest degree disheartened me', he wrote to his father from Parsonstown on 24 July 1865. 'On the contrary, in the first place my real majority will be easily restored by a scrutiny before an Election Committee of the House of Commons; but putting that aside, the affair will give me ample time to devote to my financial & professional business. A short time out of Parliament will do me no harm whatsoever.' The margin by which he had lost his seat was very small, but the truth of the matter would seem to have been that he still owed a capital sum—seven hundred pounds odd—for the hiring of 'jaunting cars' used during his campaign in King's County in 1859. Without these to take constituents to the polling stations, an Irish candidate had no hope of rounding up his rural supporters and ensuring that they lodged their vote in his favour. The men who hired out the jaunting cars in King's County refused to let Hennessy have any of them, unless he paid up his past debt and put down money in advance for the new Election.

These were not the kind of facts which my grandfather found particularly acceptable. He became convinced that an injustice had been done to him. He and his family launched a campaign to collect funds for an appeal against the Sheriff's decision. This campaign was generously supported in Cork, in Dublin and elsewhere in the South of Ireland. Still regarding himself as an MP, and doubtless claiming immunity as such, he managed to spin out his series of appeals until midsummer 1866, a twelve-month after the General Election was over.

His friends in the House warned him that his behaviour was 'injudicious' but this did not deflect him from his purpose nor calm his growing sense of grievance. In 1866 the final appeal was dismissed. The new Member for King's County, Sir Patrick O'Brien, was left in undisturbed possession of his seat. In after years my grandfather would relate that the King's County Election appeal had 'cost him' £28,000, by which it must be assumed that he meant that this handsome sum was owing in his name.

Meanwhile, before the final appeal decision, John Pope Hennessy had determined on a course open, from time immemorial, to clever young men in pecuniary difficulties. He decided to marry an heiress.

v

In the 'sixties of the last century, London Society displayed two outstanding examples of men whose political successes were largely due to their having married rich women. One of them, Disraeli, had in 1839 married the widowed Mrs Wyndham Lewis, who was thirteen years his senior, and to whom he was devoted. The other, Bernal Osborne,* who was also of Jewish extraction, had married Miss Osborne in 1844. Osborne was a notoriously bad husband. A story went the rounds that Bernal Osborne one day remarked to Disraeli: 'You and I both owe our position to our wives'; to which Disraeli is alleged to have replied: 'Yes; but *I* have never forgotten it.'

During the worst crisis of his affairs in 1866, John Pope Hennessy was discussing 'marriage as a political stepping-stone' with a friend, who has left an instructive account of the conversation. 'I would rather live in the Temple on a crust of bread than enjoy a fortune outside the House of Commons' he remarked, adding: 'If, however, I marry a rich wife, I will be to her a Disraeli; not a Bernal Osborne.' 'At a ball at the Duchess of Richmond's' [the account continues] 'Pope Hennessy met his fate.'

Now amongst John Pope Hennessy's most intimate friends in London were the brothers Lord Henry and Lord George Gordon-Lennox. Lord Henry was a confidant of Disraeli, was Member of Parliament for Chichester for thirty-nine years, and held public office in Tory administrations. He was thirteen years older than Hennessy. He and his younger brother, Lord George—who was more ne'er-do-

---

* Ralph Bernal, m. 20 August 1844, Catherine Isabella Osborne, and took the name 'Osborne'.

well and often in financial and emotional predicaments, when he would appeal to John Pope Hennessy for advice—were sons of the fifth Duke of Richmond, who had died in 1860, and consequently brothers of the sixth Duke. It was in 1866, at a ball at their sister-in-law's, the Duchess of Richmond's, in Portland Place, that Lord Henry Lennox pointed out to his young and troubled Irish friend an attractive girl, a Miss Canning, who had come to London with her mother and was said to have what was then regarded as the satisfying fortune of thirty thousand pounds sterling. 'The girl seems sweeter on you than on me,' Lord Henry remarked. 'There is grave suspicion about her birth and parentage; but none about her fortune. *I* can't marry her not knowing who or what her father was. If that's no obstacle to you, woo and win the girl.' Lord Henry's frankness seems not to have offended John Pope Hennessy, who quickly made the acquaintance of the mother and daughter. He began frequenting the supper-parties in the large suite which Mrs Canning had taken as a launching-site for her daughter in the new and fashionable Charing Cross Hotel. He was soon absorbed by the Canning family, to the neglect of his friends: 'You promised me most *faithfully* that you would join us at the Haymarket Theatre on Saturday', wrote Lord George Gordon-Lennox pettishly. 'You never came or sent an excuse which I confess I think you might have done. I hear you dined at the Charing Cross Hotel *again* last night—will you dine with *me* tonight at *8*, I am much annoyed.'

That Spring, in order to maintain an appearance if not of affluence at least of solvency, Pope Hennessy borrowed some £2,000 from a Jewish money-lender on a security 'fortified by a judgement by consent'. He gave dinners at the Star and Garter at Richmond for Miss Canning, her mother and their mutual friends. He constantly sent flowers from Covent Garden and other gifts to his prospective bride. By the end of April everything was nicely arranged: 'I was delighted to see you just now upstairs, all well and flourishing', one of the Gordon-Lennox brothers wrote to him from the House of Commons Library. 'Pray let me offer you my most sincere congratulations. . . . Will you come and have a quiet dinner with me at the Junior Club *at 8*, I am sure Miss Canning will kindly allow you *to do this* as I will let you go by *9*. *Pray* do come—.'

Although Mrs Canning agreed in principle to the engagement she proved oddly reluctant to instruct her lawyers to draw up a settlement, or herself to fix a day for the marriage. 'Pope Hennessy', his friend's narrative continues, 'had already insisted that all her fortune should be settled on the heiress.' Suddenly one Spring evening, Mrs Canning advanced upon the young couple, who were whispering together in the drawing-room of her suite and, 'placing her hands on the shoulder of either' declared that she realised that they did not wish to wait longer, and that on the next day, a Tuesday and her daughter's birthday, they could be married by special licence. 'The settlements can be completed afterwards', this unconventional parent murmured.

That night my grandfather was standing in his club in his favourite position—his little heels on the fender, his arms crossed in Napoleonic fashion, and his handsome curly head thrown well back. He was discussing Mrs Canning's announcement with three or four friends, each of whom strongly urged him to break the connection off, 'since it was evident now that there was no money in the marriage'. My grandfather replied that it was too late to draw back: 'Everyone in the House of Commons knows of it', he said. 'I should become a laughing-stock; besides', he added: 'I love the girl and will marry her, with or without money, even if I have to sweep the crossing in Parliament Street.' He was deaf to all argument. His friends consulted together, and arranged that, next morning, as the bridegroom 'a shade more thoughtful than usual' was about to step into his neatly-appointed brougham, he was arrested on a judgement debt of £2,000 and conveyed to a spunging-house in Chancery Lane.

Having thus effectively kidnapped the bridegroom, John Pope Hennessy's friends proceeded to the Charing Cross Hotel, where they casually asked Mrs Canning for the £2,000 needed to release him. 'The scene that followed', we learn without surprise, 'was simply indescribable. The bride in hysterics; the mother, in a terrible rage, ended by declaring that she had not enough money to pay the hotel bill—that the bridegroom must stay where he was.' Mrs Canning, however, recovered her self-control. She sent for the hotel manager, told him that owing to a sudden illness of the bridegroom the marriage was postponed, and that her stay in his agreeable hostelry would be prolonged. She then graciously took leave of Pope Hennessy's friends. So soon as they had gone, she hastily packed her jewellery and her lace, and taking her daughter with her, left London. 'For many a long year nothing was heard of her,' writes our informant. 'I happen, however, singularly enough, to know the tragic sequel to her fate, unknown to this day to the world at large. Let it remain so. It synchronised, I may however remark, with the death—murder, suicide or accident—of the son of Alderman Moon in a villa in St John's Wood. Her daughter was eventually married to a respectable cotton-broker.'

On this note of authentically Dickensian mystery ended John Pope Hennessy's solitary and unsuccessful attempt to gain money by marrying it.

VI

The Canning solution having rather signally failed, my grandfather's problems became grim indeed as the year 1866 waxed older. Yet he seems never to have given way to despair, and never to have lost his original self-confidence. 'I should be a very miserable fellow indeed', he wrote in April 1866 to Colonel Taylor, the Tory Chief Whip: 'if I did not know that I had ample strength in my own unaided resources to get over all my private troubles.' Evidently at Disraeli's instigation —the letter is amongst the archives at Hughenden—Colonel Taylor, through a third party, had offered Pope Hennessy financial aid: 'I cannot tell you how much obliged I am to you,' Hennessy replied: '—but I must decline, with very many thanks, all aid of the sort. Of course about fighting an Election Petition, or any similar affair, any man may accept the subscriptions of political friends. But the last thing in the world I would think of doing would be to accept such assistance in a private matter such as that which now annoys me.' It remained to be seen which, if any, of his political, and also of his fashionable, friends would continue to take any interest in a young Irishman who had swiftly risen from obscurity to a certain political position and a certain social popularity, only to plummet again, loaded with debt.

Provokingly enough, the mystery of the Cannings' disappearance coincides chronologically with a moment in my grandfather's life for which no solid documentation exists. We are not, however, left wholly to conjecture; for information on this awkward period of Pope Hennessy's existence survives in the shape of stories which he related to his eldest son, my father, in the 'eighteen-eighties, and some of which my father jotted down from memory in 1937 or 1938. According to these notes my grandfather firmly refused to contemplate taking the customary evasion route of British debtors:—across the Channel to live in poverty in Calais or Boulogne. Such a course would have been an admission of total failure, and would moreover have precluded any attempt at political resurrection in the House. He decided that he must find some quiet and moderately secret refuge in Great Britain, whence he could negotiate at leisure with his creditors, and, by letter, importune his influential friends for their aid.

The trouble was, just then, that his friends were only hypothetically influential; for the Liberal victory of 1865, with its vast increase in the Liberal majority, made Pope Hennessy's patrons in the Tory party seem more remote from office, and thus more remote from the exertion of any effective form of patronage, than ever before. And then, three months after the Election, Lord Palmerston (who did not, in fact, outlive the Pope) had died. His successor as Premier, Lord John Russell, was distinctly less adept at handling Parliament than his great predecessor had been. Was there not a faint possibility, a glimmer of hope, that the Tories might once more reach power? But where, while waiting for this happy day, was John Pope Hennessy to lie low?

As a young man my grandfather had a considerable appeal to women —both to the great ladies of London Society and to those of the demi-monde. 'I often think of you, Hennessy, of your varied genius, and talents', a successful English singer resident in Paris wrote to him at about this time. 'Unfortunately I have had much experience which has taught me a just estimation of men and believe me when I tell you among my many acquaintances I know of no one [who] possesses so much of the "savoir faire" as you do—The Americans would call you a "brick" but I call you a "trump"—I occasionally read your remarks —in fact I only look in the papers to see if I can see your name.' 'Sir', an unknown lady, who signed herself M. F. H., wrote to Disraeli, in July 1866: 'The magnificent position you have now reached by talent will have evoked your sympathy for that sort of material in others— There's little Pope Hennessy for instance—a Colossus—*with tremendously more brains* than acres. . . . Show that you stick by dawning Genius—He is worth a score of Nobles—an invaluable power to your party.' This note ended with an engaging postscriptum: 'P.S. I only *wish* I knew you—my goodness!!!'

Apart from such enthusiasts as these, John Pope Hennessy had made several true and lifelong friends in the great world of London. Two of the most faithful were Lord John Manners's mother-in-law, Mrs Marlay, who lived in St Katharine's Lodge in Regent's Park and who engaged the Manners family's interest on John Pope Hennessy's behalf, and the widowed Lady Ely, who now offered him as a bleak place of retirement a keeper's cottage upon a grouse moor on one of her young son's estates.

Jane, Marchioness of Ely, was a trusted confidante and also a Lady-

in-Waiting, of Queen Victoria. Until the day of her death she continued
to take an affectionate, maternal, interest in John Pope Hennessy,
following his career as he moved from post to post in the Colonial
Empire, applauding his marriage, and telling him of her own family
troubles—how her son was delicate and how her daughter Lady
Marion Buchanan was unhappily married. In later years Governor
Hennessy would send Lady Ely letters and Colonial information to be
shown privately to the Queen; and, while nothing more than 'a kind
message' usually resulted from these communications, they gave him,
isolated as he might be in Hong Kong or in Barbados, a comfortable
feeling of having by-passed the Secretary of State for the Colonies
and of being in some personal contact with the Crown.

Where the Elys' keeper's cottage was situated, and for how many
months Pope Hennessy stayed there, is no longer known. The
keeper's wife cooked the game which Hennessy shot, and on which,
in or out of season, he subsisted for some months. 'How long',
my father has written 'this period of seclusion lasted there is no
record but it seems to have lasted long enough to give him a distaste
for high grouse which endured for the rest of his life. In the intervals
of reading and re-reading the few books he had with him, and scouring
the moors in search of something to shoot in order to eat, he had
ample leisure to examine from every aspect the extremely unpleasant
circumstances which now confronted him.' It will have been during
this period of mental stock-taking that Pope Hennessy decided to
apply for a Colonial Governorship once the Conservative Party
should be again in power. We may suppose that the Conservative
magnates were no longer deeply concerned about the protracted
anxieties of the young Irishman—for in political, as in private, life
no one bores others more easily than a man with a grievance, and to
most people a friend's or colleague's troubles lose their interest when
they lose their novelty. Disraeli, however, promised Hennessy his
support, and remarked that in his opinion he ought to be given 'some
lucrative but quiet Governorship without any special difficulty
attached to it'.

In June 1866, Lord John Russell's Whig Ministry was defeated;
Lord Derby formed a Tory administration with Disraeli as Chancellor
of the Exchequer and Lord Carnarvon as Secretary of State for the
Colonies. In March 1867 Carnarvon resigned in protest at Disraeli's
disingenuousness over the Franchise Bill. He was succeeded by the
Duke of Buckingham and Chandos, who remained at the Colonial

Office until the fall of the Derby-Disraeli administration in December 1868. It was to the Duke of Buckingham that Disraeli spoke on Pope Hennessy's behalf.

Writing to Disraeli on 17 April 1867 to congratulate him on the Tory victory over the Franchise Bill Hennessy added: 'I can never sufficiently thank you for thinking of me on the eve of your political Sadowa. I have the best reason to know that the fact of your speaking to the Duke of Buckingham at such a moment has made him think more of my slender claims than all the other friendly hints and letters he got put together.' There happened just then to be only two Governorships to be filled—that of Malta, which could not be given to a Roman Catholic, and that of the tropical Crown Colony of Labuan, an unhealthy island off the north-west coast of Borneo. Pope Hennessy was offered Labuan. He accepted it under protest, sharply enquiring why he could not be made Governor of Queensland—an appointment which was not even vacant—and imploring Disraeli to get him a better Colonial post 'when the vacancies which are expected in the autumn occur'. 'You must not think I am inclined to grumble', he wrote, 'but the more I find out about Labuan the less I like it.—I now hear that the late Governor, Mr Callaghan, resigned from ill-health and that the few white inhabitants (about 40 in all) are constant victims of jungle fever.' In a further series of letters, he complained of being 'sent to a sort of penal servitude in Borneo', and of being 'kept at the coal-fields of Labuan'. He averred that the English and Irish Catholic Tories were outraged by his appointment and that 'the permanent officials at the Colonial Office were astonished at the Duke's having thought of giving me such a small place as Labuan'.

Whilst thus engaged in wriggling to avoid his fate, John Pope Hennessy received a telegram to say that his father had died suddenly in Cork on 26 April 1867. 'I was deeply attached to him', he wrote to Disraeli's secretary, Montagu Corry, before hurrying over to Ireland: 'and I hardly know what I am writing, but I wish to ask you to tell the Chancellor of the Exchequer that this gives the finishing blow to Labuan, for my three sisters are now thrown completely upon me, and it would be madness for me to think of taking them to such a dreadful place as Labuan.' The old hide-merchant's death could not indeed have been less opportune, for it left John Pope Hennessy's mother and three sisters very badly off indeed; he helped to support them financially for the rest of his life. Furthermore, during his thirteen years in London the vigorous little Irishman had contracted

other responsibilities which he did not mention to Mr Montagu Corry
or to Mr Disraeli. On 16 September 1867 a letter headed Lonsdale
Terrace, Barnes, reached the permanent officials of the Colonial
Office. Signed 'A. M. Conyngham', and written in a feminine hand,
this letter enquired whether 'the salary of the "Governor of Labuan"—
is paid here in London—or abroad?' Earlier in the same month this
lady had drawn up a will at a Hammersmith solicitor's, requesting and
appointing John Pope Hennessy to 'undertake the charge and to
adopt' her two children, Stella Beatrice and Mary Teodora. For many
years my grandfather paid for the education of these girls out of his
colonial salary. He would, from time to time, receive childish letters
from them at Christmas-time, addressing him as 'Darling Papa'. His
mother, and his sister Lizzie, helped to look after the children while
he was away; only their 'Aunt Mary' resolutely set her face against any
admission of their existence.

    Further pressure to accept Labuan was now brought to bear upon
Pope Hennessy. Colonel Taylor, the Tory Chief Whip, privately
warned him that the Ministry was already in so rickety a position that
they might 'go out' at any moment, in which case he would get
neither Labuan nor anything else. Lord Derby, the Prime Minister,
himself wrote a courteous four-page letter to say that 'he did not
remember' to have heard the climate of Labuan 'complained of', and
that it would in any case give the Duke of Buckingham 'pleasure to
have an opportunity, at no distant period, of offering you promotion
to a higher post'. With such promises Pope Hennessy had to rest
content. After making various arrangements for his family in Ireland,
he settled finally to sail for Labuan on 27 September 1867. He took out
with him his eldest sister Mary, a russet-haired *dévote*, selected in
family conclave as the most suitable of the three Miss Hennessys to
act as Governor's lady on a swamp near Borneo, and, as private
secretary, his Cork cousin Bryan Cody, a bald man with a hoarse
laugh and a gift for languages, already rather deaf in his early forties,
and with whom John Pope Hennessy had been involved in business
speculations.

    In Downing Street, where the Colonial Office was then situated,
the new Governor's departure for Labuan was welcomed with a
certain relief. His urgent requests that the Office should advance
money on his own and his private secretary's salaries before they had
even left London had not inspired confidence within the Office, and
although the Parliamentary Under-Secretary of State, Sir Charles

Adderley, declared that they were sending 'a very superior man to a very wretched Government', the permanent officials, with years of experience behind them, were more cynical. They noticed that Governor Hennessy had delayed paying the seventy-pound stamp duty for the Letters Patent appointing him to his post and that his financial position seemed, to say the least of it, a trifle insecure. 'Mr Pope Hennessy', minuted the Permanent Under-Secretary of the Colonial Office, Sir Frederic Rogers, 'experiences so many difficulties that one cannot help feeling apprehensive about further issues of money to him.' The new Governor had also aroused the Colonial Department's mirth by demanding an aide-de-camp on the grounds that he was 'desirous to maintain the due dignity' of his new position. In Downing Street the notion that a Governor of the tiny island of Labuan should have an aide-de-camp was curtly dismissed as 'absurd'.

Three days before he left England, John Pope Hennessy wrote to Disraeli from Hatfield House. This time it was in a tone of resignation, and to ask for his photograph: 'If your stock is not exhausted, & if you can spare me one, you may be sure it will be among my chief treasures at Labuan', he wrote. Other friends who gave the departing exile personal mementoes included Lady Ely, who presented him with a fine gold repeater watch and chain; and the millionairess philanthropist Miss Angela Burdett-Coutts who sent him an unspecified object which she hoped he would find useful 'when sitting sultry under a Banana staring at an Alligator'.

Miss Burdett-Coutts thought highly of Pope Hennessy's gifts: 'I have seen no one so likely, I think', she wrote to an acquaintance, 'to forward the best interests of the Eastern Archipelago or to interest English politicians (we scarcely possess Statesmen) in its welfare.' She was one of the few people in England who still felt any kind of optimism about the future of Labuan, a disastrous Crown Colony founded twenty years earlier at the instigation of Sir James Brooke, the first of the dynasty of the White Rajahs of Sarawak. By the autumn of 1867 Brooke, who had himself once been Governor of Labuan, was dying, but Miss Burdett-Coutts arranged a series of meetings, both in London and at Brooke's cottage near Plymouth, between the moribund White Rajah and John Pope Hennessy. In a valedictory note to the latter, giving him power of attorney to act for her in Sarawak, where she owned property, Miss Burdett-Coutts warned him that: 'The Sarawak people are all afraid you will find Labuan & the whole so much smaller than you might have supposed, but I say it is not size or magnitude which constitutes importance—*England* itself is a speck on the face of Europe.' 'My impression is', she wrote to the new Governor in a further letter, 'that you will find Labuan *a lever* for considerable objects.'

This impression coincided with the view of his tropical assignment which Governor Pope Hennessy had now decided to take. He had been confirmed in this view by the Duke of Buckingham in a final interview at the Colonial Office. 'I fear nothing can be worse than the financial state of Labuan', the Secretary of State confided. 'The greater part of its expenditure has to be voted every Session by a reluctant House of Commons. I can suggest no remedy to you. I give you however *carte blanche* to do whatever you think best on your own responsibility.' By then, Hennessy had begun to see Labuan as a personal challenge. He set off thither in the self-confident mood of the man in Kipling's *Naulahka* 'who tried to hustle the East'.

BOOK II

LABUAN

1867–1871

GOVERNOR POPE HENNESSY, his sister and his cousin, reached Singapore on 11 November 1867. In this thriving city, founded by Stamford Raffles almost fifty years earlier, they hoped to obtain transport to Labuan, which lies seven hundred miles to the north-east, out across the China Sea. In these penultimate days before the opening, in 1869, of the Suez Canal, eastward-bound travellers from Europe usually took the overland route from Alexandria to Suez; here Pope Hennessy's party had boarded the *Delhi*, a steamer of the Peninsular and Oriental Company's line, then noted for the civility and attentiveness of its cabin service, although the boats were ill-ventilated and the hatches reeked of the sweet, disquieting scent of opium. Having wound its way through the channel between the wooded islands of Singapore harbour entrance, the *Delhi* had tied up at the new P. & O. wharf early that morning, as the spire of the Cathedral of St Andrew, and the high-set Palladian mansions of the merchant princes on the hills behind the city were emerging from the steamy night-mists to face yet another stifling tropical day.

Later in the same morning, Governor Hennessy set off to pay his respects to the recently-arrived Governor-in-Chief of the Straits Settlements, Sir Harry Ord, who kept high state in his 'palace' in Singapore. The Straits Settlements—which comprised the island of Penang, with its avenues of rain-trees and of eighteenth-century houses, Province Wellesley, the charming tired old town of Malacca built by the Portuguese and the Dutch, and Singapore itself—had been reluctantly taken over by the Colonial Office from the India Office in the spring of 1867. Sir Harry Ord had been installed as Governor-in-Chief in April. With three Lieutenant-Governors serving under him, Ord's position formed an altogether enviable contrast to that of the Governor of Labuan, a flat island of only forty-five square miles in extent, off the coast of North-West Borneo.

The Colonial Office did not believe British possession of the three Straits Settlements—Province Wellesley forming an administrative unit with Penang—to be really necessary. They dreaded some consequent involvement in the affairs of the Malay Pennisula itself, that hinterland of mighty rivers and vast jungle forests. Little was then known about the Rajahs of the interior, save that they were autocratic and that they seemed constantly engaged in minor wars with one another. Scattered around in atap-roofed villages, their Muslim subjects pursued happy, indolent lives. The Malays' standard of courtesy and code of personal behaviour made the few Englishmen who had so far penetrated upriver into this twilit forest world feel like intruding boors. The Colonial Office staff rightly suspected that, sooner or later, the British Government would find itself bound to establish protectorates over these native states of the interior.

At this mid-way stage of British imperial development, Colonial policy was ill-defined and somewhat casual, but the general conviction in Downing Street was that we should not increase our Colonial commitments. This view was summed up in 1846 by Gladstone, then Secretary of State for the Colonies. Opposing the acquisition of Labuan, he had voiced a number of strong and logical objections to 'the multiplication of Colonies', his final argument being that 'we should learn to govern the Colonies we have before we acquire more'. Trade was popularly said to 'follow the Flag'; in fact it was more often the Flag which followed trade. 'Merchants press upon us new Settlements that they may try their own experiments', wrote a harassed member of the Colonial Office staff in 1856: 'it is unpopular to resist and we can always be inundated with evidence of the value of any spot on the Globe, or of its importance to national greatness—but after a time we are liable to find ourselves burthened with barren Islands like the Falklands or unhealthy jungles like Labuan.'

No sooner had he arrived in Singapore than Governor Hennessy began to make urgent enquiries as to how swiftly they could leave that city for Labuan. The result of these was discouraging. No boat was going to Labuan at the moment; in fact the Labuan community—consisting at this date of some thirty-odd Europeans, four thousand Borneans, Chinese and Malays, and a detachment of the 8th Regiment of the Madras Native Infantry—was, as usual, virtually isolated from the outside world. There was no telegraph cable to Labuan. There was no regular steamship service thither. Two sailing vessels plied monthly between Labuan and Singapore, carrying a little merchandise, European mails, out-of-date newspapers, and occasional adventurers who, having failed to make a living elsewhere in the

Straits Settlements or in Hong Kong, set off to try their luck in Labuan
as a counsel of despair. By steamer the journey took between four and
five days; by sailing ship you had to reckon on from one to three
weeks, dependent on the monsoon. Ships of the China Squadron,
based on Singapore, went to Labuan as seldom as possible, but
Governor Hennessy persuaded the naval authorities in Singapore to
give his party passages on HMS *Zebra* for the sum of sixty Straits
dollars, which he paid himself. They landed at Port Victoria, Labuan,
on the 20 November. Pope Hennessy was received in the Government
Offices by the Acting Governor, Mr Hugh Low, inspected a guard
of honour of one hundred men of the Madras Native Infantry commanded by Captain Maclean, took the oaths of office, and met the
assembled notables of the island. 'I found on my arrival', he reported,
'that the European residents were, with some few exceptions, in a state
of torpor and despondency.'

Can we wonder at this when we realise that several members of
this European community had been marooned upon Labuan for close
on twenty years?

II

In Labuan the months of November and December greet the newcomer with torrential rain, grey skies, a fierce dank heat and frequent
thunderstorms. The summits of the tremendous mountain ranges of
nearby Borneo are obscured by rain-clouds from the China Sea; the
land breezes waft these clouds down over Labuan in curtain upon
curtain of rain. It rains all night and every night. It has been known
to rain without stopping for two long weeks together. These were the
months in which one of Governor Hennessy's predecessors had complained that the public offices of Port Victoria could not be used,
since water seeped through the roofs to make puddles on the floor-
boards, and blew in through the open verandahs. The main road along
the harbour front—half a mile in length from these Government
Offices to the most westerly house—became perfectly impassable to
the few carriages kept on the island, and to the lumbering bullock-
carts. It was full of deep ruts and of pot-holes brimming with rain-
water, while heaps of decaying fruit-skins, cocoa-nut husks and fish-
heads awaited the unwary pedestrian. 'No attempt seemed to have
been made in the last twenty years to convert this place into a proper
roadway', Governor Hennessy reported soon after his arrival: 'and it
was with difficulty I was able to walk from one end to the other.'

Although he kept a couple of carriage ponies and 'a good horse for riding', Hennessy used these seldom. He went everywhere on foot: 'This climate', he wrote from Labuan, 'agrees well with Europeans provided they comply with two conditions—temperance and plenty of exercise.'

Before his departure from London, the new Governor had gathered as much available information about Labuan as he could. While not exactly misleading, gazetteer facts cannot be termed evocative. To learn, as he did, that Labuan lies six miles from Borneo and five degrees from the Equator, that in shape it is a triangle nine miles long and at its widest point five and a half miles across, conjures up no vivid mental picture of this low, hot, jungle land. Only the handful of people who had actually lived on Labuan and survived it could tell him what the island looked like; the permanent members of the Colonial Office staff had very vague ideas upon its aspect, while the Secretary of State had none at all. 'I shall be glad at all times of any information you can give me respecting your small government, its people, soil & other particulars, especially its buildings &c—,' the Duke of Buckingham wrote to Hennessy in a note of March 1868: 'I suppose photographers are not yet established there—or I shd ask for some views.'

Once he had reached Labuan, Hennessy adopted a valiant attitude to the island. He thought of it as 'about the same size as St Helena, but somewhat smaller', and recalled that, after all, it was larger than Hong Kong, Bermuda, the Gambia, Gibraltar or Heligoland. He even tried to convince himself that the notoriously unhealthy Labuan climate, the very mention of which made the citizens of Singapore shudder, was tolerable: 'it closely resembles that of the warm summer months in the South of Ireland', he reported—and what mattered a nocturnal rainfall of one hundred and sixty-six inches a year? Hennessy correctly described the island as 'extremely beautiful'.

In Labuan the midday light is blinding, and it seems hurled back into the sky by the glitter from the sea, and the stark, white, dusty surface of tracks and roads. This relentless glare, combined with a difficulty in breathing somewhat like that encountered when inhaling Friar's Balsam with a towel over one's head, is the stranger's first impression of Labuan. It is also Labuan's first and last assault; for once the shock to eyes and lungs is over, the intemperate beauty of the island shines before his eyes. The rice-fields and the mangrove swamps are a viridian green. The richness and the wildness of the tall, dense forests seem dissolute in their profusion. Black water-buffalo stand hock-deep in the swamp water, and along the roads and lanes of the island the houses of the Malays and Indians, square palm-thatched boxes, perch on stilts in glades of cocoa-nut and rubber trees, their rudimentary gardens patched with scarlet and chrome-yellow flowers. Big black and purple butterflies flop through the windless air. In the forests strident birds dart and cry.

Like most places within the tropics, Labuan is at its best in the very early morning, and, again, towards dusk. At these hours the island looks especially rural and idyllic; the untouched sand and translucent glassy water of the little coves along the southern coast round Ramsey Point surpass anything in the West Indian islands. At evening you can drive along one or other of the only two roads that cross the island, eastward or westward as you choose, and wander on the farther beaches, long and deserted, which front the China Sea. Here the tangled roots of trees stretch through the sand towards the water's edge. Beneath the cocoa-nut palms the ground is littered with dead husks and with the spiral shells, pointed like wimples, of land-snails. Mosquitoes sing happily over pools of stagnant water, a docile buffalo and its calf squelch through the mud; and under the trees, near a small stilted house, a young Malay woman wearing a cerise-coloured sarong may be lighting a fire in the hollow of a tree, while children with prune eyes and merry faces peer inquisitively at you from the shelter of the underbrush. By the roadside a shop with an open front, kept by some Chinese or Indian family, sells bananas and bright sweet bottled drinks. Along the beach the broken trunks of huge trees, grey and shrouded in seaweed, have drifted across the straits from the nearby forests of Borneo, which show dense and forbidding over the way.

Today Labuan can boast a small airstrip—partially constructed from the pounded brick foundations of old Government House, wrecked in the fighting of the Second World War—an agreeable Airport Hotel with air-conditioned bar and bedrooms, a new wharf and a string of ferro-concrete shops and offices along the waterfront of the minute port of Victoria. Yet the actual ethos of the island can have changed little in the last hundred years. There are now two metalled roads across Labuan, but hardly any motor-cars to use them. Out amongst the paddy-fields stand houses of the precise type recorded by Victorian travellers such as Lady Brassey. There are even examples of old wooden European dwellings—all shingle roofs, and fretwork gables and verandahs—which seem somehow to have survived the

Labuan climate and to have successfully withstood the rains of eighty years. It is thus not difficult to visualise Labuan as it appeared in the 'sixties of the last century, nor, indeed, the kind of life the Europeans out there led.

While somewhat exceptional in their isolation, the torpid and despondent British residents on Labuan had at any rate one characteristic in common with the members of other British communities in the East: they quite sincerely believed themselves to be superior to the people whom they governed. They waited hungrily for mails from home and they lived to go on leave. The men sought consolation in liaisons with native girls, who brought them new responsibilities in the shape of half-caste children, and they found fresh strength in the clink of the brandy decanter against the tumbler, forming alcoholic habits which brought them hepatitis and chronic inflammation of the liver. They believed that they were resisting the tropics, whereas it was the tropics which were resisting them; no sooner, for instance, was a tract of Labuan jungle cleared than a secondary growth sprang up, to become in its turn a pestiferous swamp. The frame houses of the Europeans stood at the mercy of the rain, the white ant and the carpenter-bee. At least two forms of virulent fever were rampant in the island, and, in the first days of the settlement, the gravediggers were kept as busy as the convicts who felled the giant camphor-trees. In those earliest days a colleague or a crony with whom you had been cheerfully drinking on your verandah on one evening might quite likely be dead and buried on the next. Even the Anglican Bishop of Labuan hardly ever visited his diocese, preferring to live outside British territory—in the busy little river-town, Kuching, capital of Rajah Brooke's Kingdom, Sarawak.

III

The uninhabited island of Labuh-an—as purists amongst the first British settlers there spelled the name—had become British territory in December 1846. This was as the result of a treaty signed on board HMS *Iris*, lying off Labuan, by Captain Mundy, RN, representing Queen Victoria, and by a Malay nobleman, one Pangiran Munim, deputising for his cousin, the weak-minded, ugly old Sultan of Brunei, who had pleaded that sea-sickness precluded his coming to Labuan to sign the treaty himself. The terms of this Treaty were threefold: the first clause proclaimed eternal friendship between the Queen and the Sultan of Brunei; the second gave the British Crown possession of the island of Labuan in perpetuity; the third consisted of a promise by the British Government that, in return, they would undertake to patrol the Sultan's territorial waters, and to protect his subjects in their upriver settlements from the raids of the native pirates who were ruining Brunei's trade.

The British Government's decision to take over Labuan had come suddenly, after many months of laborious discussions between the Foreign Office, the Colonial Office, the Treasury and the Admiralty. The idea of turning Labuan into a British Colony had originated in the romantic mind of James Brooke, who was simultaneously engaged in obtaining for himself sovereign rights over the Sultan of Brunei's territory of Sarawak, of which he soon became the first White Rajah. Brooke had found support over Labuan amongst the merchant community of Singapore, as well as, more significantly, in the City of London and in Manchester; for a seam of coal had been identified upon Labuan, and it was believed that, properly exploited, this would prove commercially profitable, while at the same time converting the island, with its fine natural harbour, into a convenient coaling station for the China Fleet and for mercantile steamships plying the trade of the China Sea. Deceptive analogies between the islands of Singapore and Hong Kong on the one hand, and of Labuan on the other, had been drawn by those who urged the Labuan settlement. These enthusiasts overlooked a cardinal fact: that although the prosperous cities of Singapore and of Hong Kong had indeed been created by the British, both places had always had villages of native fishing people. No natives—fisherfolk or otherwise—had ever dreamed of living on Labuan. In the Malay language the name means 'Beautiful Harbour', but the subjects of the Sultan of Brunei were well aware that from time immemorial Labuan had been a beautiful and pestilential swamp. The Sultan Omar Ali of Brunei, who had indulged in much wily prevarication before the actual signature of the 1846 treaty, must have known quite well that he was getting the best of the bargain. He had sent over a flock of ornate Brunei notables to attend the hoisting of the Union Jack upon the island on 24 December 1846. This unfurling of the British flag upon Labuan automatically brought with it the posting of a guard there night and day. A small wooden guardhouse for the Marines was erected near the flagstaff by the sea-shore. This was the first house built on Labuan as a British Crown Colony.

'Labuan, its dependencies and islets, are now part and parcel of the

British dominions', a Singapore merchant wrote in January 1847 to a friend in London who was financially interested in the Eastern Archipelago Company, a questionable concern with insufficient capital which had been floated in the City to exploit Labuan coal: '. . . HM ship *Wolf* is at Labuan; her commander, Gordon, died and is buried there. . . . The crew of the vessels suffered considerably from some unknown cause, probably from eating too much fruit and cucumber, which the Jacks are too prone to do when opportunities offer.' 'The *Columbine* and *Nemesis* are at Labuan', he wrote again, later in the year. '. . . The crew of the former has been very sickly. I suspect reports have been submitted home, ascribing the sickness to the insalubrity of the island.'

Amongst the reports submitted home had been the health return of the ship's company of HMS *Columbine* for the spring months of 1847, which showed that 'jungle fever', diarrhoea, and a fatal disease during the course of which the body broke out into a mass of suppurating nodules, were rife amongst the ratings of *Columbine*, many of whom had died. *Columbine's* surgeon, Mr Campbell, attributed this sickness to the 'peculiarly unhealthy' climate of Labuan. 'The island', he wrote, 'is covered with forest jungle, with the exception of a small swampy plain occupying about 300 acres, on which water is stagnant, long rank luxuriant grass grows in profusion . . . at the back part begins a dense jungle of large trees, growing in a swampy soil, impenetrable from thick underwood, from which a body of water at one point comes into the plain. . . . After a few days dry weather the greater part of the water disappears, some remains stagnant and a large portion of the channel through which it sluggishly flows is left covered with vegetable matter exposed to the action of the sun. . . . Rain is frequent, particularly at night, during nearly every one of which it falls in torrents and does not cease until towards daylight, soon after which the sun comes out causing a noxious and pestiferous exhalation from the adjacent swamp and jungle, to which may be added that emanating from the decomposing bodies of myriads of insects destroyed by the heavy rain.' This report was submitted by the Admiralty to the Colonial Office, where it caused some dismay. However, the treaty with Brunei had now been signed and it was too late to withdraw from its commitments. Plans for the civilian settlement of the island, and for the opening up of the coal seams, were well under way.

In November 1847 Queen Victoria had signed the warrant appointing James Brooke first Governor of Labuan. He was at the same time given the post of Her Majesty's Consul-General for Borneo, with the duty of looking after British trading interests in the Sultanate of Brunei and Dutch Borneo. After Brooke's resignation in 1854 the Consul-Generalship was separated from the Labuan Government. In 1867 the two jobs were once again combined, with the object of giving Governor Pope Hennessy a modest Foreign Office salary to add to his Colonial Office stipend.

James Brooke had set sail for Singapore and Labuan in February 1848, travelling on HMS *Maeander*, a frigate uncomfortably converted into a passenger vessel for this voyage. He was accompanied by his Lieutenant-Governor, William Napier, the latter's wife, two daughters and baby boy, as well as by a young London botanist, Hugh Low, who had just published the first book written on Sarawak. Other members of the party included a competent engineer named Scott, and certain other civilian volunteers destined to be the first European colonists on Labuan.

The voyage of *Maeander* was, in Brooke's own words, 'speedy but somewhat disastrous'. Soon after the ship had left Cork Harbour, the Napiers' youngest child was found dead in its cot. William Napier was one of the nine sons of Walter Scott's friend Macvey Napier, editor of the *Edinburgh Review*. He had followed a brother out to the Straits Settlements, and began by living in Malacca. When Singapore was founded, the Napier brothers had proceeded thither, where they made fortunes in land-conveyancing. They had commissioned their friend Thomas Coleman, the distinguished architect of the new city, to build them two fine country houses on the hills behind it. It was a moment, in Singapore, when money was easy to make. Coleman himself was growing rich, when, in 1844, he suddenly died. In October of the same year his well-off widow married William Napier, a bachelor who already had a fifteen-year-old daughter born of his liaison with a Malacca lady of Malayan blood. This daughter, christened Catherine but known as 'Kate', celebrated her nineteenth birthday on board *Maeander* and shortly afterwards became engaged to the young botanist from Clapton, Hugh Low. Married at 'a cheery wedding' in Singapore in August 1848, Kate Low followed her husband to Labuan, where she died of jungle fever in 1851 at the age of twenty-two.

So soon as *Maeander* had reached Singapore, Brooke and his companions busied themselves with final preparations for settling on Labuan. Prefabricated wooden houses were constructed and sent across to the island with an advance party to erect them. At the end of

September Brooke himself arrived in Labuan to be sworn in as Governor. He found the Colony and its inhabitants in a miserable state. The little houses had been set up on an unhealthy plain close to the sea-shore, but below sea-level; more marines had died, and several of the other Europeans were gravely ill. By late November the whole colony was down with fever. Governor Brooke himself seemed to be on his deathbed, and his young medical attendant, Dr Treacher, was almost as bad. It was now decided to shift the wooden huts to higher ground, 'where they ought to have been from the beginning'. Some improvement in the health of the Europeans resulted; but the Colony of Labuan had got off to a bad start. It was already gaining a sinister reputation as a plague-spot. Singapore, in particular, was swept by what one of its leading newspapers described as 'an insane panic' over Labuan: 'an insane panic caused by the appearance of a local fever, common enough in new tropical localities, and readily removeable by drainage and ventilation'.

Insane or not, the panic was widespread, affecting Chinese as well as European immigration to the island, for the Chinese, a people as prudent about their health as about their money, had discovered that they seemed even more susceptible to the fever than were Europeans. In later years a small though prosperous Chinese trading community did develop upon Labuan, but in these earliest days the native merchants of Borneo and the Straits Settlements preferred to wait and see whether the fetid swamp-lands round Port Victoria, Labuan, could really be made healthy by drainage before risking their own lives and those of their families in the new Crown Colony.

IV

From the very start, Labuan was ill-administered. In September 1849 Captain Harry Keppel, of HMS *Maeander*, described Sir James Brooke's Government as 'a mis-shapen, useless structure'. 'And what a selection!' he wrote. 'My friend Brooke has as much idea of *business* as a Cow has of a clean shirt, Napier is no better, and although a fairish Proctor while at Singapore, his head is completely turned where he is, he is so entirely eaten up with his own importance that he can attend to nothing else.' Napier pursued squatters with a 'ridiculous zeal', and demanded such exorbitant rents for plots of uncleared land that prospective settlers were deterred from building. 'In fact under his administration the island is already made ridiculous and will, very shortly, be altogether ruined', wrote the first manager of the Labuan coal-mine, who was himself incompetent and soon took to drink.

The coal-mine, situated at Tanjong Kubong on the northernmost point of the island, had quickly proved a disappointment to its London lessors, the Eastern Archipelago Company. The seam of coal was genuine enough, but it ran in a ravine through the primeval jungle. Small quantities of it were tried out in ships of various nationalities: the general verdict was that Labuan coal burned more quickly than Welsh coal, made much more smoke, and was badly hewn and badly washed. For some years there was no road to link Tanjong Kubong and Victoria, the sole means of communication being by rowing-boat along the coast, which was dangerous after dark and expensive in rough weather. The European miners were neither a contented nor a respectable community, and allegedly suffered from 'moral and social evils' arising from 'the disparity of the sexes at Coal Point'. By 1860 the coal-mines wore such a desolate air that the survivors from a large ship, the *Fiery Cross*, wrecked that April in the China Sea, thought, when they landed at Coal Point from a lifeboat, that they had reached an uninhabited island. In 1868 the Eastern Archipelago Company went into liquidation.

Since the Eastern Archipelago Company had made no money, it had paid no royalties to the Government of Labuan, which thus remained dependent on a Parliamentary Grant. In Downing Street Labuan was already regarded as an embarrassment and a burden; from time to time, inside the Colonial Office, it was even suggested that the best solution of the Labuan problem would be to leave the island altogether. Hearsay knowledge of this defeatist proposal only added to the deep sense of frustration felt by those victims of Labuan, its successive Governors.

The first Governor of Labuan, Sir James Brooke, left the administration of the Crown Colony to a deputy—initially to the Lieutenant-Governor, William Napier, and after his dismissal to the Surveyor-General, John Scott. William Napier had quarrelled with every member of the small European community on Labuan, and had finally come to grief for disobeying Brooke's explicit instructions in the case of a young half-caste adventurer from Singapore, who occupied an official post as Napier's salaried clerk. This youth, whose name was Meldrum, had bought a dram shop in Victoria, and had engaged in trade, activities naturally enough forbidden to Government servants. Napier, obsessed by his youthful employee, sanctioned this irregularity and even lent Meldrum money; as a result he was suspended from his position as Lieutenant-Governor by Brooke and subsequently dismissed by the Secretary of State. The Surveyor, Scott, succeeded him, becoming, on Brooke's resignation in October 1854, the second Governor of Labuan. In 1856 Scott, who after nine long years on Labuan developed a chronic liver complaint, was promoted to be Governor of Natal; the Hon. George Edwardes, a retired Household Cavalry officer and a third son of Lord Kensington, was chosen to succeeed him in Labuan. Dismissed in 1860 after a tempestuous four-year term of office, Edwardes was followed as Governor by a Colonial servant from Hong Kong, Mr Callaghan, who soon became ill and, quitting Labuan on sick leave in 1866, did not return. Callaghan was Pope Hennessy's immediate predecessor.

These were still the days of patronage, although the theory that Colonial Governorships should properly be given to men who had proved themselves efficient public officers within the Colonial Service was very slowly gaining ground. The first twenty-five years of Labuan's history shows the two systems running concurrently. Of the four men sent out to govern the Colony between 1854 and 1871 two—Scott and Callaghan—were experienced Colonial servants, and two—Edwardes and Pope Hennessy—were appointed from the Private Patronage ledger, called within the Colonial Office 'the Secretary of State's list'. In other words, Labuan, during this period, was governed twice by professionals and twice by amateurs.

John Pope Hennessy had no doubt heard enough of the case-histories of Labuan's Governors to justify his reluctance to take up his post. Quite apart from the question of health and climate, there was a deadening monotony about life on Labuan, where European society was as restricted as at the Captain's table of some small passenger schooner. Aimless and demoralising, it induced acute melancholia and created hectic squabbles. By the time of his dismissal in 1849, William Napier, for instance, had ceased to be on speaking-terms with any other European on the island, including his own son-in-law. His successor, Scott, was less hysterical but wrote uniformly querulous despatches to the Secretary of State: these dealt with the incidence of dysentery, with rheumatism, with remittent as well as intermittent fever, with the high death-rate and the 'intemperance' at the sepoy barracks, with the inertia of the Coal Company and with the extravagant freight charges from Singapore. Scott concentrated what energies he could muster on building: he replaced the shacks of Port Victoria with 'structures of a more durable kind' and erected for himself and his wife 'one of the finest and most spacious Government Houses in the East'. The next Governor, Edwardes, reported that Scott had neglected land drainage, so that the jungle had 'regained possession of the plain', and that fever was once more raging. 'In the present state of the Victoria District', wrote Edwardes, 'the strongest may fall at any time.—With the mind distressed or the body afflicted from any cause no one can be safe from Fever.'

Governor Edwardes, described by a friend within the Colonial Office as 'a man of the world, possessing polished manners' soon found himself at loggerheads with a number of his subordinates on Labuan, chief amongst them the Surveyor-General, a bouncing young man of twenty-nine called St John, in whom he induced a kind of persecution-mania and who complained of him to the Secretary of State in London. Inside the Colonial Office the Governor's conduct towards St John was considered 'monstrous' and 'singularly unjust and tyrannical'. Edwardes's disputes with his subordinates created a bad impression in Downing Street; and when he embarked on a public quarrel with the Brookes of Sarawak he was recalled.

The reign of Edwardes's successor, Governor Callaghan, was calmer, although one of his first actions on reaching Labuan from Hong Kong was to apply for six months' leave of absence in England, so that he could be married there. This 'embarrassing application' met with a refusal: 'There was little use in sending him to Labuan if he is at once to come home again', minuted the Permanent Under-Secretary at the Colonial Office, Sir Frederic Rogers.

This, then, was the history of Labuan and its Governors up to the moment of my grandfather's appointment to that place. It was a Colony with hardly any past and, seemingly, no future; its European inhabitants lived there in a state of nervous stagnation, cut off from most ties with the outside world. The absence of a telegraph cable, together with the fact that it took despatches six or seven weeks to reach London or to be received from thence meant that if a Governor or Administrator chose to act tyrannically he could so do with some impunity. Any complaint from a subordinate about his actions could only be submitted to the Secretary of State for the Colonies through the Governor himself. If such complaints were detailed and lengthy, so became the Governor's written defence: and thus it came about that the overworked staff in Downing Street were sometimes faced with page after page of manuscript, copied out in an elaborate oriental hand by the confidential clerk, and dealing with such important questions as to whether the young Surveyor-General had or had not given Governor Edwardes's pony 'a sharp hasty blow' while His Excellency was inspecting a cocoa-nut plantation. The climate, the isolation, the general sense of purposelessness made the Labuan community tense and obsessive. Gossip was rife, and quarrels were frequent. 'One of the unpleasant personal disputes which from time to time reach us from the smaller Colonies, and of which the Islands in the China Sea appear at the present time to be specially productive' ran a typical Colonial Office comment on a typical Labuan row not long before Pope Hennessy's appointment to the Colony. Energy, suavity and detachment were the qualities most needed in a Governor of such a place as Labuan. Pope Hennessy had two of these.

———————

A T FIRST, all went well on Labuan under the new régime. To the young Governor it must have seemed like a repetition of his initial successes in the House of Commons. His self-confidence grew.

Pope Hennessy lost no time in putting into practice his own theories of Colonial policy. These were but tenuously related to the official views of Downing Street, or to the way the Crown Colony had hitherto been run; but since the old system had produced no results and had brought the colonists neither prosperity nor even a sense of purpose, the Colonial Office were prepared to wait and see: 'Mr Hennessy seems very active, but I shd. like to wait & see what his activity comes to', Sir Frederic Rogers noted on a Labuan despatch in April 1868. A year later Rogers was less sceptical: 'I really begin to think Mr Hennessy as capable a man as he thinks himself' he minuted on another Labuan report. 'Sir Frederic', scrawled his chief, Lord Granville, beneath this comment, 'grows rash.'

In a series of laudatory articles on Labuan affairs, the *Straits Times* (the main English-language newspaper of the Archipelago) lavished praise on Governor Hennessy for the 'immense stimulus' he was giving the stagnant little Colony. The newspaper especially congratulated him on being 'quick to discover' the 'talisman of success in eastern colonisation'—the value of resident Chinese traders in any Colonial community. In the speech he made at the swearing-in ceremony on the day he landed, Governor Hennessy had gone out of his way to refer to 'that industrious population, the Chinese'. At this time the Chinese community on Labuan was probably no larger than five or six hundred persons. Amongst these were several wealthy merchants, who traded with Brunei and owned sago manufactories. Others were shopkeepers, others again were employed as clerks or servants. The Europeans on the island regarded them as useful though inferior beings; the only concession so far made to them had been to grant them five acres of land for a Chinese Burial Ground. Chinese and Klings had incessantly petitioned the Labuan Government to let them establish and financially support a hospital for their sick; but nothing had been done. Similarly there was no Chinese school, just as there was no wharf at Victoria Harbour, no proper fish or fruit market, and no well for supplying fresh water to the town. All these defects Pope Hennessy decided to remedy in one fell, spectacular swoop.

When he had been on Labuan for just over one month the new Governor ordered a public celebration of the twenty-first anniversary of the Colony's acquisition. This anniversary fell on Christmas Eve 1867. Governor Pope Hennessy began the day by liberating a dozen prisoners from the gaol—a favourite gesture, which, together with his strong disapproval of flogging and of the death penalty, led him later to be accused of 'a diseased sympathy with criminals'. From the prison the little Governor went in a procession 'composed principally of the Chinese and native inhabitants' to the site for a Chinese school. Here he laid a foundation stone, and proceeded onward to the water-front where he drove two stakes into the beach—one to indicate the site of a wharf to be named Albert Wharf after the Prince Consort, and the other to mark the position of the projected fish-market to be hygienically built on piles over the sea-water, with sufficient space at each side for the sale of fruit. He also turned the first sod on the site of a proposed freshwater well. The party then trooped back to the Government Offices 'which were decorated with flags, several tables were found spread with an ample *déjeuner*, at which the Governor and Miss Hennessy entertained all the officials, the inhabitants of Coal Point, and the principal inhabitants of Victoria, Chinese and Malay'.

After loyal toasts and the singing of songs, the Governor invited all his guests to another party that very evening. It was the first occasion in the Crown Colony's history that Chinese, Malays and Indians had been asked to a Government House party. This innovation was one small but signal proof of the new Governor's firm belief in racial equality.

II

Government House, Labuan, in which Governor Hennessy received every morning from seven till ten o'clock, and his sister Mary was 'at home' on Wednesdays and Saturdays from twelve till three, no longer exists. Its elegantly planted English park is now a mess of secondary jungle growth, and the semi-circular carriage drive, which led up to the house from one gate on the North Road and back again to a further one, is bumpy and overgrown. In its heyday British travellers compared the Labuan Government House to 'an old-fashioned West Indian planter's residence of the best class'.

Completed in 1854, six years after the initial settlement of Labuan, the house replaced the dilapidated native structure of palm mats and thatch in which the first Governors of Labuan had lived. New 'GH' was sited on a piece of slightly rising ground one and a quarter miles inland from Port Victoria, and just below the military cantonment. Since no good building stone was available on Labuan, the house was made of wood on brick foundations. To obtain the necessary bricks a local brickyard and kilns had been set up by a Singapore speculator who lost his money and later died of Labuan fever. The bricks were of clay, trodden by buffaloes, and were not of good quality.

Far superior to any other building on Labuan at that date, and reckoned one of the finest Government Houses in the Archipelago, the new building may have been the expression of an earlier Governor's optimism—or merely of his lack of occupation. In any case neither money, labour nor ingenuity had been spared. The main features of the house were a neat carriage porch, a trellised verandah ten feet wide running all round the building and supported by no less than one hundred and fourteen carved posts, two very large drawing-rooms and an impressive dining-room which could seat forty persons. A wing contained five big bedrooms, each with its own bathroom connecting with it by a private stair. The brick foundations, which raised the house four feet above the ground, were plastered and painted white. The exterior of the building was of white-painted weather-boarding, the roof was tiled, there were several gables with ornamental 'pendants' and more of these pendants decorated the verandah. The windows opened outwards and were 'Venetian' or slatted. Walls and ceilings of all the main rooms, including the bedrooms, were panelled in polished redwood, and the heavy redwood doors had mouldings on both sides and were finished with finely wrought brass locks and handles. The cook-house, servants' sleeping-rooms, stables and other offices at the back were of native construction.

Successive Governors had complained that the furnishing of the house was sparse, although this is hardly the impression we derive from the lists of furniture—much of it second-hand—which they would compile for the Colonial Office to prove that more was wanted. Rattan mats covered the floors, lamps and punkahs were suspended from the ceilings. The three-piece dining-room table was of redwood, as were several other circular tables, sofa-tables, bookstands and music-tables. There were quantities of ottomans, armchairs, easy chairs, bamboo chairs, satinwood chairs, maraboo couches, and 'whatnots'. In the chief drawing-room hung that important adjunct of tropical life—a standard thermometer.

In 1864 Pope Hennessy's immediate predecessor as Governor, Mr Callaghan, had reported that all this furniture was 'quite shabby and unsuitable ... the reception rooms still remain in a very unfurnished condition as regards the most necessary articles'. He was allowed to spend one hundred pounds on further couches and chairs, on chintz for the sofas, on cushions and on ten hanging lamps with self-adjusting chains. The permanent staff of the Colonial Office did not take social life on Labuan too seriously. One of them underlined the words 'reception rooms' in Callaghan's application, and cynically queried in the margin: 'to receive *whom*?' In January 1868, seven weeks after Pope Hennessy's arrival, he in turn proposed to spend a sum of money 'absolutely required to render the building habitable for the present'.

My grandfather seems to have found no difficulty in filling the rooms of Government House with guests. At the end of his term on Labuan he told the Secretary of State for the Colonies that he thought the next Governor's salary should be raised. As there was no hotel on the island all visitors had to stay at Government House: 'I have had the honour of receiving under my roof at the same time, the Admiral on the station and his family, and the officer in command of a new detachment of Troops and his family; and on looking through my household accounts, I see that in nine days I spent on unavoidable entertainments more than two months' salary.'

Admitted even by his enemies to be a considerate and charming host, my grandfather was very hospitable and liked entertaining. The anniversary party on Christmas Eve 1867 was the first which he and his sister supervised at Government House. The *Straits Times* reported that the house was 'brilliantly illuminated', and the rooms 'crowded—for the first time in the history of Labuan—with Chinese and other Oriental costumes as well as with the whole of the European community'. There was 'an abundance of good things in the way of eating and drinking; a small military band was stationed in one of the verandahs, and dancing was kept up till a late hour'.

This gathering, with its novel feature of Orientals welcomed on an equal footing with the other guests, seems to give us a good opportunity to acquaint ourselves cursorily with some of the personalities of Labuan.

III

In 1867 the total population of the island of Labuan was thought to number between three and four thousand persons, the great majority being Borneo people—Mooruts, Dusuns and Kyans—with some Malays from the Straits Settlements, six hundred Chinese, a group of Indian stallkeepers, and about forty Europeans. These last included the handful of officials who administered the Colony.

Acting under the Governor's orders, these colonial servants were also at his mercy. The Governor could promote them or suspend them. He could switch their jobs and increase or curtail their salaries. His decisions had ultimately to be confirmed by the Secretary of State in London, but London was a long way off; and the Colonial Office liked to support a Governor's decision whenever they could decently do so. Except that the Governor of Labuan did not have the usual Executive Council to advise him, and that the Legislative Council was absurdly small, Labuan was in every other way a microcosm of any British Crown Colony of that day.

The European community fell into certain distinct and conventional categories. First came the officials, with the Governor at their head. Then came the Services—the military represented by three or four European officers in charge of the detachments of Indian or Malay or Singalese troops which might be stationed on the island as a nominal defence against attack; and the Navy, represented by the officers and men of the gunboat HMS *Leven* patrolling the Borneo coast. The spiritual needs of the few Christians on Labuan were taken care of by the Anglican Colonial Chaplain, and by a Spanish Catholic priest, who had been despatched thither from Manila in 1857 with the impressive title of 'Apostolic Prefect for Micronesia and Melanesia'. Medical men who strove to preserve life on this unhealthy island comprised the Colonial Surgeon, who had an Apothecary to aid him; the Military Assistant Surgeon attached to the troops in the Cantonment; a Naval Surgeon on board the gunboat; and a civilian doctor paid by the Coal Company to cope with the ailments and excesses of the miners at Coal Point. There was also, in 1867, the remaining staff of the bankrupt Coal Company, who, like their miners, lived on the northern tip of the island, at Tanjong Kubong, now linked to Victoria by a jungle road eight miles long.

All, or almost all, of these gentlemen (and the wives and daughters of those who had any) were disporting themselves in the lofty redwood reception rooms of Government House that evening of December 1867, until in the damp and warm small hours of Christmas Day, the Governor's aide-de-camp, Lieutenant Cherry, gave the infantry band on the verandah the signal to terminate the entertainment by playing *God Save the Queen*. As, exchanging merry greetings on that Christmas morning long ago, they depart homewards down the curving drive of Government House in their carriages, on horseback or on foot, we shall try to identify some of their faces by the light of the tropical moon.

We may first approach two men waiting in the carriage porch for a young girl who has gone to find her cape. One of these men, whose sunken cheeks and white side-whiskers give him a premature air of great age, is John Treacher, the Colonial Surgeon of Labuan, a doctor more physically infirm than the majority of his patients. The other gentleman, whose hair, moustache and drooping whiskers are of dark luxuriant growth, is Mr Hugh Low, the Colonial Treasurer, oriental linguist and expert on the fauna and flora of the island. For Dr Treacher and for Mr Low the day's anniversary ceremonies will have held a special and nostalgic interest, for they are the last representatives in Labuan of the original European colonists who settled there in 1848. But Dr Treacher and Mr Low have much more than their memories in common. They are co-owners of the offshore plantation islet of Daat, which lies between Labuan and Borneo; and on Labuan itself Dr Treacher now boards with Mr Low, living in a small detached bungalow in his twelve-acre garden. Mr Hugh Low's garden is famous throughout the Archipelago for the beauty and the rarity of its shrubs, flowers and plants. It also contains, screened by a clump of orange trees, a tombstone which marks an European grave.

When the girl for whom they have been waiting steps into the circle of light cast by the oil lanterns of Government House porch, we see that, slim and graceful, she has long raven-dark hair and piercing, pale grey eyes. This is Mr Hugh Low's only daughter, Kitty. In October of this same year, 1867, she has celebrated in Labuan, in her father's house near the coral sea-shore, her seventeenth birthday.

We shall see more of Kitty Low, and in no distant future; for she must already be aware, and with a pleasant sense of conquest, that at this ball she has captivated the most important personage upon the whole island of Labuan—the bachelor Governor himself.

IV

During the year-long interregnum between the departure of Governor Callaghan from Labuan in November 1866, and the arrival of Governor Pope Hennessy in 1867, Hugh Low had administered the Colony. It was the third time that he had acted as stand-in for an absent Governor, and he was justified in having expected that he would have been given the full position himself. Without any influential friends at home to press his claims upon the Secretary of State, Low found that he was once more passed over, and this time in favour of a much younger man who knew no Eastern language, was quite ignorant of the Orient, and had obtained his appointment through an exercise of political patronage of the most blatant kind. An honourable and high-minded public servant, Low was human enough to feel angry disappointment and, no doubt, its ally, jealousy.

Years afterwards, as British Resident in the jungles of Perak, Hugh Low was instrumental in creating the Federated Malay States, for he had an intuitional understanding of the oriental mind as well as 'the gift of creative genius which only a few administrators possess'. To this day his name is legendary in Malaya; but on Labuan in 1867 he was merely Colonial Treasurer and Police Magistrate, a man chafing with resentment at the Colonial Office's neglect. As an official of the Crown Colony of twenty years' standing, he would naturally distrust Governor Hennessy's innovations, for they formed in fact an open criticism of the policy which he himself had long upheld. It was repeated to Governor Hennessy that one of his predecessors had declared that Low 'would sooner poison a Governor than see him improving the Colony'; and though this characteristic piece of Labuan hearsay was not necessarily true, it should have served the new Governor as a warning to tread warily with Mr Low.

When Governor Hennessy took over from him, Low and his daughter retired from Government House, where they had been living for the last year, to their own house some two miles west of the shack-town of Victoria, and not far from the sea-shore and the gaol. Low was an erudite naturalist and botanist, endowed with 'a constant sense of beauty' and 'a love of watching things grow'. His garden was the finest on Labuan, and he was responsible for many beautiful plantations and vistas in the island, including the 'miniature English park' round Government House. He was also interested in economic forestry, and in the cultivation of tropical fruit-trees; the pomolos, mangoes and mangosteens he grew on Labuan were considered the most luscious in the Archipelago. He had a private aquarium and a tropical aviary, as well as important collections of sea-shells, butterflies and moths, snake-skins and stuffed animals. In Labuan, as later in Malaya, he kept pet monkeys in his house. He preferred the company of Malays to that of Europeans, and of his pet animals to either. He once wrote to his daughter Kitty that he loved only two creatures in the world—his wah-wah monkey, Eblis, and herself.

In the spring of 1867, the year of Hennessy's appointment, Kitty Low had 'come out from home' to join her father, who was a widower. Her mother who, we may remember, was the Eurasian daughter of Labuan's first Lieutenant-Governor William Napier, had died of the fever in 1851 after three years on Labuan. At her death she was only twenty-two. She left her husband, who was four years older, with two small children, a boy and a girl. These infants were sent home to the family of Low's brother, the part-owner with his father of an old-established and extensive nursery garden in the then rural London suburb of Clapton. In twenty years of life on Labuan, Hugh Low had only been back to England once, and that was for twelve months' sick leave in 1861.

Hugh Low had every reason to feel aggrieved at his present situation and at his salary of five hundred pounds a year. Both in Labuan and inside the Colonial Office, he was recognised as an able and experienced public officer, as well as a good oriental linguist. Born in Clapton in 1824, he had been educated privately and then trained as a botanist, making his first expedition to the East in search of orchids at the age of nineteen. In Singapore, or possibly in Borneo, he had fallen in with James Brooke, who engaged the young man as his secretary and took him out to Labuan as one of the first settlers in 1848. Before sailing on the *Maeander* with Brooke, Napier and their companions, Low had completed and published his book *Sarawak, Its Inhabitants and Productions*, a far less ponderous work than its title suggests, containing much sensitive, accurate yet picturesque description of the Borneo jungle. The book likewise reveals the gentle, humorous and diligent character of its author. The shimmering domain of tropical nature had been the first love of his youth. He loved it still.

Perhaps from fidelity to his dead wife's memory, perhaps from lack

of opportunity, Low had not married again. He had buried his wife in
the garden of his house, in a grove of orange trees, for at the period in
which she had died of fever the Christian cemetery at Labuan was
raided after nightfall by the headhunters of the Borneo mainland, who
would dig up the bodies of the newly-buried to hack off their heads.
The graveyard was railed in, locked and guarded; new graves were
filled with broken glass; but nothing would deter the eager native
amateurs of European heads. It was Low's natural anxiety to save his
young wife's corpse from desecration and her skull from joining those
which hung, shells in their eye-sockets, from the rafters of the long-
houses on the mainland, that made him determine to bury her secretly
in his own garden near his house. There is no longer any trace of Kate
Low's gravestone on Labuan, but the story of her burial, which had
passed into island folk-lore, is preserved in a short story by that
admirable writer, Sir Hugh Clifford, entitled *A Tale of Old Labuan*.
Low's brief marriage seems to have been idyllic, if we can conceive of
an idyll on a fever-ridden swamp. Small wonder that he had wished to
rule Labuan or to leave it, since Labuan had taken first his happiness
and then his youth.

In 1867 Low was forty-three, a man of medium height with abun-
dant glossy dark hair, parted at the right side, kept long and curling at
the neck, but brushed back in a wave from his sloping and intelligent
brow. His nose was rather hawk-like, his eyes sagacious but too weak
to permit him to write by lamplight. Long Dundreary whiskers
flowed to his coat collar. He habitually wore sponge-bag trousers of a
thin material, a dark cutaway coat and, in the sun, a high-crowned
Homburg hat.

Hugh Low was happiest gently trapping some new, brilliantly-
coloured tropical fish for his aquarium, collecting on the slopes of
Mount Kinibalu rare azaleas and unknown orchids for his garden,
watching the loud flight of the giant hornbills of Borneo, or despatch-
ing his native servants to the coast of Brunei to catch butterflies with
nets they made themselves from muslin he supplied. Always inquisitive
about the tropic world he was determined to penetrate its every secret.
On one occasion on Labuan an European couple who had crossed to
an offshore islet hoping to start a cocoa-nut plantation 'abandoned it
after a few nights saying that the place was haunted by demons, and
that it was impossible to endure their cries, moans and screams which
lasted the whole night through'. Low immediately repaired to this
island 'and' he tells us, 'heard the screams during the moonlight night

without being able to identify them, until by accident a bird uttered its cry quite close to me in the daytime, and rushing to the spot I put up a menambun which had just come out from the burrow of its nest'.

Lest we should too much incline to picture Hugh Low as the Gilbert White of Labuan we may here briefly mention that, in 1867, he had at least one other daughter on the island. This nine-year-old child and her mother, a Sarawak lady who was known as Nona Dyang Loya, lived in a native house standing in its own compound at Sagumau on the Coal Point Road, which ran northwards to the colliery at Tanjong Kubong. The house belonged to Hugh Low, and there he would visit the mother and child, whom he supported from motives which he termed those of 'honour and justice and duty'. Such irregular unions between Malay women and Europeans were widely recognised throughout the Archipelago, and the courtesy title 'Nona' was accorded to these ladies by natives and Europeans alike. Dyang Loya lived peacefully with her mother and her daughter in the Sagumau house: 'In the evenings it was a common thing for the family to play on rebanas as they recited pantuns to each other.'* On other evenings the Nona and her friends would enliven the tropical night with the silvery sound of tambourines. Neither Hugh Low, nor anyone else who had lived long on Labuan, could imagine that the existence of this contented little household at Sagumau would one day be used against him.

To sum up, the Colonial Treasurer and Police Magistrate of Labuan may well have been embittered, but he remained a sensitive, well-instructed and highly original man. None of these three epithets could be applied to his close friend and tenant the Colonial Surgeon, Dr John Gavaron Treacher.

v

As well as being Colonial Surgeon of Labuan, Dr John Treacher was a Magistrate and the Senior Member of the Legislative Council. Once upon a time during the absence on sick leave of the then Governor, Scott, in 1855, this seniority had automatically brought him the Acting Governorship of the Crown Colony; but within the week he had resigned this position in favour of Low, whom he thought more suited to the exercise of power than he himself. Dr Treacher was a modest and not over-active man.

In 1843, at the age of twenty-eight, Treacher had gone from Singapore to Sarawak aboard HMS *Royalist* to join, as surgeon, the

* Malay rhymed couplets which are improvised by each speaker.

staff of Rajah James Brooke, with whom he had already sailed about the Celebes. Five years later he had been amongst the first Europeans to settle on Labuan. On Labuan, with several periods of sick leave in England, he had remained ever since.

While technically still in his middle-age, Treacher looked much older, for he had not borne the climate well. By 1867 the long, fan-shaped whiskers which framed his friendly face were, like his hair, snow-white. He suffered badly from rheumatic gout and from malaria. He said he was 'unable to walk or ride any great distance', and that if he did any medical work in the morning he was sick for the rest of the day. He had come to depend more and more upon the Apothecary who was his assistant, and to delegate almost all his duties to this robust young family-man, whose name was James McClosky and who, 'a native of the East', had first been stationed with the Army of India at Masulipatam.

At a Sanitary Enquiry instituted and conducted by Governor Pope Hennessy in 1870 Dr Treacher agreed that for the last two years he had confined his ministrations to the southern end of the tiny island of Labuan, that he seldom went even as far as the town of Victoria, that he had been used to calling in at the Public Offices only two or three times a week but that since Mr McClosky's arrival he had not found it necessary to go there at all. He also admitted that it was a long time since he had visited Coal Point, that he never went to the police station on the Coal Point Road, nor to the Plain, nor to Howards Road nor to the Batu Arrang district. He said that he knew nothing of the conditions in the native village of Raucha-Raucha, which lies just across the bay from Port Victoria, that he had no ideas about drainage, that the farthest he could ride in a day was one or one-and-a-half miles, that he had never been inside the military barracks except sometimes to go to the military hospital, and that his patients were limited to four or five officials, their servants, the convicts and occasional civilians in Victoria. Dr Treacher had 'never been in the habit' of taking notes of his cases, he kept no meteorological register, and had not heard of Beri-Beri (from which the soldiers of the Singalese garrison were at that time dying like flies). He had never mastered the proper use of the stethoscope, and his most recent medical books were twenty-five years out of date. At this enquiry he showed some mental confusion over the death of a Singalese soldier which had occurred at the military hospital only the night before.

If Dr Treacher was a victim to the Labuan climate—a living

monument to lethargy and physical decay—he was just as much the victim of the hesitant, casual policy of the Colonial Office, which grudged every penny of each annual Parliamentary Grant for Labuan and yet could not decide to evacuate the island altogether. For sixteen years, from 1848 until 1864, Dr Treacher had been paid a salary of £417 a year, which was finally raised to £500. He was a bachelor, known in his youth as the adventurous medico of HMS *Royalist* who had a weakness for Sarawak girls; but, even for a bachelor, life on Labuan was not at all cheap. Hugh Low had written to the Secretary of State for the Colonies in 1863 that Labuan salaries were 'so inconsiderable in comparison with those of the neighbouring Straits Settlements, although the expense of living is no less, and the risks and deprivations are much greater'. There was no incentive to encourage Dr Treacher to be more industrious. His chief aim was to hold on to his job until he would qualify for the meagre pension of £241 13s. 4d. a year.

In 1860 the Colonial Office had circulated to all their Governors a questionnaire drawn up by Miss Florence Nightingale who wished to compile a report on *The Sanitary Statistics of Native Colonial Schools and Hospitals*. From Labuan no answer to this questionnaire was ever sent: 'no doubt', Low wrote in 1863, 'owing to the fact of there being no Schools for native children, or Hospitals into which native patients were received, on Labuan. . . . There are very few diseases to which natives are subject except the fever endemic in the Island, which chiefly attacks newcomers. Poor patients, who desire it, are visited at their houses by the Colonial Surgeon or his Apothecary, and medicines are dispensed daily, to those who apply for them, at the expense of the Government. The evils frequently arising from the contact of Europeans with native races which Miss Nightingale so justly reprehends and deplores, are not likely to prevail in this Settlement, which can never become a focus of indiscriminate European immigration.' One of Governor Pope Hennessy's first steps on Labuan was to set up a Committee to establish a hospital in an unfinished building originally designed as a gaol; the Chinese community undertook to provide food and bedding, and to pay the Colonial Apothecary an extra twenty Straits dollars a month for his attendance. By October 1868 this hospital was already in operation with twenty beds permanently occupied and room for more. 'Heretofore', wrote my grandfather, 'the destitute-sick of Labuan have been treated like criminals', for, when ill, they were allotted convict cells in the civil prison, where they were

visited daily by the Apothecary and where Doctor Treacher peered in
on them once a week.

Pope Hennessy's predecessor, Governor Callaghan, had reported on
Dr Treacher as being 'a most respectable officer, and in every way
suitable for the position he fills, although there are symptoms percepti-
ble of his long residence in the tropics beginning to tell upon his
constitution'. The yet previous Governor, Edwardes, said that he had
'ever' found himself 'placed . . . in most unsatisfactory relations with
the Colonial Surgeon'. In the first flush of the 1848 colonisation of
Labuan, many officials had bought up considerable areas of undrained
swamp-land as a speculation, hoping to make money in the future by
building villas for the expected influx of wealthy European and
Chinese settlers. Treacher was amongst them, having acquired fifty-
one acres, which commanded 'the whole drainage of the Government
Grounds. . . . So ill-assigned', wrote Governor Edwardes, 'were the lots
disposed of, that the approach to Government House was included in
the sales . . . all ventilation was impeded and both sides of Government
House were swamped by the neglected drainage.' Although he had
kept two acres in a decent state and had built 'a good substantial house
with premises . . . upon an elevated portion' Treacher, despite the fact
of being the chief medical authority in the island, declined to have the
rest of the malarial ground drained or cleared, concentrating his time,
energy and any money he had managed to save on the establishment
of a private cocoa-nut plantation on the island of Daat. The cocoa-nut
oil produced was then marketed by the doctor to the Coal Company.
Meanwhile, Treacher had sold his house and land on Labuan to a
Chinese merchant on a mortgage of twelve hundred Straits dollars.
The Government had felt obliged to buy it back again at the same
price, and to drain and clear it in the vague hope of one day turning
the house into a school. It was some time after this sale of 1859 that Dr
Treacher moved, as a permanent resident, to a cottage in Low's garden.

Working together these two old hands, the Colonial Treasurer and
the Colonial Surgeon, formed a conservative team. They would be
liable to distrust and probably to oppose abrupt changes on Labuan,
and to wish, in their tired way, to tarnish any brilliant new scheme
laid before them as Legislative Councillors. We have seen that Low
felt that he should himself have become fifth Governor of Labuan.
Dr Treacher, who had absolutely no ambitions, simply wanted to be
left in peace. Both, perhaps, had long ceased to wonder just what they,
or any of the other officials, were really doing on Labuan at all. Over

twenty years a waning faith in Labuan's future had slowly dwindled to a cheerless recognition that this island Colony was at once their destiny and their home.

VI

If Governor Hennessy was unlikely to find allies in either Mr Low or Dr Treacher, he might have expected to do so in the person of the new Colonial Secretary, Mr J. G. Slade, who reached Labuan from England shortly after the Governor himself. In the hierarchy of a Crown Colony, the Colonial Secretary ranked next to the Governor. He was his chief adviser and at times his mouthpiece, for the Governor, as Queen's representative, was supposed to keep aloof from his subordinates and staff. Mr Slade had married his wife Frances 'on the strength of his appointment'. The optimistic pair arrived in Labuan in January 1868. The island climate made short work of both. Slade, already a subject to what his wife termed 'old attacks of liver', speedily became an invalid. By April he was so ill that he could no longer do his work and by July he was unable to use his eyes 'either for reading or for writing'. Mrs Slade, who was herself ailing, told the Governor that her husband was 'at times quite insensible, and at other times so light-headed that I fear to allow this worry about office duties to continue'. The Governor readily granted Slade three months leave on half-pay, and persuaded the Colonial Office to transfer the couple to a post in Western Australia.

The fact that the position of Colonial Secretary was thus once more vacant suited the new Governor well, for already in his first weeks in Labuan he was experimenting with the highly personal system of Colonial government for which he later became notorious. This system was based on the replacement of existing officials with more sympathetic candidates of his own choosing, and at first involved a process commonly known as 'clearing the decks'. 'One of the Complaints against Mr P. H.', minuted Lord Granville on a Labuan despatch of October 1869, 'is that he gets rid of the place holders in order to fill them with his friends, but this is a charge which it is easy to make, & most difficult to decide upon.' In any case Mr Slade's early removal from the Crown Colony was not unwelcome to the Governor. We may ourselves feel that the withdrawal of Mrs Frances Slade from the small island community was no bad thing either, for during her brief residence there her husband had had to complain that one of the very few walks that Labuan afforded was automatically out of bounds to

Mrs Slade. His wife, Slade declared, 'was unable to walk up the Coal
Point Road because she found there were high officials who did not
scruple to salute her when they were in company with their Malay
mistresses. He begged me', the Governor reported to the Secretary of
State, 'to try and check this public scandal.' The part played by such
Englishwomen as Mrs Slade in spreading racial prejudice throughout
the mid-Victorian Empire should not be overlooked by students of
British imperial rule.

Chief among these courteous offenders on the Coal Point Road was
the carefree young Colonial Surveyor, Mr James St John. In fifteen
years on Labuan St John had raised a numerous Eurasian family in
his house, which stood in its own compound near the Roman Catholic
Chapel on North Road, just opposite the Military Cantonments. Like
Mr Low, St John also had a lodger, his intimate friend the tall and
bearded Captain Maclean, who commanded the detachment of Madras
Native Infantry stationed on the island.

Described in a previous Governor's confidential report as 'quick
and intelligent', 'an active healthy man' but 'decidedly unfit for the
position of Surveyor', James St John was one of the earliest of the
European settlers on Labuan. He had left England at Christmas-time
in the year of the Great Exhibition, 1851, when he was twenty years
old. Except for local leave, he had been stationed on the island ever
since. He had never again seen his mother, who lived in the St John's
Wood district of London and regarded her son as a 'precipitate' but
'reliable and truthful' young man. St John was now thirty-six, had
become proficient in the Malay language and had a longstanding
liaison with a Malay lady, Nona Singin, whose brother, Ersat, was
recognised in the island as the best local pimp and 'pander to the vices
of others'. St John seems to have been high-spirited and happy-
natured, but like all his colleagues on Labuan he would often express
the trite desire to quit the island for ever. He would have liked to find
himself a niche as clerk in some department of a larger Crown Colony,
or as Auditor in another small one.

Governor Edwardes had reported James St John to the Home
authorities for cheekiness, and Governor Callaghan had alleged that he
was 'not an efficient officer in his present position'. He had been
reprimanded by the Colonial Office when it was found that, granted
leave from Labuan 'to restore health and vigour', he had remained in
the sickly Colony as surveyor to the Labuan Coal Company. In 1867,
when Governor Pope Hennessy reached Labuan, St John was not only

Surveyor-General but Acting Colonial Secretary, Auditor, Superintendent of Convicts and Registrar of Lands; for the shortage of European officials on Labuan frequently involved such a multiplication of duties by a single individual. He was not a trained auditor, kept his accounts vaguely and 'often pleaded a defective memory'. With the initiation of the new public works programme by my grandfather in December 1867, St John found himself responsible for building the Albert Wharf and the Lord Grey fish-market (both soon swept away by a cyclone), the police station at Tanjong Kubong, for sinking the new well and for completing the new hospital. As he himself wrote afterwards he had indeed 'at that period . . . very many causes for preoccupation of mind'. St John's salary, like all Labuan salaries, was derisorily small. Of his physical appearance we have no record, although it is tempting to identify him with the short thickset gentleman holding a sword-stick in the photograph of Labuan notabilities reproduced in this book. He is seen standing on Mr Hugh Low's left, just behind Mr Claude de Crespigny who is seated cross-legged beside old Dr Treacher on the grass.

Mr Claude de Crespigny was, like St John, a pluralist. He combined the three jobs of Harbour Master, Post Master and Superintendent of Farms—superintendent, that is to say, of the Government monopolies or 'farms' of opium and spirits. In 1867 he was in his later forties. His beard was strong, dark and crisp, but his hair was already receding and gave to his forehead an intellectual look. He had the clear gaze of a naval officer which is precisely what, for much of his early life, he had been. After fifteen years in the Navy he had ended up as commander of a gunboat, been granted two years' special leave to explore Borneo and had become 'known everywhere in these seas'. After resigning his commission in 1858 he had spent four years in unsuccessful commercial speculations in Singapore where his associates were 'among the secondary society and ships' chandlers'. In the summer of 1862 he had made his way to Labuan, to present himself as candidate for the vacant positions of Harbour Master and Post Master. Since he possessed 'a pretty correct knowledge of the Malay language' and was well acquainted with both entrances into the harbour of Labuan, he proved a godsend to the reigning Governor, Mr Callaghan, who declared that 'it would be difficult to find a person so suitable as he seems to be in every respect to fill the appointment', adding that de Crespigny struck him as 'a very gentlemanly and intelligent man'. De Crespigny was somewhat more sophisticated than other Labuanites and he quickly gained the esteem of Governor Pope Hennessy. He did not keep it for long.

The twin positions of Harbour Master and Post Master on Labuan were not as onerous as in other larger, healthier and richer Colonies, but none the less the holder of them had to be fairly spry. 'They involve personal attendance on the commanders of ships and the personal waiting for & reception of the letters of the community as they gradually come in previous to the departure of the Mails', wrote Hugh Low. 'This attendance is sometimes prolonged far into the night and at other times the officer is ordered to take letters which have been too late for the Mails on board personally, chasing the ship in a canoe into the open sea outside the Harbour.' The Post Office itself was run on a credit system. The account books and printed forms sent out from London had headings and columns which did not tally with the Labuan system of postage. The Post Master had also to maintain 'a rather intricate account with Singapore owing to the different postage rules in the two Colonies' and to use Straits Settlements stamps. Mail to and from Labuan was transhipped at Singapore, and the postal authorities in that Colony were lax: 'The last ship that brought letters to Labuan brought four English mails', Governor Pope Hennessy wrote in February 1871. 'Whilst these mails were lying at the Post Office at Singapore, two steamers and a sailing ship left for Labuan, without bringing any letters.' The arrival of a mailboat in Labuan was 'an event . . . so rare that it creates quite a "sensation" [wrote the Labuan correspondent of the *Straits Times* in 1868], 'everybody rushing for letters and papers, and eagerly devouring the news, especially that from Home'. Since no telegraph cable linked Labuan to Singapore, no one could predict on which day some expected ship would actually reach the island. This meant that, in his capacity as Harbour Master, Claude de Crespigny had to hold himself available at all hours. As Harbour Master he had two native boatmen to help him, but much of his work—the placing of beacons and piloting of vessels in particular—demanded his constant personal supervision.

Together with the Treasury Clerk, whose surname was in fact Clark and whom Governor Hennessy termed 'one of the most inoffensive and good tempered officials in the country' while others called him a hypocrite and 'a low mean fellow', the gentlemen with whom we are now acquainted were the main European officials of the Crown Colony of Labuan in 1867. With the exception of the infirm Dr

Treacher, they would go down each weekday morning, by buggy or on horseback or on foot, to the Public Offices in Victoria town. Here in their leaky rooms they would sit at tables covered with dark blue cloth, gossiping and waiting for something to do. The wooden walls of these rooms stopped short of the ceiling, so that it was easy to eavesdrop from one room on what was being said in the next. Chinese clerks with shaven heads and gleaming pigtails flitted stealthily to and fro, as the rain pelted into the verandah and beat down upon the small stone memorial which stood in the grass outside the Offices to remind the passer-by that the glorious Crown Colony of Labuan had been founded in the ninth year of the reign of Her Majesty Queen Victoria. In two sentry-boxes saturated sepoy soldiers stood on guard.

VII

The officers in charge of the Indian troops stationed on Labuan had even less to do than the civilians. The detachment's primary duty was to man three guardhouses—at Government House, at the Convict Prison, and at the Public Offices on the unhealthy plain by the sea-shore. The troops' rate of sickness, much of it fatal, had always been the highest on the island; this was due to bad sanitation, unsuitable food, the heavy use of opium and the fact that sentries who had been patrolling all night in the tropical rain went back to sleep in barracks in sodden uniforms. The Indians were demoralised as well by home-sickness. After rain the barrack-square became a marsh. In 1867 the sepoy latrines had not been cleared for a twelve-month.

Governor Pope Hennessy had no knack for getting on with the Services. In his first months on Labuan he had little contact with the military beyond appointing the youngest subaltern, Lieutenant Cherry, to act as his aide-de-camp, despite direct Colonial Office instructions that he was not to have one. Lieutenant Cherry operated the only camera on the island. He spent part of his time photographing the Colonial Secretary's pretty daughter Kitty Low upon her pony, Beauty, or his brother-officers lounging on the grass by the Cantonment wall.

The new Governor's relations with the naval officers at Labuan were even more intermittent, for the gunboat nominally based upon Port Victoria was seldom seen there. Labuan offering no amusements for naval officers, they would invent excuses to take their ship to Kuching, the capital of Sarawak. This township had an hotel, a bandstand, and tiled shops. It had even once been likened to a minor Mediterranean resort. As Governor of Labuan, Pope Hennessy was also its Vice-Admiral. He could thus commandeer a naval vessel to take him across the Straits to Brunei, down the coast to Sarawak or, farther still, to Pontianak in Dutch Borneo. He never lacked physical courage, and on one occasion in November 1868 he much impressed the commander of HMS *Dwarf* by personally leading an expedition to avenge an insult to the British flag by pirates of Ubean Island in the Tawi-Tawi Group. For the naval officers Labuan might well prove dull but their prospects were not entirely dismal—they could temporarily escape from the Crown Colony when they felt inclined to do so. Moreover each ship's turn of duty on the Labuan station had set limits.

Even more disillusioned, if possible, than the civilian officials, or the military or the sailors, were the European coal-miners up at Tanjong Kubong, where, in dense steaming jungle, amidst conditions of heartbreaking squalor and disease, some fifteen young Scotsmen were still struggling to work the coal-face. The mine passages were flooded with monsoon water, the pit props were rotting. The actual temperature in the mines was cooler than in the rain forests above them, and my grandfather was informed that it was 'a most agreeable change to a person habituated to mining to go underground'. The manager declared that the mines were 'free from all noxious gases' and that 'the air at the exit shaft is as pure as when it first entered the workings'. Soon after he reached Labuan Governor Pope Hennessy visited Tanjong Kubong, and penetrated into the galleries of the mines at every level, working some of the coal with his own hands. He also narrowly inspected the account books and was shocked by the very large salaries drawn by the managerial staff and by the 'reckless extravagance' with which the failing Company's money had been spent. For the last six months the miners themselves, and the native labourers at the coal wharf, were being paid with promissory notes, which were then bought from them by astute Chinese traders at a discount of 40 per cent. The young miners imported from Scotland to work the coal—Jimmy Baird, Alexander Watson, John Gillespie, John Gillies to name some of them—were doubtless tough; but they hated the jungle. They had learned to dread the fever and the tropical sun. They were frustrated by the lack of women at Coal Point. They especially loathed and distrusted their medical attendant, a certain Dr Barry who was even less qualified than old Dr Treacher, and was cruel and unscrupulous into the bargain. The miners were frequently ill. Several of their mates had died.

The hopeless condition of the coal-mines was the cancer which had long been destroying any chance of a healthy Labuan economy, for the coal-seam was the Crown Colony's real *raison-d'être*. 'The maintenance of a Colonial Establishment at Labuan is justified only on a consideration which a cheap and sufficient supply of coal in that quarter of the world would confer on the mercantile marine of this Country, as well as on Her Majesty's ships', the Land Board in London reminded the Colonial Office in a harsh minute in 1868. So far, the coal supply was seldom cheap and never sufficient; in twenty years the Company had spent a quarter of a million pounds and had not made one penny, nor had they got around to paying the Colonial Government the annual rent for the land. Even the gunboats on the Labuan station, which, under a cut-price contract, could, in theory, coal at the rickety wharf at Tanjong Kubong, would steam away to load up with 'Welsh Hartley' at Kuching.

Governor Hennessy had arrived on the island determined to make the coal-mine pay. By skilful arbitration he wound up the affairs of the China Steamship and Labuan Coal Company, thus paving the way for the arrival of the managerial staff of a new Company, the Oriental Coal Company, just floated in the City of London. The manager of the new Company (which was very soon in as bad a financial state as that which had been wound up) was a Mr Alexander Lumsden, who quickly proved himself an adept in the manifold intrigues which riddled Labuan life. Mr Lumsden became *persona grata* at Government House. The Governor's red-haired sister Mary Hennessy would often be his guest for days together, knitting with persistence in his house up at Coal Point. This friendship added a fresh scandal to the many simmering in the small island community. It was concluded by the Labuan public that Miss Hennessy must have married Mr Alexander Lumsden secretly.

VIII

The new Coal Company had undertaken to pay the Labuan Government one thousand pounds a year, quite apart from royalties on the coal. They also promised to build a new wharf at Port Victoria and to run a railway line to it from Tanjong Kubong, a distance of seven miles. In point of fact neither the annual rent nor any coal royalties were ever paid. The railway track was built, and did at least diminish the miners' sense of isolation. Mr Lumsden, as lavish of promises as his employers, even said that he would run an engine with one truck along the line on Sunday mornings, so that the Anglicans and Presbyterians among the miners could attend service at the Cathedral of St Saviour, 'a handsome and commodious building' made of wood. This promise, like the others, remained unfulfilled.

The congregation of the Anglican Cathedral of Labuan was, to say the least of it, select. Of 127 Christians on the island, 86 were Roman Catholic, 20 were Presbyterian, 4 were Baptist, and exactly 17 (including 4 children) were Anglican. The small number of Anglicans revealed in a rough census taken on Labuan in 1869, came as a shock to the Colonial Office, which was paying the Colonial Chaplain three hundred and fifty pounds a year. 'The Chaplain therefore costs £20 a head!' minuted the Secretary of State, then Lord Kimberley. 'This continuance certainly cannot be justified'.

The religious set-up on Labuan was as bizarre as most other aspects of the colony's administration. Not long after the island's settlement it had been elevated to a Bishopric, which came directly under the Archbishop of Canterbury at home. Dr Francis McDougall, described as 'an odd rollicking mixture of Bishop, Surgeon & sea captain . . . a man of a good deal of shrewdness & observation', had been consecrated first Bishop of Labuan in 1855. Bishop McDougall was an imposing rather oriental-looking personage with a bald head and a spade beard. He and his wife resided at their mission station and school in Kuching, Sarawak. The Bishop visited Labuan as seldom as he decently could. The objects of his occasional descents upon the Colony were very characteristic of Labuan life—he would order one over-crowded European graveyard to be closed and consecrate a new one, or try to combat the Spanish and Italian Catholic missionaries 'whose sole business', he declared, 'is to make proselytes of our people'.

As in other parts of the Eastern, and the African, Empire there were unseemly sectarian squabbles over native converts. In 1859, for instance, Bishop McDougall paid one of his flying visits to Labuan: 'My visit was well timed, and I hope did good, especially as regards the Roman Catholics', he reported. 'They had got hold of a lad I baptised last year, whom I recovered, and baptised two others, whom, if I had not gone up, they would have had.' The Catholic Church in the Philippines had indeed sent a strong team to Labuan, considering the size of the Colony. Four Italian priests were under the charge of an able Spaniard, Don Carlos Cuarteron, who was given the grandiose title of 'Apostolic Prefect of Micronesia and Melanesia'. They had immediately constructed 'a large and well-built Roman Catholic chapel', as well as a church in the Sultan of Brunei's capital on the Borneo coast. Don Carlos had also imported a number of 'Manila-men' —servants and sailors—whose children were taught in the small Catholic school. Worse still, from the Bishop's viewpoint, was the fact that, since they had no clergyman of their own, the Anglicans and Presbyterians on the island attended Don Carlos' Sunday mass and had 'often been glad to accept his ministrations'. It was to counteract this Catholic influence that Bishop McDougall had persuaded the Colonial Office to subsidise a resident Colonial Chaplain on Labuan: 'It is most desirable', he wrote, 'that those whose duties call upon them to reside in so isolated a station sd [sic] have a clergyman resident among them, to remind them of their Xtian duties & prevent them deteriorating in a moral & religious point of view, until they become a curse instead of a blessing to the Natives around them.'

The delicate task of turning the disgruntled officials and scallywag merchants of Labuan into a blessing to the natives around them was first entrusted to the Reverend Julius Moreton, who arrived in Labuan with his wife in 1861. Mr and Mrs Moreton and their two children lived in one of the three largest houses in Victoria. Amongst Mr Moreton's duties was that of ministering to the sick and dying ratings on such Royal Navy ships as put in at Labuan. He and his wife also took the trouble to learn Malay and to set up a school for native, non-Christian children whose education had hitherto been totally neglected. When Governor Pope Hennessy reached the Colony, Moreton had been Chaplain for six years. Granted sick leave a few months later, he was then promoted to be Chaplain on the pleasant Straits Settlements island of Penang. He was succeeded by Mr Flower, a portly man of forty-five who wore a wedding-ring and had arranged for his wife to follow him out to Labuan. Mrs Flower planned to make the voyage with five of her younger daughters who, children themselves, were none the less judged capable of giving instruction in the school. The Reverend Mr Flower reached Labuan on the fourth of July 1868. On the fifteenth of that month he went to pay a call on young St John, lying sick in his house on North Road. While mounting his pony to return homewards he was thrown from the saddle and dragged. Spared the attentions of Dr Treacher, who deputed the Colonial Apothecary to look after him, Mr Flower lingered on for just over a week. Unable to eat or sleep, he died on 26 July, in the

Governor's presence, of congestion of the brain. Twenty-two days between landing on the island and dying on it formed a record even for Labuan.

After unsuccessful efforts by Governor Pope Hennessy to get an Anglican missionary sent along the coast from Sarawak, a new Chaplain came out from England. This was an indolent and excitable old party from Norwich, the Reverend William Beard. During his brief time on the island Beard's predecessor, Mr Flower, had continued to operate the school for native children and had even begun to take steps to persuade English officials to marry their Malay mistresses (it was, no doubt, with this object in view that he had visited St John that fatal July evening). Mr Beard, on the other hand, closed the school for Malay and Kling children, since he resented their passing through his living quarters to their schoolroom, and since he neither knew nor wished to learn Malay. Far from having a soothing influence on the European community, the new clergyman soon became embroiled in the local feuds and once wrote acidly of Governor Hennessy as an 'utterly despicable' character. But we must not anticipate events. For the moment it is enough to remember, when surveying the Labuan scene, that Christianity was represented in the Colony by an inactive English clergyman and an energetic Spanish priest. The non-Christian inhabitants of the island were Mahommedan, Hindu and Buddhist. They had built themselves their own places of worship, which included a brick mosque with a tiled roof, a Hindu temple and two Chinese temples in wood, and a new Chinese joss-house in brick.

Any evocation of life on Labuan at this period would be incomplete without a reference to the most industrious and most scheming community in the Colony—the Chinese. The Labuan Chinamen, whom Governor Pope Hennessy astutely courted, were split into two Secret Societies, headed respectively by two wealthy merchants, Choa Mah Soo and Lee Cheng Ho. Choa Mah Soo was the richest man on the island, owning extensive sago factories, the best trading-schooners and a series of shop-houses. He was a stout man with silver spectacles, wore ostentatious silken robes and kept a carriage and pair 'far superior to those of the Governor'. Lee Cheng Ho, the son of one of the first Chinese settlers, was tall for a Chinaman. He had an affable manner and an eternal smile. Anxious to establish racial equality in his little kingdom, Governor Pope Hennessy soon appointed Choa Mah Soo and another Chinaman to the Bench, though whether the new Magistrates were well versed in British law seems open to question. He also took to consulting the leading members of the Chinese community upon such subjects as the new hospital, the drainage and the lighting of Victoria, as well as on taxation and trade. He relied considerably on their experience for advice, which for some reason he assumed to be disinterested. As we know, his policy earned the praise of the *Straits Times* of Singapore which congratulated him in a leading article on being quick to discover that the Chinese were 'the back bone of commerce and industry in the Far East' and that to treat them with kindness and give them protection was the 'talisman of success in eastern colonisation'. Together with a handful of well-to-do Arab traders, the Chinese merchants were the most fruitfully taxable members of the community of Labuan.

CHAPTER THREE

———————

'FROM THE MOMENT of Your Excellency's arrival everything in the Colony appeared to change. Your energy and personal example dispelled the gloom that universally prevailed.' These sentences from an address presented to Governor Pope Hennessy by the retiring staff of the bankrupt Coal Company suggest the early impact of his flamboyant character upon the moribund Colony. This general satisfaction did not last, for, happy to charm and praise, the Irish Governor proved just as swift to criticise and to condemn. Determined to show the Colonial Office that he could succeed where all his predecessors had failed, he set himself the task of turning Labuan into what he called 'a little Singapore'. His attention darted hither and thither. He pounced on any sign of laxity (and they were many) like a falcon on its prey. To increase the revenue he stringently increased the taxes, raising the price of the only two commodities which had made life on Labuan tolerable to Europeans—tobacco and alcohol. Slowly but surely the climate and atmosphere of Labuan affected him: he tended to become quickly overwrought, and began to give rein to his native talent for dramatising small events. His was a brilliant but an obsessional mind. Tiny faults in others were magnified in a flash, rather as we are told that a speck of paper blowing along a road looks menacing and gigantic to the sideways eye of a horse. It was not long before the Secretary of State for the Colonies was reminding him that a Colonial Governor's duty was 'to set an example of temper & moderation to his subordinate officers, & by the exercise of justice & forebearance to establish that harmonious cooperation which is so essential to the well being of a Colonial community.'

'Temper and moderation' had long been at a discount on Labuan, which offered almost limitless opportunities to test and fray the nerves. Governor Hennessy was a man of the world and it might have been possible for him to view his subjects on Labuan with detachment and with humour. But, though he managed to look a dignified, even distinguished little personage, with his head thrown back, his friendly smile and a walk which was once unkindly described as 'a strut', he

succeeded during his first Governorship in inspiring fear and bewilderment rather than respect. All his life he indulged in favourite causes
and favourite people, and, while the latter might change suddenly, the
former never did. It would be imprecise to say of him that he was
governed by his heart and not his head, for he was swayed first by the
one and then by the other, so that to cool English minds his behaviour
seemed to lack logic to a singular degree. A confirmed humanitarian
he was also an autocrat; an avowed Conservative his views were
really Liberal; a British Colonial Governor he believed that Colonial
peoples should be free to govern themselves. Intoxicated by his own
powers of persuasion and by his conversational gifts, he would make
promises which it was not always easy, and was sometimes downright
impossible, to keep. Arriving on Labuan he must have assessed the
situation and have seen that to do real good there he should keep aloof
from his subordinates and from their several cliques. Instead of this,
within ten weeks of landing in the Colony, he married the Colonial
Treasurer's daughter, Kitty Low.

Although rain-drenched Labuan in December might not seem
propitious to the *coup de foudre* we must assume that such a burst of
emotion inspired a marriage in all its aspects reckless. Kitty Hennessy
was barely seventeen; her husband was thirty-four. She was the
daughter of the only man in the Colony who nursed the grievance
that he should have been made Governor himself. Low, the Governor's
subordinate, now became his father-in-law, which gave rise to jealousy
amongst the other colonial officials, who fancied that his would be a
privileged position. Kitty Low had no dowry and was a staunch
Anglican. The marriage caused dissension within the Governor's own
family, for his sister Mary, as ultramontane a Catholic as himself,
resented it. Brought all the way out from Dublin to act as châtelaine
of Government House, Labuan, Miss Mary Hennessy now found
herself suddenly superseded by a beautiful girl of character, who
moreover had Malayan blood. When news of the alliance reached
London it aroused the sympathetic, slightly wondering, interest of
his friends. 'I am glad', Miss Burdett Coutts wrote to the Tuan Muda
of Sarawak, 'he makes a marriage likely to provide *Brio* to the East.'

So far we have only caught a glimpse of Kitty Low leaving the
Christmas ball at Government House, on the very evening perhaps
that the Governor had made his proposal of marriage. Now she is
aboard as a permanent passenger on the voyage through this book we
may study her more closely. From the frightened girl whose quarrels

with her husband were manna to the gossips at the Labuan Club and whose simple frocks led a Governor of Singapore to mistake her for her own child's amah, we shall see her change in London into an elegant young woman of whom Lady Ely wrote: 'Hers is not a common character & her beauty is quite out of the ordinary, I could not help admiring her peculiar grace & a charm which few people have.' A devoted wife on the Fever Coast of Africa, an admirable hostess in Barbados, a dreamy, moody beauty who inspired at least one dangerous passion in Hong Kong, we shall take leave of her in Mauritius where she is remembered for her educational zeal and for her piety—she was by then a Roman Catholic convert—and where she was recognised as the most generous of human beings, a sort of ambulant image of Charity, secretly selling her jewellery to relieve the poor. On occasion the involuntary instrument of her husband's enemies, Kitty Hennessy's life was, like her character, restless and uneasy. On the one hand she was thoughtful, truthful, dutiful, religious, and, at times, very energetic. On the other, she was extravagant, prone to anxiety and indecision, and given to precipitate action and bursts of temper, followed by silence and regrets. She would become interested in some subject only to drop it again. She was musical, with a passion for dancing, at which she excelled. In appearance she was tall and slender, with a graceful carriage and a pleasing manner. Her remarkable facial beauty, her dark silken hair and the set of her eyes bore witness to her strain of Asian blood. Such was the complex young person whom John Pope Hennessy now impulsively asked to accompany him through life.

Catherine Elizabeth Low had been born on Labuan in October of 1850, the fourth year of that island's settlement. She was the second child and only daughter of Hugh Low by his wife Catherine Napier, whose background reflected a strange amalgam of scholastic Edinburgh and Malacca Malay blood. Mrs Low died of Labuan fever shortly after her daughter's birth and the two babies, Hugo Brooke Low and Kitty Low, were sent back to England where they grew up in the family of Hugh Low's brother, Stuart, a leading nursery gardener and botanist in Upper Clapton. Uncle Stuart and Aunt Lizzie Low themselves had a numerous family, so that the Labuan children experienced a normal, happy upbringing. On leave from Labuan, their father visited them for some months in 1861, but otherwise there was nothing to remind Kitty Low of the country of her birth. The only surviving anecdote of her childhood records how two ladies, peeping into her perambulator in Clapton, cried out that the child had 'the most extraordinary eyes' that they had ever seen.

Kitty Low's education was completed at a small boarding school in French Switzerland kept by a pious Swiss pastor and his wife. Here she mastered French and German thoroughly, and made close friends among her schoolmates, girls with such names as Minnie Matilda Detmolds, Maria Miraflor, Ida Dammam, Josephina Gabel and Lizzie Hingshound. In all these girls she seems to have aroused considerable affection, to judge by the sentimental contents of an autograph album which she packed in her trunk when leaving trim and tidy Montmirail for the atap-thatched huts of the Conradesque island of Labuan in December 1866. To a sixteen-year-old girl brought up in Europe, the change must have been marked indeed. She went to join a father whom she scarcely knew in a small tropical outpost which she could not remember. As Acting Governor, Hugh Low was at that moment resident in Government House. He gave his daughter a fat little pony, Beauty, and provided her with a personal maid or 'amah' who was sister to Arnat, the Government House gardener. He led her to stand beside her mother's grave in the orange grove of his garden and he told her of the existence of his mistress Nona Dyang Loya, and of her child who was Kitty Low's half-sister. This latter piece of information was an early lesson in the stark facts of Colonial life and might have startled Pastor Richard-Ohrenberg of Montmirail. Without her brother Hugo, her Clapton cousins and her Swiss school-friends, Kitty Low may well have felt trapped and lonely on Labuan. Except for Lieutenant Cherry, the junior officer of the Madras Native Infantry detachment (who took the photograph of Miss Low upon her pony reproduced in this book), there were no other young Europeans on the island. It is small wonder that when the forceful, fashionable, persuasive new Governor demanded her hand she and her father acceded at once. Apart from any personal leanings—and there is no reason to suppose that this sheltered seventeen-year-old girl did not fall in love with him—Governor Pope Hennessy was asking her to share with him the most prominent position in the Colony. There was the prospect, moreover, of almost immediate escape to some larger and livelier place—for at this time Hennessy refused to believe that Labuan was to be his four-years' fate. 'I am in daily expectation of hearing of some change', he wrote to Lord Henry Gordon Lennox about this time.

On 4 February 1868 two wedding ceremonies, Catholic and

Protestant, were performed by the Reverend Mr Moreton and Don Carlos Cuarteron respectively. In negotiations before the marriage, the Governor found himself obliged to reveal to Mr Low that he had no income save his Labuan salary and that he could not afford to insure his life in his bride's favour for more than fifteen hundred pounds. Since old Dr Treacher was a witness to this contract, the news of the Governor's poverty would soon have circulated in Port Victoria. The bride's father and his future son-in-law exchanged other confidences, Low telling Hennessy about his Nona and her child, to which my grandfather candidly responded by telling Low about his illegitimate little girls at Barnes. Low added that his daughter knew all about the Nona, and it is likely that Pope Hennessy then told Kitty of his own offspring, to whom she used later to send notes, Christmas cards and money, signing herself 'Mamma', for it seems that their mother, Miss Conyngham, had died. Thus, to the farther East of Suez, were Victorian conventions much relaxed.

The marriage was enlivened by a crowd of the Governor's Chinese admirers, who joined the bridal cortège beating drums and waving banners. After the wedding breakfast in a large beflagged tent in Hugh Low's garden, the couple steamed away on board HMS *Leven* for a honeymoon across the straits in Brunei, where the Sultan gave the Governor his own kris, while the Sultana pressed 'some valuable diamond rings and brooches' on the bride. Pope Hennessy wrote to Disraeli offering him the 'handsome blade' presented to him by the Sultan, and assuring his patron (by then Prime Minister for the first time) that Labuan was 'really becoming, at length, a little Singapore; and neither you nor the Duke will have any cause to regret sending out a Tory Governor'. He pleaded to be promoted to another and better Governorship at once. When the news of Disraeli's elevation to the Premiership reached Labuan the Governor ordered that a nineteen-gun salute be fired and that every flagstaff should be dressed with flags—unorthodox proceedings which caused consternation on Labuan and surprise in Singapore. The salute was effected with 'some old buried guns' and was 'not quite to regular time' since Captain Reed of HMS *Rifleman* would not allow his gunboat to be used for the purpose. 'As I was not able to give a cheer from behind the Treasury Bench, it has been some comfort to me to waken the echoes along the shores of Borneo', the Governor wrote to one of Disraeli's friends.

In his sanguine way John Pope Hennessy was convinced that one of Disraeli's first actions as Prime Minister would be to arrange that the Colonial Office promote his Irish protégé, the Governor of Labuan. After six months on the island he shared at least one aspiration with his subordinate officials—like them, he longed desperately to get away. But when he told the Home authorities that 'Labuan is now, & for ever, financially independent' it had, of course, the opposite result to that expected—for who would remove from the Colony a Governor who had seemingly performed this economic miracle, and in so brief a time? In later years the staff of the Eastern Department of the Colonial Office, men dreadfully down to earth and not easily impressed, began to question the wisdom and the efficacy of Pope Hennessy's fiscal reforms, which had a trapeze-artist quality all their own. But in 1868 they were still grateful for his seemingly successful measures. The Secretary of State congratulated him on 'the intelligence and activity which you have shown during your brief administration of the affairs of a Colony, which has for so many years been a burden on Imperial Funds'. This was all very nice, but it did not imply promotion, for which he had asked. He next asked for a knighthood, again without success. It was in a mood of some petulance that Pope Hennessy settled down to the totally new experience of married life— married life in a tropical Government House in a monsoon.

II

Despite its lofty rooms, its airy verandahs and its spacious park, Government House, that monsoon season of 1868, was not a comforting place to live in. The Governor fretted with impatience at the apathy of his subordinates as well as at their covert opposition to his plans. His sister's anger over the Governor's marriage created emotional tensions; it was already murmured in Port Victoria that she and the Governor's first cousin and private secretary, Bryan Cody, were collaborating to break up the marriage. Then the inmates of Government House kept falling ill. Labuan fever invaded the panelled bedrooms. Diarrhoea was rife. Those members of this disunited family who inhabited the north-west wing complained of the 'extremely offensive' tainted air which penetrated through the slatted windows. The Governor had begun life as a medical student and it was he who identified the source of the infection: fever and stench were both traced to the Sepoy Lines.

The Military Cantonment, or Sepoy Lines, lay behind Government

House, but on slightly higher ground. The soldiers' latrines were situated within the actual boundary of Government House Park, polluting the stream which wound through gentle grassland at the back of the house to feed its drinking well. Further investigation showed that the latrines at the Military Hospital, also adjacent to Government House, had not been cleared since 1866. The Governor at once sent a stiff note to the officer in charge of the sepoy detachment —the smart and popular Captain Maclean—to say that he had reported him to the War Office in London and had demanded his instant dismissal. He then ordered the Surveyor-General St John, in whose house Captain Maclean was lodging, to turn the Captain out. When St John refused to do this, the Governor started a campaign against the young Surveyor which began with his suspension and ended with his resignation from the Colonial Service some months later. Governor Hennessy also accused St John and the Colonial Treasurer, Hugh Low, of withholding information on an old report on the sanitation of the barracks, writing to Low, who was his own father-in-law, a twelve-page letter of sarcastic tone. This was the first of the many bitter quarrels between Pope Hennessy and Low. In these the Governor's wife sided with her father and not with her husband.

Labuan, like Sarawak, had long been notorious for the squabbles of its European denizens, but the sepoy latrine row of 1868 sparked off a chain reaction of explosions of a violence unparalleled in the history of the Colony. The tiny community split into rival parties. Delation became fashionable, and several people ceased to be on speaking terms. 'No doubt they all get on very ill among themselves', a puzzled civil servant in Downing Street wrote on the minute sheet of a despatch from Labuan. As the years passed the permanent officials of the Eastern Department became more and more bewildered by the methods and the results of Governor Hennessy's rule. In many ways they found his policies admirable and at one time spoke of raising his salary—and then a voluminous letter of complaint would reach them from some Labuan official or another, accompanied by an equally voluminous and far more skilled defence from the Governor himself. They began to realise that they had on their hands a highly unorthodox and unsettling Governor, who would disobey the Secretary of State's directives if he did not like them, and would take independent action which he seldom bothered to explain. The meaning of events and changes in Labuan became, within the Eastern Department at Downing Street, a parlour guessing game. 'Tho' the object is not apparent I see no objection to this arrangement as Mr Cody agrees', one of them, Mr Cox, minuted on a Labuan despatch of July 1871. 'Everything is mysterious in Labuan', Mr Herbert, the new Permanent Under-Secretary, musingly added to the page. 'It is not everywhere that we have a Hennessy to weave these mysterious webs. Approve', wrote the Secretary of State for the Colonies, Lord Kimberley. At any rate nobody could now call the Labuan community 'torpid'. It resembled rather an ants' nest or a hive of bees when either has been disturbed.

The germinal row over the sepoy latrines emphasises two basic truths of Victorian Colonial life which we should not forget: ignorance or carelessness over sanitation, which rendered tropical outposts of Empire far more lethal than they need have been, and the considerable power of a Colonial Governor to make or break subordinates at will. It seemed to the Colonial officers on Labuan, for instance, that their fate—advancement, increase of salary, promotion to another Colony or bleak dismissal without pension—rested on the Governor's good or bad opinion of them. The most feared of a Governor's weapons was his power of suspension—the power 'to suspend from the exercise of his office and the enjoyment of his emoluments' any subordinate whom he judged inefficient or dishonest. Suspension, or any other punitive measure, had ultimately to be confirmed by the Secretary of State in London. His staff in Downing Street tried scrupulously to assess the rights and wrongs of colonial quarrels submitted for their Chief's arbitration; yet they had largely to depend on what a Governor chose to tell them, and even if he were clearly in the wrong they were (as we have noticed) reluctant to undermine his position by a public censure. Moreover, as we have also seen, mails from distant places like Labuan took many weeks to reach London, and it was many weeks more before the Secretary of State's decision could be received in reply. A suspended official in such a colony might thus remain five months without work and without a salary while waiting for the London decision to arrive. Just as the lack of drains and ignorance of hygiene bred sickness and mortality, so the fear of a Governor's power gave birth to the grossest forms of hypocrisy and of intrigue. Both were corrosive to Colonial life.

III

If, to the Permanent Under-Secretary of State seated before his snug coal-fire in Downing Street, the goings-on in Labuan seemed mysterious, how much more so must they seem, distant as they are in time, to us. In one sense we are almost as well-informed as Mr Robert Herbert, for we can still read the inward Labuan despatches on which he would tender his advice to the Secretary of State. But for Herbert these were supplemented by private letters, which have disappeared, and also by occasional interviews. He and his colleagues had talked to Labuanites on leave. They knew John Pope Hennessy—'more persuasive than most Governors'—in person. They knew Mr Low— 'not without his faults . . . [but] a public officer of great intelligence'. They had seen decrepit old Dr Treacher on his numerous sick leaves. They liked Mr de Crespigny. They had not been favourably impressed by the new Colonial Chaplain, Mr Beard. Over us they had, and have still, the advantage. We can only watch—and listen.

So confusing become the motives and activities inside the great white Government House of Labuan as well as at the enemy head-quarters, Mr Hugh Low's verandah, that often we seem to be peering into a thick mist—the mist rising each hot damp dusk from the Labuan swamp-lands to obscure the wooden house-fronts of Victoria town and the silent rain-forests behind it. Scraps of conservation, discordant voices, reach us through the mist. Some of the voices are narrative: 'Mrs Hennessy came out on the verandah and asked me what I wanted.' Or: 'I told Major Tranchell that he had put his foot in it considerably.' Or: 'as we walked towards the gate at the foot of Church hill he said that 'there was no occasion to stand on professional etiquette with Dr McClosky as he is a nobody'. Or, again: 'Dyang Loya was a witness to an occurrence in the Coal Point Road on the 30th of July which the Governor imagined might at any time be turned up against him in our bitter family quarrels.' Other voices have the clarity of direct speech: 'The case will look very ugly both for you and for Mr Beard', for instance. Or: 'Mr Warren's constitution is breaking up.' Or: 'I do not want soft words, I want power.' Or, a last example: 'Have you never heard it spoken of amongst the lower orders at Coal Point?'

Some, though happily not most, of such remarks have forever lost their context. We do, as it happens, know that 'it' was certainly discussed by the Scots miners. We know why the Governor suddenly declared his former protégé Dr McClosky to be 'a nobody'. We can agree that Major Tranchell had indeed put his foot in it considerably. But we do not know what was the incident which Nona Dyang Loya saw through her hibiscus garden hedge at Sagumau on the Coal Point Road. Such oblique documentary references to happenings off-stage

give to the tale of Labuan in the time of my grandfather touches of
ambiguity almost reminiscent of some novel by Henry James.

It is, at any rate, perfectly clear that many of the disputes which
bedevilled Governor Pope Hennessy's otherwise enlightened rule in
Labuan were complicated by his hasty marriage. The new Governor's
strong programme of reform, his profound belief in racial equality,
and his stinging comments on the way the Colony had previously
been run by what he termed 'a set of incapables' did not endear him to
the old timers. A sullen opposition party formed. At its head was Hugh
Low, the Colonial Treasurer, who even went to the length of writing
a long article in a Singapore newspaper criticising the new Governor's
tax policies. Since Low was now the Governor's father-in-law any
disagreement between them upon official matters ended by becoming
an acrid family quarrel, while purely family rows, which broke out
very soon after the marriage, influenced and impeded official work.
The Governor accused Low of using 'domestic pressure'—the
influence of Low's young daughter on her husband—to advance his
own ambitions. He found Hugh Low impervious to his charm. The
most cajoling eloquence would merely goad his father-in-law to
reply that he wanted power and not 'soft words'. Low, on the other
hand, accused the Governor of knowing nothing of colonial administration and of trying to force through a set of showy measures of
reform. He also stated that the Governor was a bad husband, and that
his daughter was 'most unhappy' in her marriage.

That Kitty Hennessy was not happy in these early years of her
married life we can only too easily believe. Any romantic girl of
seventeen married to a man just twice her age might find adjustment
difficult under ideal circumstances. Those of Labuan were far from
that. Once the Brunei honeymoon was over she can have been but
seldom alone with her husband in Government House. She knew that
John Pope Hennessy's sister and his cousin did not like her. Later,
when the Governor's spendthrift younger brother Willie Hennessy
came out from Cork City to work as private secretary at Government
House her opponents inside the family rose to three. Her husband
criticised her father, and her father criticised her husband. After seven
months of marriage she left her husband's house and went back to
live at her father's. She was indeed between the Devil and the deep
blue Sulu Sea.

Kitty Hennessy was soon persuaded to return from this first of her
fugues. In March 1869 she gave birth at Government House to a son,

John Patrick—'my Johnnie'. On this child she concentrated her affection and for the next half year all went well. In August 1869, however, the Governor refused to recommend Hugh Low for a rise in salary. Low then asked for leave to go to Sarawak, and Mrs Hennessy said she wished to accompany her father as her brother Hugo had recently arrived in Kuching. Both requests were refused, whereupon the Governor's wife once more withdrew to her father's house, sending the baby, with its nurse, its child attendant and all the luggage in the Governor's carriage, while she herself put on her bonnet and walked down 'by the road and by a private path'. The Governor, who asserted that his wife loved him, believed her latest flight to have been a form of blackmail engineered by Low and by the clique of officials who disliked his administrative methods. Low contended that he knew nothing about his daughter's plans until, riding home from the Public Offices in Victoria, he found his hallway blocked by 'packages containing lady's paraphernalia' and his verandah occupied by his grandchild and the nurse. He said that he told his daughter that her step was quite illegal. She replied 'in the strongest manner' that she could never live with her husband again.

Three months went by, during which the wife and husband corresponded. Then, in the first week of November, Governor Pope Hennessy issued a writ of Habeas Corpus against his father-in-law, on the grounds of his illegal detention of the Governor's child. After some unsavoury scenes in the Labuan court-room, and some equivocal intervention by the Colonial Chaplain, Mr Beard, Mrs Hennessy and her son returned once more to Government House.

All this was bad enough for a Governor aiming to raise the tone of life in a depressed colonial station. But it had almost worse repercussions outside the Colony. Low sent, through the Governor, a very lengthy account of the proceedings to the Secretary of State in London. The Governor sent an even longer, and extremely intricate and legalistic, refutation of Low's statement. This despatch, which reached Downing Street soon after another in which Governor Hennessy explained that he had been obliged to suspend the Harbour Master and Post Master, Mr Claude de Crespigny, caused a disastrous impression on the Colonial Office staff. The Secretary of State 'altogether declined' to give any consideration to 'this wretched affair'. Low was officially reprimanded, and Pope Hennessy was privately reproved. 'The only thing that seems quite clear', the Parliamentary Under-Secretary of State minuted, 'is that Mr Hennessy and Mr Low cannot be left together in the same place. I suppose Mr Low hoped to have governed the Colony through his son-in-law and failing in this has declared war against him.' The general feeling was that the affair reflected little credit on either party.

The Labuan Habeas Corpus case gave the Downing Street authorities further food for thought. Were the manifest advantages of having, in Hennessy, a galvanic and on occasion brilliant Governor, who had modernised the town of Victoria, attracted shipping and trade to its harbours, apparently increased the revenue and enlisted the co-operation of the Chinese, offset by the fact that he was evidently an angry young Irishman who could not, or would not, get along with his English subordinates?

IV

Punctuated by rows and by monsoon weather, year after year jolted by. The Governor's hopes rose with each mail, only to fall again when he found that the Colonial Office bag brought him no order of release from his island purgatory. At times he found relief in crossing on consular business to the court of Brunei, or in spending a few days alone in his 'wild hut' on an islet at the entrance of Victoria Harbour. He paid a state visit to Dutch Borneo. He organised race-meetings on the Plain, gave evening parties at Government House, or improvised an expedition to study an eclipse of the sun. From Singapore he imported glazed street-lamps to light the silent streets of Victoria at nightfall, and from Dublin he secured four improbable types, teetotal Irish constables, to overhaul the expanded police force so that the costly military contingent on the island could become superfluous and be withdrawn. Vaccination against the smallpox was made compulsory. The opium and spirits monopolies were sold and re-sold. The Coal Company still did not pay.

There were changes in the European personnel, and in their posts. St John and Captain Maclean had gone. De Crespigny was suspended and left the island. The Chief Constable was dismissed. Dr Treacher was persuaded to retire upon his pension after a gruelling investigation into his incompetence. The Governor's cousin Cody was made Colonial Treasurer. William Hennessy came out from Cork to replace him as Private Secretary, after lingering for expensive weeks in Singapore. A young Irishman, Captain Hervey, who had become Chief Superintendent of the new police force, and a great favourite of the Governor, acted as tale-bearer to Government House. Hugh

Low, having resigned the Treasurership, remained Police Magistrate, but was forced also to tackle the jobs of Harbour and Post Master. The room he had used in the Public Offices for the last twenty years was taken from him. What the Colonial Office staff recognised as 'the vicious state of antagonism' between son- and father-in-law was now overt. The Governor referred to Low in conversation as 'The Plague'.

As ominous and unfriendly as the indifferent rain-forests, this was the background to the last scene we shall witness before we, too, leave Labuan for good. The setting for this scene was a thatched house, with steps leading up to a verandah, at the hamlet of Sagumau on the Coal Point Road.

This house had been bought by Mr Low in 1868 and given by him to his Malay child's mother, the Nona Dyang Loya, otherwise the Nona Tuan Low. It stood in a garden-compound amidst fruit trees. Nearby were green paddy-fields in which the Nona's buffaloes would wallow and graze. The house, which boasted a billiard-room, was inhabited by the Nona, her mother, her brother and her little girl. They were a family of Sarawak origin. A sister, Nona Dyang Kamariah, was living respectably with a wealthy European in Singapore. When she visited her sister on Labuan she would trave lwith a retinue of three servants, and she herself was richly dressed in semi-European, semi-oriental clothes, with smart Balmoral boots. There were two more brothers, one of whom, Jelludin, baptised as 'John' by Bishop MacDougall, had been despatched to England to be trained as a Christian missionary; the boy had, however, displeased the religious authorities. Shipped back to Labuan he was made a turnkey in the local gaol.

We may recall that on his daughter Kitty's arrival in Labuan, Hugh Low had told her about this quiet liaison, and that he had also told his future son-in-law shortly before the marriage. While he was Acting Governor prior to Pope Hennessy's arrival the Nona Tuan Low would bring their child to see him on Sunday afternoons, driving up to Government House porch in a hired carriage. He said that he had never permitted any familiarity between his legal daughter and his natural one. In Low's own opinion his conduct had been both normal and discreet.

One day in late September 1870, when Hugh Low had arranged to take his daughter Mrs Hennessy out riding, he got a message to say that his child at Sagumau was ill. He therefore called at the house on the Coal Point Road, dismounting and holding his horse's bridle while he spoke to the little girl on the verandah steps. Mrs Hennessy meanwhile remained outside the house, but inside the compound, upon her pony, Beauty. Unluckily McClosky, the Colonial Apothecary, happened to be riding along the Coal Point Road, that same evening. He saw the Governor's wife in the compound of her father's mistress. More unluckily still he repeated what he had seen to the Governor's sister, Mary Hennessy. '*Hinc illae lachrymae!*' the Secretary of State, Lord Kimberley, has scrawled in the margin of the narrative at this point.

Putting down, no doubt, her knitting, the devout Miss Hennessy hastened to tell her brother the Governor of this fresh scandal. The Governor said nothing about the incident either to his wife or to his father-in-law for nearly six months. Low subsequently alleged that this silence was due to the fact that the Governor had put himself in an awkward position by having taken his wife, Kitty, under protest, to call on the Malay, Ersat, who had a very bad reputation in the island. It seems more probable, however, that he at first resisted the efforts of his sister, his brother and his cousin to use the episode as part of a full-scale campaign against his father-in-law. His relatives were much abetted by the Chief Police Superintendent, Captain Hervey, who had no respect for truth and whose carefree Irish nature had recently been warped by discovering that his own wife had been granting rendezvous to another European in the house of a Malay named Baboo. Finally, unwise counsels prevailed, and Captain Hervey set to work to show that the little Sagumau household was in fact a gambling den and a place of ill resort. Could this be proved, it would then logically follow that Mr Low could be brought to book for having, while Police Magistrate, kept up a connection with the Nona's house.

Nothing could be proved. A police watch on the house only revealed that gambling went on in several other houses at Sagumau, but not at Nona Tuan Low's. Her neighbours all testified to the restraint and dignity of her life. Apart from music and poetry in the evening, and the distribution of oranges to young friends, the house was an undisturbed haven of peace. Once only the Nona had given a large feast, with dancing, but this was in discharge of a religious vow. A police raiding party found one single playing card in the house, and that was used as a reel for silk-embroidery thread. But in June 1870, a man was arrested at Coal Point for illegally peddling tobacco. He admitted having sold five cents' worth of it at, or outside, the house of

Nona Dyang Loya. This was enough for Captain Hervey, who, aided by the Governor's cousin Cody, drew up a series of indictments against Hugh Low, accusing him of owning a house inhabited by persons 'known to the police'. At a curious enquiry which followed, Low was suspended from his offices and his emoluments. He retaliated by charging the Governor with conspiracy, and spoke of 'perjury and tyranny' being used against him.

Throughout the Labuan community a species of hysteria now prevailed. It was only calmed by what the Colonial Chaplain called 'the welcome, or rather joyful, news' that a new Governor had been appointed by the Secretary of State. John Pope Hennessy had received promotion—the Governorship of the Bahamas. This post was another insular one, but it was more important, more lucrative and more healthy than that on Labuan.

The new Governor, Henry Bulwer, reached Labuan in September 1871. Mr and Mrs Pope Hennessy left the island three days later. Travelling alone with their child (Miss Mary and her brother William had already withdrawn from the Colony), they passed through Saigon and Singapore. Early in the voyage my grandmother celebrated her twenty-first birthday. In Singapore she distinguished herself by insisting, against her husband's wishes, on attending a Government House garden-party on the day they landed. When he pointed out that, after four years on Labuan, her clothes were out of fashion, she commandeered a Government House carriage and an aide-de-camp to go shopping. The strong-willed couple reached London at the beginning of December. They put up at the Grosvenor Hotel. Away from Labuan and free from all family pressures, they could get to know one another at last.

BOOK III

THE FEVER COAST

1872–1873

———

W HEN, WITH JAUNTY STEP and ready smile, Governor Pope Hennessy called on Mr Herbert at the Colonial Office that December he found an urbane welcome. Despite the quarrels that had marked his rule in Labuan, it was generally felt within the Eastern Department that he had done a good job. He had abolished the imperial subsidy, saved the War Office twelve thousand pounds a year by replacing the military contingent by native policemen and left the Colony apparently self-supporting. His successor in Labuan soon discovered that Pope Hennessy had much over-estimated future revenue and that the imperial subsidy would once more be required. But in December 1871 the Colonial Office staff still considered that, although eccentric and perhaps a trifle difficult, Pope Hennessy was an asset. When, some months later, an unfriendly letter to *The Times* newspaper referred to 'Mr Pope Hennessy the late and unsuccessful Governor of Labuan', the Secretary of State, Lord Kimberley, minuted on it 'This is quite untrue'.

At this period the British Colonial Empire was run from 'an ordinary family residence' at the top of Downing Street. The whole staff comprised sixty-seven persons, of whom fifteen were copyists and twelve were office messengers. Until 1877 this staff was recruited by patronage and not by open competitive examination. All 'gentlemen of family and position', the mental calibre of the clerks who sorted and made précis of the despatches as they came into the office in white sealed canvas bags was high, and they were famous for their courtesy to visiting colonial officials and colonists. Though small in scale by modern standards, the amount of work was considerable: in 1870 a total of some twenty-six thousand despatches, letters and telegrams were received or sent out from Downing Street, and at this period three-quarters of them were still seen personally by the Secretary of State, whose room on the first floor overlooked St James's Park. Also on this floor were the rooms of the Permanent Under-Secretary, an official who did not change with the Cabinet, and of the Assistant Under-Secretary. On the ground floor the Parliamentary Under-

Secretary of State had his office next to the library. The rest of the staff were housed in comfortable little rooms on the second floor and in the attics. Work did not begin until eleven o'clock in the morning. Some of the more hard-pressed senior officials of the permanent staff would take papers back to their own homes at night, but on the whole the atmosphere of the office was calm and leisurely. The Governors most popular within the office were those who had a gift for 'keeping things quiet' in the Colonies they governed. The spirit of the Colonial Office at this moment was all against the acquisition of new colonial territories. It was dedicated to the maintenance of the *status quo*.

The moment at which my grandfather returned to London, December 1871, found the Colonial Office staff, and in particular the men who worked in the African Department under old Sir George Barrow, in a state of some perplexity about the West African Settlements—the Gambia, the Gold Coast, Sierra Leone and Lagos. The Governor of these settlements was coming home on leave, and had no wish to return to the most notoriously unhealthy of all our territories overseas. Simultaneously negotiations were proceeding with the Dutch Government, which wanted to transfer its possessions on the 'fever coast' to the British flag. This transfer had been under discussion since the year 1869, when Lord Clarendon, then in charge of the Foreign Office, had told the Secretary of State for the Colonies, Lord Granville, that 'the Dutch appear anxious to be quit of their *damnosa possessio* in Africa'. These discussions had been shelved when the King of Holland intervened against the transfer: 'I suppose that stupid pig the King will not part with his costly & useless African possessions', wrote Lord Clarendon, to which Lord Granville replied next day: 'I am not surprised at the King of Holland declining to part with Elmina—as he probably does not know where it is, or what an impossible problem it is for him.' It had already been made clear to the Dutch that the British Government would not acquire the territory by purchase: 'There is no care in this country for our African possessions', Lord Clarendon had written to Admiral Harris, the British Ambassador at The Hague. 'I believe that an announcement of intention to get rid of them would be popular and I am sure that it would be exceedingly difficult to get a vote from the H. of Commons for extending them.'

When negotiations were resumed the Dutch reverted to an earlier suggestion that the British Government should pay only the value of the stores left in Elmina and the other forts. Terms had been agreed,

and the Colonial Office were now seeking a 'capable man' prepared to
go out to West Africa, effect the smooth transfer of the territory from
one flag to the other, and administer the settlements for six months.
This was the problem facing the African Department in December
1871. No unemployed Colonial servant of suitable rank would consent
to go to Africa for so short a period. Then John Pope Hennessy,
Governor-designate of the Bahamas, appeared in London. He was
known to have got on markedly well with the Dutch authorities in
Borneo, and to have a passionate sympathy for the coloured races.
Asked to defer his assumption of office in the Bahamas for six months
he readily agreed.

At the end of January 1872 Pope Hennessy and his wife crossed to
The Hague, where he consulted Baron Gericke, the Foreign Minister,
Mr van Bosse, the Minister for the Colonies, and Colonel Nagtglas, the
Dutch Governor of Elmina. It was known in London that the people
of Elmina, who owed an ill-defined allegiance to the inland kingdom
of the Ashanti, were not anxious to be transferred to British rule. The
Colonial Office had made it clear that the British Crown could not
accept Elmina if there were any risk of riots or carnage. The Dutch,
who were longing to get rid of Elmina and their other Gold Coast
forts, minimised the potential dangers, Colonel Nagtglas telling
Hennessy that the Elminas were 'easy to manage' and that all that
would be needed was 'a great show of force' without the actual use of
it. All the same the 'King' of Elmina had sent a special envoy to The
Hague with a violently-worded protest against the transfer. Pope
Hennessy arranged a 'friendly interview' with this envoy, a native
Elmina shopkeeper named Mr David Mills Graves. He judged Graves
to be 'a sensible person' who might 'ultimately cooperate in carrying
the Treaty into effect'. Optimistic as ever, he made light of the opposition of the Elminas, as well as of the dark tales of war preparations at
Kumasi, where, in the depths of the Ashanti forests, the young
Asantehene Kofi Karikari had five years previously succeeded to the
Golden Stool. The idea of West African administration appealed
strongly to John Pope Hennessy, who once more felt that here were
misunderstood colonial problems with which an enlightened mind
could deal.

The treaty of transfer was ratified in February 1872. In that same
month Mr and Mrs Pope Hennessy, their child and an Irish nursery
maid, sailed from Liverpool for Freetown, capital of Sierra Leone and
headquarters of the Governor-in-Chief of the West African settle-

ments. At the time of this voyage aboard the steamship *Benin* little Johnnie Hennessy was just on three years old. The wise septuagenarian head of the African Department, Sir George Barrow, had implored the boy's father not to expose him to the fatal climate of Freetown, then known as 'the White Man's Grave'. Perhaps because he and his wife could not bear to be parted from the child whom they adored, perhaps because he thought that he knew far more about the tropics than Barrow, Governor Pope Hennessy took no heed.

On 27 February 1872 the new Governor-in-Chief and his family landed at Freetown, to the fluttering of flags and the boom of shore batteries and of naval guns firing a salute. They took up residence in the Governor's house, Fort Thornton. Here, less than a month after their arrival, the boy Johnnie contracted dysentery and died. He was buried in the chapel of a small local convent. At five-thirty every morning his parents went to hear mass beside his grave. In his book on Equatorial Africa, the Marquis de Compiègne describes the black marble plaque in the convent chapel. It was heaped with fresh flowers daily, and engraved upon it was the single word: *Baby*. He found the Governor and his wife 'brisés par la douleur' and wearing permanent mourning. He calls Hennessy 'homme d'une politesse et d'une bonté exquises, catholique fervent marié à une charmante jeune femme.' Both husband and wife were forever helping the nuns' mission, and formed what Compiègne termed 'the edification' of this body.

II

The quick and meaningless death of their only child in the fetid, sodden African port of Freetown was a thunder-stroke of fate which crushed his parents. Remorse was added to their sorrow, for they could so easily have left the boy at home. 'In truth no change, work, or anything else can make me forget my little boy', John Pope Hennessy wrote to Sir George Barrow. 'How often I have reproached myself for not taking your advice about him!' His wife, who had become a convert to Roman Catholicism during their stay in England, took refuge in aiding the charitable work of the Christian missions in Sierra Leone, while the Governor immersed himself in the myriad administrative problems of the West African Settlements, giving a high priority to a scheme for reducing by sanitary reform the notorious death-rate of Sierra Leone.

The settlements of Gambia, the Gold Coast, and Lagos had only been made appendages of Sierra Leone as recently as 1866. This was done on the recommendation of the West African Committee of 1865, of which Pope Hennessy's close friend Sir Charles Adderley had been chairman. The Committee had also recommended the ultimate withdrawal of British rule from 'all West African Governments except, perhaps, Sierra Leone'. In its cautious, vacillating way, the Colonial Office had neither rejected this latter recommendation, nor put it into effect. No one in England thought that the Settlements had much of a future. Indeed very few persons in England thought about the West African Settlements at all.

Sierra Leone, in those days merely a small coastal strip comprising Freetown and its immediate surroundings, formed an incisive contrast to the other British West African Settlements. These still remained what they had always been—small fortified trading outposts strung along the shore-line of independent native African 'kingdoms'. The attitude of the native 'kings' or tribal chieftains to the Europeans in these forts was complex and not easily predictable, especially since the abolition of the slave trade on which these chieftains and the European merchants had grown rich. Whereas Cape Coast Castle, Elmina and the other European stations on the coast had long ago been founded as depots for the despatch to the West Indies and the Americas of herds of manacled Africans, Sierra Leone had, since 1791, been organised as an experimental settlement for escaped or liberated slaves. After the abolition of the Slave Trade in 1807, Great Britain had taken over Sierra Leone as a Crown Colony. With the final abolishment of slavery itself thousands of negroes from the West Indies and the United States had been shipped into Freetown. These former slaves were English-speaking, had largely forgotten their tribal beliefs and allegiances, and were many of them nominally Christian. Soon there evolved a middle-class of educated and semi-educated negroes who aspired to service under Government. Some of these 'educated Africans' found in the new Governor-in-Chief their most ardent champion.

My grandfather's enthusiasms were as full-blooded as his antipathies. He now began to urge the Colonial Office to appoint distinguished negroes such as Dr Africanus Horton to important administrative positions. This policy had been recommended by the 1865 West African Committee, but the Colonial Office were not prepared to implement it, rejecting Dr Horton's claim, for instance, because he was 'perfectly black'. In spite of one or two small scandals about native cashiers Pope Hennessy wrote that he remained convinced that 'as respects the custody of public money or any other responsibility the Negro is as trustworthy as the white man'. He was soon busy making plans for 'the higher education of the African race', for he believed that the system of sending a few children of the wealthier Africans to be educated in Europe had the effect of spoiling their characters: 'It is painful', he wrote, 'to notice the contrast between such young men, who ought to be the natural leaders of public opinion in their own country, and the Chiefs and people of the Interior who have been untouched by Europeans. The latter have a manly bearing, a natural courtesy, a very keen intelligence and a frank and honest disposition. The negroes who have been educated in Europe, or who have been forced here into a sort of semi-European mould, are the very reverse of all this.' The coast negroes who had been to Europe had learned to drink, to lie and to be idle. How much more rewarding would it be to have facilities for higher education on the West Coast itself: 'I think a West African University founded on a very humble basis, ought to be established, where not only the sons of rich Africans could be educated, but where, like in the early Irish Universities, and some of the Continental Universities of our own times, even the poorest youths who had talents and a real taste for knowledge might by sizarships or fellowships have an opportunity of cultivating learning', he wrote.

The Secretary of State, Lord Kimberley, found this suggestion 'extremely interesting': 'we should study what is doing in India to promote education, & endeavour to introduce a similar system into these African settlements. Mere missionary education will never effect much.' His subalterns inside the Office were listlessly sceptical, doubting 'whether such a plan would succeed' and considering such a University 'more easily conceived than established'. Lord Kimberley's detached attitude soon became an outraged one when, in December 1872, Governor Pope Hennessy treated him to a dissertation on what he called the 'Superior Being' theory held by the Europeans in the Settlements. 'I can assure your Lordship that the Natives know very well that the white men sent to the coast of Africa are not Superior Beings. The fact that the Negroes are keen enough to detect the real characters of the white men renders this "Superior Being" assumption a frequent source of difficulty to the Government.' He quoted his predecessor, Sir Arthur Kennedy, who had written that 'the moral influence of this Government depends more upon the men than measures. The Negro is quick in discovering the quality of his master's morals and breeding.' He added that Sir Richard Burton had believed that 'in intellect the *black* race is palpably superior'. Lord Kimberley categorised these statements as 'rubbish': 'It is impossible not to distrust the judgement of a man who can write in this strain.' Distrust Governor Hennessy's judgement or no, the Secretary of State could not deny that the new Governor was making rapid improvements in Sierra Leone. For these there was much scope.

It had not taken Governor Hennessy long to decide that Freetown was 'radically unhealthy'. Built upon the southern side of a broad river estuary, the capital of Sierra Leone lies in a plain backed by high wooded hills. In my grandfather's day the river-mouth was choked with vegetable decomposition, which, driven back into the town twice a day by the tide, filled the streets with noxious vapours. Daily at dawn, and all through the rainy season, the Governor and his wife would take a brisk walk up Leicester Hill behind the town. From this eminence, he wrote, they could 'observe the river vapours lying motionless over the houses of Freetown'. Pope Hennessy had discovered that when, some fifty years before, European officials had lived in the hills there had been much less illness amongst them, and far fewer deaths. He therefore suggested to the Colonial Office that the administrative capital should be moved up to Leicester, a small dirty village with but a single street, well situated on Leicester Hill. 'The removal of the residence of the Europeans to a healthy spot would if practicable be of inestimable advantage', agreed Lord Kimberley. The Colonial Office toyed vaguely with the project, but in the end it came to nothing.

Although boasting a stone Anglican Cathedral, and a number of solid old official residences, the capital of Sierra Leone at this epoch was a shanty town of ineffable squalor. Some twenty-one thousand persons were living in 'houses' the floors of which were always under water in the rainy season. Too many people slept packed into one room, 'inhaling poisoned air'. Many parts of the town were undrained and covered with rank vegetation. Sanitation consisted of open cesspits; one corner in the yard of every house was piled high with a mountain of human excrement. Certain houses occupied by Europeans were in the same state, and their lavatories sometimes consisted of a hole cut in the boarded floor of the sitting-room with a chair frame placed over it. The old cemetery in the centre of the town was described by Governor Hennessy as 'a mass of filth and weeds—dangerous to public health and painful to look at'. The number of bodies buried in this and in the town's one other cemetery was 'incalculable'. In the Colonial Cemetery, just to the east of the barracks, and encircled by native huts, nearly eight thousand corpses had been interred in the last fourteen years.

The new Governor had the cemeteries put in order. He set about the introduction of sanitary education and of the dry earth system; it was the same story as that of the sepoy latrines at Labuan, but on a civic scale. He also directed that the fish, meat and vegetable markets be cleared of the accumulated refuse of years, and that the numerous carcases of dogs, goats and hogs which lay rotting in the streets and water-courses of Freetown be removed. He was not sanguine as to the results of his campaign, for he found that the Mahommedan inhabitants alone had any basic idea of cleanliness. The handful of European traders in Sierra Leone had degenerated and lost their more civilised habits. They set no standards to which the negroes might attempt to conform. Since horses could not live in the climate of Freetown the Europeans kept small curricles drawn by harnessed Africans; my grandfather particularly objected to the sight of 'European Missionaries dragged about by pairs of negro boys in lieu of horses'. He concluded that, even could it be made a sanitary paradise, Freetown with its hot, moist, demoralising climate could never really suit Europeans—a view which brought him back full cycle to his wish to fill the administration with intelligent and well-educated men of African stock.

Governor Pope Hennessy liked his West African work—'great variety & activity, great power & responsibility' he wrote to Governor Bulwer, his successor in Labuan. He was at his desk from eight o'clock till five, with half an hour's interval for luncheon. He governed with a Legislative Council, the most useful members of which, he asserted, were natives. He soon found his Colonial Secretary, Captain Kendall, 'incapable of doing his duty' and suspended him for striking a native messenger. His confidential secretary was a 'useful & trustworthy' young negro named Lewis and, with the exception of Mrs Hennessy's Irish maid, the little household at Fort Thornton was, of course, run by African butlers and boys. Originally an old fort, the house stood in restricted grounds on a slight hill, with a splendid view over the harbour. At its back, on a higher hill, were the barracks, occupied by West Indian troops. Apart from adding a staircase and having running water laid on, Governor Hennessy did nothing to renovate Fort Thornton which he described as plainly furnished and comfortable with a good drawing-room, a good dining-room, one large bedroom and five attics. The Governor's office gave off the dining-room and the Council Room opened off that.

Life in Fort Thornton was lonely. 'As to society, there is really none', wrote Hennessy. 'I like the Colonial officials—but, except on business, I never see them. The Bishop, Dr Cheetham . . . is the only person I visit. He is a sensible and interesting man.' Apart from missionaries' wives and some nuns there were hardly any European women in Sierra Leone. The two ladies who had tried to comfort Kitty Hennessy after the death of her child—Mrs Harriet Spencer, and Mrs Cheetham, the Bishop's wife—were both dead of African fever within the year. In 1872 to 1873 the death-rate in the tiny European community in Freetown was two or three deaths a month. As in Labuan Pope Hennessy himself kept healthy by abstinence from alcohol, by frugality and by exercise. Steamers putting in at Freetown usually brought news of fresh outbreaks of yellow fever on the Oil Rivers to the south, or of deaths from the same scourge at Bathurst in the Gambia. His early medical training in Cork City enabled Hennessy to remain calm where cases of the dreaded yellow fever were concerned. When two of its victims were isolated in Freetown hospital in December 1872 he visited them himself to make sure that the ward was clean and the nurses doing their duty.

The government of Sierra Leone was, however, only one part of Governor Pope Hennessy's West African assignment. We may recall that he had been sent out from England primarily to take over the Dutch forts on the Gold Coast. The solemnities of this transfer were slightly delayed by the death of Hennessy's child, but five days after the funeral the Governor-in-Chief, accompanied by his young wife in deep mourning, left Freetown for Cape Coast Castle aboard his official steam yacht, the *Sherbro*. From Bishopscourt, Sierra Leone, Bishop Cheetham sent a valedictory note to 'wish you both a safe & pleasant trip, tho' it is hardly a voyage for a lady'. The journey along the coast of Africa took five days. During it we may examine the origins of the curious, the ominous situation which lay waiting for Governor Pope Hennessy on the Gold Coast, in the cruel old slaving forts.

III

Of the forty-two teeming European forts which had at one time stood, white in the African sun glare, along the Guinea Coast, twenty were still in use in 1872. Originally there had been Portuguese, Dutch,

English, French, Danish, Swedish and Brandenburger fortresses; now there were only the English and the Dutch. By a transference of sovereignty in 1867 certain of these forts had been exchanged between the Dutch and the English, but the natives of Kommenda and other former English outposts to windward had refused to raise the Dutch flag and had plunged into open revolt. Tired of the profitless local wars in which they had thereby become involved, the Dutch Government had at length decided to withdraw altogether from the Coast, handing over their nine forts—Elmina, Kommenda, Shama, the two Sekondis, Butri, Dixcove, Axim and Beyin—to the somewhat reluctant British Government. By the treaty signed at The Hague in February 1872 the British became the only white power on the Gold Coast. They thus automatically assumed responsibility for the safety of all the European traders and missionaries in the area, inheriting as well the complex tribal feuds with which the Dutch had found themselves unable to contend. The British had long exercised a tacit form of Protectorate over the natives in the neighbourhood of the British forts. They now took on the additional role of protecting power to tribes which, allies of Holland for many generations, had a long history of anti-British skirmishes behind them. It was a situation which looked simpler viewed from Downing Street than from Elmina or Cape Coast Castle.

The headquarters of the British were at Cape Coast Castle, where Pope Hennessy's deputy, Governor Ussher, held sway. The Dutch had their headquarters at Elmina, the most imposing and the oldest of the surviving coastal fortresses (many of which are being carefully restored by the Ghanaian Government today). The great castle of St George d'Elmina is, like that of Cape Coast, built on blackish rock above the tumbling sea. It gives an impression of monumental dignity and determination. Within its white-washed curtain-walls and beyond its drawbridge, the huge oblong central courtyard lies exposed to the blinding heat of the West African sun; only the old slaving quarters, where the newly-bought negroes were herded before being shipped to the Americas upon 'the Middle Passage' are shady, dank, sinister and cool. The Palaver Hall itself is on the first floor of the square central building, and commands a fine view of the courtyard. Eastwards of the castle there stretches a curving sandy coast, belted by cocoa-nut palms and dotted with the long surf-boats of the fishermen. Upon the eastern horizon, just visible in the setting sun, rises the bulk of Cape Coast Castle, where L.E.L. lies buried in the sloping, rhomboid castle yard.

The Portuguese had built Elmina in 1482, allegedly shipping it from Portugal in cut and numbered stones, together with a gang of workmen to erect it on the chosen site. The Dutch, led by Count Maurice of Nassau, had captured Elmina in 1637. Now, after two hundred and thirty-five years, the Dutch flag was to be lowered from the castle for the last time, and the Union Jack run up in its place. When it came to the actual ceremony of the transfer of sovereignty Governor Pope Hennessy most tactfully arranged that both flags should fly from the same staff until sundown. On the following morning the British flag was hoisted alone.

The Gold Coast forts had been built on ground leased from whichever native King ruled in the locality. The leases granted a European power permission to construct a fortress, but did not give it extra-territorial rights. Through three and a half centuries the Europeans on the Guinea Coast had thus lived and traded in the anomalous position of tenants of the native tribesmen. They had no jurisdiction outside the walls of their citadels, yet they were expected and indeed obliged to protect the people on whose land they were living, and they had frequently intervened to stop the tribal wars. These wars were themselves largely engendered by the very presence of the Europeans, since only by victory over an enemy tribe could a local King procure in sufficient quantities the young and virile human merchandise which the Christian white men bought. Although the slave trade was ultimately abolished, the habit of warfare persisted down the coast.

The notes, or 'bonds', by which an European power agreed to pay tribute in gold to some specified native kingdom were highly valued. In time of war they passed by right of conquest to the victor. By the defeat of the Ashantis and their allies at the bloody battle of Dodowa in 1826, the English had won back from the enemy their own promissory bonds. Henceforth they ceased to pay tribute for Cape Coast Castle and their other forts. They claimed the land on which these stood, and could have asserted, though they did not do so, that they now owned the land occupied by the Dutch forts as well. In fact the Dutch continued to pay tribute for Elmina to the inland kingdom of Ashanti, for the Asantehene still held the Elmina bond. The Asantehene regarded the Elmina people as his vassals, and Elmina itself as his one legitimate outlet to the coast. For these and other perfectly valid reasons, Kofi Karikari and his advisers in Kumasi opposed the transfer of Elmina to the British crown. Here was the crux of the problem which John Pope Hennessy had been sent out fresh from London to solve.

It was not an easy problem. West African administrators of far longer experience still knew very little about the Ashanti kingdom and its capital of Kumasi, shrouded in dripping forests. It was known that the kingdom was held together by a mystical belief in the power of the Golden Stool, a seventeenth-century object never used by the Asantehene as a throne but carried before him in its own litter, attended by its own retinue of musicians, priests, servants and slaves. Very few white men had ever penetrated to Kumasi and when they had done so they had only been able to communicate through interpreters of dubious reliability, whose knowledge of Dutch and English was, to say the least of it, faulty, and whose healthy fear of the Ashantis made their own attitude to European employers ambivalent. The subtlety of the Ashanti constitution escaped these Europeans. They regarded the Asantehene as a despot and his subjects as savages, whereas in fact the Ashanti King, whose claim to the throne was invariably matrilineal, was merely the mouthpiece of his assembled councillors, could not take personal decisions, and if he displeased his subjects was told to abdicate. Europeans did not realise that, if bound by certain oaths and most notably by the Great Oath of Ashanti, the Asantehene and his councillors could be trusted absolutely, nor that their ambitions were limited to gaining access to a single seaport on the coast. European prejudice against Ashanti was not indeed surprising, for a constitutional monarchy allegedly based on human sacrifice was not acceptable to western minds. The demise of each King of the Ashanti was marked by the wholesale slaughter of his chief courtiers, attendants and slaves. In the Death Grove on the forest's edge at Kumasi were heaped the bodies of tens of thousands of victims of almost daily ritual murder. In a sumptuous hall of the King's palace the stools of his ancestors stood caked in human blood and swarming with flies.

Kofi Karikari, the youthful Asantehene with whom Governor Pope Hennessy now began to negotiate by messenger, had succeeded to the Golden Stool in 1867. He was not in himself an especially warlike young man, and when subsequently deposed for theft and sacrilege he disappointed his subjects by omitting to commit ritual suicide. He consistently declared that he did not want to fight the English or their protected tribes, but that his Council, and the Queen Mother—a conservative and jovial matriarch—insisted on it. Kofi Karikari had inherited the indecisive state of truce which had terminated the Fifth Ashanti War. His subjects expected him to resume the war, the chief

results of which so far had been the closing of the roads—or, more
properly, of the forest tracks—to Ashanti from the coast, and the
capture by the Asantehene of a small group of German and Swiss
missionaries who had been kept hostage in Kumasi for three years. The
release of the 'Basle missionaries' soon became a major object of my
grandfather's activities. They were not unkindly treated in Kumasi,
for to the Asantehene these pious white captives were a source of
modest pride. In Cape Coast Castle the British held some Ashanti
hostages of importance. In the town of Elmina there was an Ashanti
force, sent down there with an Ashanti ambassador to announce the
accession of Kofi Karikari to the Golden Stool. When he had presented
his credentials to the King of Elmina, this envoy had been sacrificed as
protocol required. His attendants stayed on, spying and making
trouble in the town.

IV

From the deck-rail of the Governor's yacht Sherbro, as she glided
down the Guinea coast, the old Renaissance and seventeenth-century
fortifications, standing high on their rocky promontories above the
restless surf, had a romantic air. Once you were ashore this illusion
vanished. Soon after landing at Cape Coast that April my grandfather
performed the 'disagreeable duty' of telling the Administrator, Mr
Ussher, that he found the town 'to be the most filthy and apparently
neglected place I had ever seen under anything like civilized government'.

The town of Cape Coast clustered round the castle. It was larger
than the other British stations on the coast, and had wide main streets
which, though macadamised, were ill-drained and dirty. The European
residents and the better-off natives lived in whitewashed clay houses
with overhanging balconies and verandahs painted green, while the
bulk of the Cape Coast people were crowded into a warren of thatched
mud huts. Beneath these they buried their dead relatives in shallow
graves scratched in the earth floor. Some of the negroes and half-castes
wore European clothing, but most of them were dressed in ample
cotton togas of brilliant colours. The women sported copper and
silver bangles, and heavy gold ornaments thrust into their plaited hair.
As Fantees these natives were the traditional enemies of the Ashanti,
for protection against whom they had long relied on British aid.

Government House, Cape Coast, was rented from a commercial
firm in the town. A capacious building, it was now virtually uninhabit-

able during the rainy season, since the roof, and the ground floor ceilings, leaked 'like a sieve'. The dining-room alone was fit for use. Mr and Mrs Ussher had laid out a vivid tropical flower-garden. They kept up a strip of level green lawn on which they gave croquet parties for the native ladies. In a cage on the verandah was coiled a puff adder eight feet long.

On his return to the Gold Coast, Mr Ussher had left his wife in England. When my grandparents, to the chanting of native boatmen, were carried ashore from the flat-bottomed surf-boats used for landing passengers at Cape Coast, they were introduced by Mr Ussher to a Mrs Finlason who was doing the honours at Government House. It was not until 'each gentleman among the officials' at Cape Coast came to the Governor to express 'his indignation and horror' at her presence that the Hennessys realised that she was one of Ussher's numerous mistresses. A bull-necked, lascivious man, whom the Colonial Office had begun to regard as 'another casualty of the climate', Ussher had been appointed Administrator at Cape Coast in 1867, and had previously served for many years at Lagos. Cited in a number of African divorce suits, he was held responsible for several broken marriages, amongst them that of the son of the coloured Bishop of Nigeria, Bishop Crowther. This last scandal had occurred in Lagos, where Ussher used to move into young Samuel Crowther's house whenever he left the town: 'he with Mrs Crowther made my hat a shuttlecock of kicking it about the room', the aggrieved young husband wrote in a long petition to Governor Pope Hennessy. 'Mr Ussher having been the first to tread on the threshold of my domestic comfort with impunity, my wife Mrs Crowther has since sunk deeper and deeper into unfaithfulness and has committed herself with many other parties at Lagos.' Mrs Crowther, by birth a Miss Lemon of Sierra Leone, was divorced in 1872.

Ussher was not at all the sort of Colonial official with whom his new chief, Pope Hennessy, was liable to get on. They had already conferred in London and in Sierra Leone. Now, seeing him in action at Cape Coast, Hennessy judged him to be incompetent and timid— 'the only official who thought it necessary to carry a loaded revolver'. The youth and vigour of the new Governor, together with his sympathetic attitude both to the natives and to the Dutch, probably aroused Ussher's hostility, which my grandfather certainly did nothing to allay. The Colonial Office staff thought it was time that Ussher was moved from the coast: 'Mr Hennessy', wrote Knatchbull Hugessen, 'has gone out as a new broom to sweep clean places which have become foul, & the old brooms & old housemaids (however respectable) will be better away as soon as it can be done.' Ussher, who suffered fearfully from dysentery, was at this time an extremely ill man.

With the other Cape Coast officials, though not with the English merchants, Pope Hennessy established fairly amiable relations. The Colonial Secretary, Mr Salmon, became an admirer of the Governor's 'singular patience and wonderful tact'; but the most picturesque personality was that of Colonel Foster Foster, an ex-soldier who expressed himself so violently that some of his phrases had led the Colonial Office staff to suggest that 'his sanity appears doubtful'. Like every other European on the coast, Colonel Foster Foster was frequently down with fever. 'Colonel Foster is I have heard very ill', Lord Kimberley noted on an application for an increase in the police inspector's salary, '& tho' this is probably his misfortune, not his fault, it wd not be a very good moment (if he is ineffective) to increase his pay.'

Two days after his arrival in Cape Coast, Governor Hennessy went by sea, alone and unarmed, to consult the Dutch Governor and the Chiefs of Elmina, which lay eight miles from the British settlement. Although Ussher and other men with long experience on the coast declared that the Elminas and the native tribes generally would only respond to a show of military force, Pope Hennessy had made up his mind that the pacific, conciliatory tactics he had pursued with the Sultans of the Eastern Archipelago would prove equally effective amongst West African Chiefs. When, on 6 April 1872, the transfer of sovereignty was solemnly and publicly performed at Elmina he again adopted the same civilised attitude, landing in full uniform but without an armed force. Once the Dutch Governor had departed by sea, Pope Hennessy moved into Count Maurice of Nassau's apartments in Fort George d'Elmina. Ussher, who was staying with him there, carried his own revolver from room to room inside the castle, but Governor Hennessy would wander about the streets of the town each evening, chatting to the natives through his interpreter and carrying only an umbrella. Like all his other habits the little Governor's persistent use of his umbrella, to give shade in sunshine and shelter in the rain, was reported back through the forests to Kumasi, where the young King of the Ashanti and the bellicose Queen Mother welcomed the news scornfully as a sure sign that the new Governor was infirm. They themselves had umbrellas galore at Kumasi, but these were huge and ceremonial, and made of silks and velvets shimmering with gold.

The quiet and evidently successful transfer of Elmina delighted the Colonial Office. They had feared riots and bloodshed, and they attributed the absence of these to the ingenuity and suavity with which Governor Pope Hennessy had negotiated with those Elmina leaders opposed to British rule. He was publicly thanked in the House of Commons by the Parliamentary Under-Secretary to the Colonial Office. Sir George Barrow, Knatchbull Hugessen and Lord Kimberley himself all agreed that he had shown 'great tact, ability & discretion'. The Permanent Under-Secretary, Robert Herbert, wrote a private letter congratulating Hennessy in the same vein: 'I am very glad', Herbert ended, 'that you have thus early had an opportunity of showing so conclusively that the Colonial Office (in this case at all events) knew how to put the right man in the right place. Lord Kimberley, and indeed "all hands", are much pleased with your success.' Hennessy was rewarded with the companionship of the Order of St Michael and St George.

After a few more days in the castle of Elmina, the Governor decided that it was time for him to board the *Sherbro* and proceed to a further dependency of his Government, the islet of Lagos lying in its lagoon off the coast of what is now Nigeria. Before leaving he appointed a civil administrator for Elmina. Mr Ussher urged the choice of a British military officer for this ticklish post, but my grandfather decided on an imaginative dramatic gesture. He announced that he had chosen an educated negro of Elmina, Mr Eminsang. There were several things about Mr Eminsang which Hennessy could not know, amongst them the fact that he was busy divorcing Mrs Eminsang on the grounds of her adultery with Mr Ussher.

The Bishop of Sierra Leone had warned Governor Pope Hennessy not to try to take the yacht *Sherbro* across the Lagos bar. Landing once more by surf-boat, my grandparents were met by a new specimen of officialdom, Captain Glover, the Administrator of Lagos. In Captain Glover the Governor encountered a man whom he soon found to be even more distasteful than lusty Mr Ussher. Before he could more fully develop this antipathy, however, he was hastily summoned back to the Gold Coast by bad news from peaceable Elmina. The riots which he and the Colonial Office were convinced he had forestalled had broken out on his departure. A promising young Dutch lieutenant from the flagship *Admiral de Wassenaer* had been murdered, in broad sunlight, in the streets.

CHAPTER TWO

THE FACTS OF THE murder of poor Lieutenant de Joost are much more certain than the motives for the crime. Sent ashore with money promised to some skilled Elmina workmen by the Dutch, de Joost had finished paying out and was walking back towards the landing-stage in the company of other Dutch officers and of the new Civil Commissioner, Mr George Emile Eminsang. They were all at once confronted by an armed mob brandishing Dutch flags. De Joost was felled by a blow from a rifle butt and then shot as he lay on the ground. His colleagues lugged him into the castle, where he died next day. The drawbridge of St George d'Elmina was raised. The Europeans were besieged within the castle walls.

Eminsang, who had himself narrowly escaped capture by the rioters, took refuge in a private house in the town. Here he stayed hidden, only sending an appeal for help to Captain Turton, who commanded the tiny garrison of Elmina. His appeal was ignored, since Turton thought it madness to try to quell a large-scale revolt with the sixty-odd men at his disposal. Mr Ussher hurried over from Cape Coast, but made no attempt to take charge, to trace the murderers or to institute any sort of enquiry into the crime before the return of Governor Pope Hennessy from Lagos.

When he reached Elmina on the *Sherbro*, the Governor-in-Chief was in a trenchant mood. He accused Ussher of slackness, Captain Turton of cowardice, and accepted Eminsang's resignation. Colonel Foster Foster was ordered to track down the murderers, while a legal expert brought from Lagos opened a judicial inquiry. The Governor's interpreter collected witnesses to prove that de Joost had been murdered by discontented workmen. The evidence of these witnesses was extremely important, for an alternative theory was already abroad. Propagated by Ussher and his supporters, it was favoured by all those in England who later connected Governor Pope Hennessy with the outbreak of the Sixth Ashanti War. This theory was that Lieutenant de Joost had been murdered accidentally. The intended victim was said to have been Eminsang.

To Ussher and his school of thought, Hennessy's appointment of
George Emile Eminsang as Civil Commissioner of Elmina was not a
brilliant stroke of diplomacy, but a ghastly and ignorant blunder. It is
clear that, far from being charmed by the liberalism of the appointment,
the Elminas took it as an insult. For centuries their town had been the
proud seat of the Dutch Government on the coast. The Elmina
people had dreaded English rule lest it demean them. They had been
largely persuaded to accept it by Governor Pope Hennessy's eloquence
and by his promise that their freedom, their 'customs' and their
prestige would not be affected. They then learned with amazement
that the Governor's deputy was to be a half-caste—and they knew well
that in the past only the most insignificant of all the coastal stations
had ever been entrusted to a man of coloured blood. Ussher believed
this discontent to be the cause of the riot and that Eminsang had been
the crowd's real target. In Holland, where the British Ambassador had
some awkward explanations to make, the *Staats Courant* and other
newspapers linked Eminsang's appointment with de Joost's murder.
Although he replaced Eminsang by an European Civil Commissioner,
Governor Hennessy would not allow that his first choice had been an
error. He continued to look upon the appointment of Eminsang as an
intelligent and enlightened step, for he had wished to free the Gold
Coast natives from the 'Superior Being theory' and to show them that
the Queen's representative was willing to delegate his powers to one of
themselves. That the experiment had not worked seemed to him to be
patently due to sabotage by Mr Ussher.

By this time my grandfather had unearthed the old story of Ussher's
share in Eminsang's divorce suit, using this not wholly relevant
episode to try to discredit Ussher with the Colonial Office, and
urging that it altogether accounted for Ussher's attitude towards
Eminsang. Ussher's defence of his inactivity after the murder of de
Joost was to say that the Governor had left him no instructions about
Elmina affairs, and that he had been made to feel that he was never to
interfere in the newly acquired territory. Tired, and ill with dysentery,
he had in fact worked himself up into what a member of the Downing
Street staff called a state of 'sensitive nervousness' over his relations
with his new chief. Pope Hennessy had made it very plain that, to him,
Ussher's long experience of Africa was without consequence. Stiff
and rusty old methods of government must be replaced by flexible
new ones. The ultimate aim would be racial equality, my grandfather's
lifelong ideal.

Even idealists, however, cannot let murderers get away with murder. Colonel Foster Foster produced four suspects in the case of young de Joost. One was acquitted, but three, despite doubts as to their guilt, and impassioned pleas for mercy, were hanged in public from a gallows erected on Elmina castle walls. When they realised that their fate was sealed, they swallowed quantities of gold dust provided by their relatives to ensure that, in the next world, they could at least begin by paying their way.

The Colonial Office staff were not greatly impressed by Hennessy's efforts 'to damage Mr Ussher'—which included an allegation that his bad example had taught the innocent natives of the Gold Coast the 'evil practice' of adultery—but they did feel that the time had come to withdraw Ussher as having 'rather out-stayed his utility on the Gold Coast'. The Governor-in-Chief believed his subordinate to be sensible of the 'leniency and even kindness' which he had showed him. In fact Ussher left Cape Coast the bitter enemy of Pope Hennessy, to whom he managed to do immediate harm in London, and, years later, in Manila and Hong Kong.

Long before Ussher's departure from Cape Coast Castle, he had seen his policies reversed by Governor Pope Hennessy. Ussher and his supporters were certain that the Ashantis were planning to attack the Fantee and other native allies of the British, and to sweep down upon the coast. According to this theory, only the 'closing of the roads'—more precisely the blocking of the narrow forest tracks with fallen tree-trunks and military strong-points—was delaying Kumasi war preparations by denying the Ashantis arms and ammunition from the coast. Two weeks after the transfer of Elmina, and just before the riot in which de Joost was killed, Governor Hennessy sent an amiable letter to the Ashanti King. He told him that he would continue, and moreover double, the annual stipend which the Dutch had paid the Asantehene for Elmina, and that as an earnest of good faith he would open the roads at once. By the same messenger he sent the King one hundred yards of embroidered silk as a gift from Queen Victoria, adding to it a golden ring ornamented with the signs of the zodiac as a present from himself. Beneath each of the signs was engraved a letter of the alphabet forming the name *POPEHENNESSY*.

My grandfather reported happily to London on the negotiations for the release of the Basle missionaries which he was then personally conducting with some ambassadors from Kumasi. He found these envoys refreshingly easy to deal with, especially, he noticed, after he

had announced to them that he was opening the roads. He wrote that
he had become 'almost intimate' with Cotico and the other members
of this Ashanti embassy. Having at first refused to offer a ransom for
the missionaries, he subsequently agreed to the sum of £1,000.
Thereupon the Ashantis demanded £2,000, with delivery of the
money at Kumasi before the missionaries could be set free. To sweeten
up the Asantehene still further, Governor Hennessy released the
distinguished Ashantis held hostage in Cape Coast Castle. This
gesture enchanted the Asantehene's ambassadors, but in the Colonial
Office in London it created nothing but dismay. The negotiations
over the missionaries dragged on from month to month. The Governor
remained bright and optimistic. In November of 1872 he wrote to
Count Perponcher (the German Ambassador to Holland whom he
had met while in The Hague) that their release was imminent and
certain: 'On Christmas Day', he added, 'they will be able to drink
Prince Bismarck's health in freedom & perhaps they may add the
health of the ultramontane Governor who worked for their freedom!'
As it turned out, Yuletide 1872 found the emaciated party from Basle
and Hamburg—Herr Kühne, Herr and Frau Ramseyer, and baby
Rosie Ramseyer—still confined to their hutches in Kumasi, singing
French and German hymns, eating fu-fu and moodily watching the
interminable procession of wailing victims headed for the Death Grove
through the relentless rain. It was over a year before the missionaries
were set free, and then only because the Ashanti chieftains hoped to
placate Sir Garnet Wolseley and to stop the triumphal march of his
British troops from the coast to sack Kumasi at the climax of the
Sixth Ashanti War.

During the enquiries into the murder of Lieutenant de Joost,
Governor Hennessy had suddenly restored to power the King of
Elmina, whose deposition had been voted by some but not all of the
Elmina chiefs before the transfer, and had been confirmed by the Dutch.
This was the potentate, by name Kobina Edjan, who had resolutely
opposed the transfer, and had even sent an envoy in protest to
The Hague. Kobina Edjan had been de-stooled for his unswerving
objections to the British take-over of Elmina. He remained as anti-
British and as pro-Ashanti as he had ever been. Critics of my
grandfather's policy declared that he never bothered to find out
Kobina Edjan's real opinions, nor to make him take a loyal oath.
Mr Pope Hennessy had merely declared, in the great inner courtyard
of Fort George d'Elmina, that he recognised Kobina Edjan as King.

He sent him forth from the gates with royal honours and in a palanquin of state.

Appointing an inexperienced Irish Roman Catholic doctor as new Civil Commissioner in Eminsang's place, the Governor-in-Chief once again boarded the *Sherbro* and returned to Lagos, there to scrutinise Captain Glover's administrative methods and ideas.

II

Arrived off Lagos, Governor and Mrs Pope Hennessy lived on their yacht, doubtless owing to the discomfort of Lagos Government House. This building, described by Sir Richard Burton as 'an iron coffin', and called 'deplorably makeshift' by Pope Hennessy, was so sizzling hot that its inmates would spend sleepless nights wandering with mattress and pillow about the cast-iron verandahs or up and down the shadowy central corridor, where the Houssas' arms were stacked, seeking a shaft of air. The Lagos climate was worse than that of Cape Coast, and few Europeans could endure it.

A recently acquired Crown Colony, the sandy island of Lagos, three miles long, had been ceded to the British Government by King Docemo in 1861. How much of the adjacent territory had also been ceded had not yet been properly defined, although the British claimed rights at certain points along the mainland, and had established customs stations in tin huts at Badagry, at Leckie and at Palma. They likewise considered that they owned the glassy, worm-filled waters of the Lagos lagoon, which was crossed by three ferry-services. As a British enclave in the hostile countries of the Egbas and the Jebus, Lagos was in a vulnerable position and could easily be starved out. To the Egbas the presence of the British in Lagos was peculiarly exasperating, since it not only deprived them of the main slave-market on the Bight of Benin, but also meant that any 'domestic slave' crossing to Lagos from the mainland became automatically free by setting foot on British soil. King Docemo, who had been deposed since the cession of Lagos, held feckless court in his palace in the British town. 'A man of low intellect and weak character', Docemo was playing a double game—outwardly friendly to the British, but inwardly as anxious as the Egbas to see them leave the coast for good and all. The King's ambivalence was clearly shown by his behaviour—at one moment giving European-style breakfast parties for Captain Glover, the Administrator, at another ordering his fetish priests to invoke the aid of the Goddess of the Sea against him. The state of affairs at Lagos was every bit as cloudy and potentially as dangerous as that on the Gold Coast itself.

By 1872 Lagos had become a comparatively neat, up-to-date trading port, with an esplanade, 'The Marina', with wharves, warehouses, shops, a court-house, a hospital, three Christian churches, a race-course and some well-built villas for the Europeans, who were ninety-four in number amid a native population of some fifty thousand odd. The port represented an achievement of which, on a superficial glance, one could be proud. Governor Hennessy admitted that 'the satisfactory appearance of Lagos makes it a striking contrast to the other African Settlements of Her Majesty', and recognised that this was largely due to Captain John Hawley Glover, late RN, who had been in charge of the settlement for nine years. Nominally held in check by the Colonial Office, where he was judged 'a trifle *too energetic* for our peaceful non-interference policy', Captain Glover really ruled in Lagos as an uncrowned King. Lagos was eleven hundred miles from the seat of the Government-in-Chief at Sierra Leone, and the Captain had grown used to having his own way. The rapid descent upon Lagos of the sprightly and inquisitive Mr Pope Hennessy was no more welcome to Glover than it had been to Administrator Ussher, his counterpart at Cape Coast.

When he first encountered my grandfather, in April 1872, Captain John Glover (afterwards knighted, married, and made Governor of Newfoundland) was a bachelor of forty-three who had been crossed in love in early life in Cologne. Physically and mentally Glover was cast in an heroic mould—an ox of a man with a massive bullet-shaped head, clipped dark hair going grey, a thick drooping moustache and an imperial. His expression combined the friendly, the formidable and the self-confident, and he religiously believed that it was Great Britain's mission to colonise Africa. Although he wore undervests of pink spun silk he was otherwise a being of spartan habits, enduring long days in the sun with his head protected only by a little dark blue forage cap, and damp nights in the forests of the Niger sleeping on the ground on his black ram-skin rug. Down the coast Glover was a by-word for his horsemanship, for his hairbreadth escapes from assassination, for his skill in palavering with hostile tribesmen, and for his recruitment of the Houssas, a race of tall, fierce warriors whom he had formed into the famous Cape Coast Constabulary. Instead of puff-adders he kept antelope, ostriches and secretary-birds in the grounds of Government House, as well as the 'clock-bird', the horses' friend, which would march out daily with the mounted police as far as the gates of the town, say goodbye to its favourite horse, Gunner, and then scuttle swiftly home. Captain Glover gave dinners, dances and, inevitably, croquet parties at Government House; at Christmas he mixed the plum-puddings himself. Much of his day was spent smoking cigarettes on his verandah as he adjudicated solemnly between the noisy contestants in witchcraft, matrimonial and property cases. The Houssas called him their Father, and the natives of Lagos called him 'Obba Golobar'. A romantic and, as even my grandfather agreed, 'a thorough gentleman', Captain Glover claimed descent on one side of his family from Egbert, King of the West Saxons, on the other from Charlemagne's wife, Hildegarde of Swabia.

Taken all round, Glover was a perfect example of the type of adventurous imperialist which John Pope Hennessy least liked. He began by treating Obba Golobar with courtesy, but he had made up his mind that Obba Golobar must go. 'Another Administrator going home!' he wrote with glee to Mr Robert Herbert of the Colonial Office once he had achieved this aim. 'We gave him three cheers as he stepped into the boat. Lagos is already reviving & in a few days I hope to be able to report that the trade is flourishing again.' To Lord Kimberley he recommended the late Administrator for a decoration, but to Glover himself he gave scant praise. 'You know nothing of the country, the place or the people', was but one of His Excellency's comments which rankled. Like Mr Ussher, Captain Glover sailed for Liverpool in a surly and defamatory frame of mind. Meanwhile the Governor-in-Chief returned to his task of exercising personal magnetism on a deputation from the Egbas, a rational and interesting people whom 'poor Captain Glover' had ruffled and had misunderstood.

When Governor Hennessy first reached Lagos, the Treasury was empty and trade at a standstill. In good years the annual revenue, chiefly from customs dues, had been as much as forty-five thousand pounds. Such staple products as ivory, palm-oil and gold dust were supplied by the natives of the mainland, who obtained Lancashire cotton goods, casks of rum and quantities of tobacco in return. But by April 1872 trading had virtually ceased. Pope Hennessy found a dozen large vessels lying outside the Lagos bar, while many smaller ships were moored upon the gleaming surface of the hot lagoon. All were waiting for cargo—waiting, that is to say, for produce from the

African mainland. No produce was forthcoming, since, in an effort either to strangle Lagos trade altogether, or at any rate to force the British to accept their terms, the Egbas had 'stopped the roads'. To the Egbas' older grievances was added the fresh one that, at the request of the French Government—which was engaged in a local war on the Upper Niger—the British had forbidden the import of arms through Lagos. The Egbas determined to blackmail the British authorities into lifting this ban. There was also the question of Yoruba trade.

Just as, in the hinterland of the Gold Coast, there sprawled the vast empire of the Ashanti, so to the north of Lagos there had grown up over the centuries the great kingdom of the Yoruba, bounded on the east by the Niger river, on the west by the kingdom of Dahomey. Yoruba, with its capital at Abeokuta, was a land of great potential wealth, but to exploit its resources the Lagos traders must rely on forest tracks which wound through Egba territory. By closing these tracks, and themselves refusing to trade with Lagos, the Egbas were reducing that city to stagnation. Captain Glover, who had learned by experience that the Egbas were shifty and hostile, had sent an expedition to explore the possibilities of an alternative eastward route to Abeokuta, which would avoid Egba territory entirely and thus undercut the Egbas' schemes. Pope Hennessy insisted that the Goldsworthy Mission—so called from Captain Goldsworthy, its leader—was a main cause of Egba hostility. The Colonial Office staff also had doubts about the mission, but for other reasons: they dreaded the extension of British influence and responsibility north of the coast, just as later in Malaya they sought to avoid the inevitable spread of British power among the native states of the interior. To them the British Empire was essentially a commercial enterprise. They clung to the illogical conviction that trading stations on the West African periphery could be maintained in the face of the hostility of powerful inland tribes. 'Administrators are not sent to "open roads" and create trade', wrote Mr Herbert; their duty was 'to maintain order and good government. . . . If for the sake of the English merchants we are not allowed to retire from the coast, at least let us stick to the coast proper & to our own boundaries on it.' The Secretary of State, Lord Kimberley, agreed heartily: 'Captain Glover's policy', he noted, 'has been too ambitious.'

From talks in Downing Street and from despatches he had received since, Governor Pope Hennessy was well aware of this official point of view; but when he reversed Glover's policy he did it with such haste, and with such evident animus, that he agitated the Colonial

Office in his turn. 'Speaking, not officially but as a friend', Mr Knatchbull Hugessen wrote to him in a private letter from Downing Street, 'I am rather inclined to fear that you have been at least a little *quick* in the reversal of the policy adopted by Capt. Glover and I fear the consequences. Even if a policy has not been entirely what might have been wished, its sudden reversal is to be deprecated, when the consequence may be to . . . weaken British "prestige". It is difficult, however, to judge accurately of these things at a distance.' If Pope Hennessy was an unnerving public servant, gifted with what Lord Kimberley called 'a marvellous power of creating quarrels out of small matters', it cannot be denied that the Colonial Office was at times an inconsistent and variable master.

Ignoring the officials at Lagos, whom he regarded as a backward, Gloverite clique, Pope Hennessy now embarked on serious negotiations with the Egbas. In these he was aided by a small group of disgruntled British traders who told him that Captain Glover's policy had meant their ruin, as well as by certain educated Africans such as Captain James Pinson Lablo Davies, a rich Egba merchant whose negress wife, Sally, had been brought up in England at Queen Victoria's expense. 'Mrs Davies is the leader of fashion at Lagos', my grandfather wrote to Lady Ely, for the Queen's eye. 'She wears, like all the other negro ladies, an immense chignon of black wool; but she dresses with better taste. She is always doing good . . . I am about recommending Lord Kimberley to let me put Mr Davies on the Legislative Council of Lagos. Sally will (in Lagos) be "The Honourable Mrs Davies" if this is done. In any case the Queen has every reason to be satisfied with the result of the protection she gave many years ago to the little curly-headed negress who escaped being killed at Dahomey. I enclose you a photograph of a Lagos baby.' Many people in Lagos suspected that Captain Davies, by origin an *ogboni* of the Egbas, was already a sworn member of the Egba secret council and earnestly anti-British. He was one of the persons whom Captain Glover said had 'succeeded in working upon the vanity and culpable weakness of Mr Pope Hennessy'. If this were true, the Egbas could not complain of the effects of his advice.

Governor Hennessy's first step was to lift the ban on the importation of arms and ammunition. Finding that this move made the Egbas much more amenable he next agreed to discuss the mainland boundary dispute, and to restore deposed King Docemo to a position of limited authority within Lagos, announcing in a public speech that the King's stick was to have precedence over the Government stick on all official occasions. In return for these substantial gains the Egbas promised to open the roads to the interior. Accounts conflict as to Pope Hennessy's attitude to the Egbas' demand for the return of runaway slaves, but it is probable that they assumed that his sharp reversal of previous policy included this question also. When he had left Lagos for Sierra Leone conditions in the former town deteriorated fast. King Docemo held councils at two in the morning, sent his bellman round the streets and had his gong-gong beaten publicly as though he were once more a sovereign. Back in London Captain Glover received full reports of these activities and sent them on with relish to the Secretary of State. The Colonial Office staff were mystified as to what was really happening in Lagos: 'I think there can be no doubt', wrote Mr Hugessen, 'that a change in the policy of the Lagos Govt. as regards slaves *did* take place upon Glover's departure, that authority was foolishly given to Docemo & that abuses occurred in consequence.' Hugessen recognised that employment of Docemo was 'of course part of Mr Hennessy's plan of conciliation & governing *through* the natives, but it may be dangerous in the case of a man who claims sovereignty over the country. Time will show.'

Having removed the import duty on gunpowder and shored up Lagos finances by borrowing four thousand pounds from the local British trading community Governor Pope Hennessy left for Sierra Leone in July. The fact that, owing to what he came to term 'hitches', the Egbas never fufilled their promise to open the roads did not lessen his self-confidence any more than the total failure of the Asantehene to send the Basle missionaries down to Cape Coast. 'I still believe the roads will soon be opened', he wrote to the Acting Administrator of Lagos at the end of October, '& that this is only the usual attempt to haggle over the bargain & get more. The King of Ashantee has just acted in the same way, but by firmness & patience he gave way & is doing what I wanted & releasing the captive missionaries.' This was no longer the belief in Downing Street, where confidence in the diplomatic skill of a man who made solid concessions in return for airy promises was on the wane. At home, backed by the bankers and manufacturers of Manchester, who had watched their West African markets dwindle, Mr Ussher and Captain Glover were virulently criticising Mr Pope Hennessy. Letters began to appear in *The Times*, questions were threatened in the House of Commons. Glover was predicting a massacre in Lagos, whilst Ussher warned that an Ashanti conquest of the Gold Coast was imminent. From having been 'far from comfortable about Lagos affairs', Lord Kimberley became frankly anxious: 'Mr Hennessy has I fear been bamboozled', he minuted, 'and it will be fortunate if we escape serious trouble.'

III

The speed and efficiency with which Governor Pope Hennessy had got rid of Administrator Ussher and Captain Glover placed upon the Colonial Office the onus of finding successors for these two officials. This time men with African experience were passed over in favour of persons who had served across the Atlantic. Lieutenant-Governor Berkeley of St Vincent was appointed to Lagos; and the Gold Coast was allotted to a Colonel Harley who had commanded a regiment of West Indian troops in British Honduras and now resigned from the army. As neither of the new Governors reached their posts before the late autumn of 1872, Pope Hennessy left the Gold Coast in the hands of an Acting Administrator, Mr Salmon, an ardent supporter of his own, and promoted Mr Henry Fowler, the Collector of Customs at Lagos, to administer that settlement. Both these men were Irish and Roman Catholic. Salmon had spent three years in Lagos, while Mr Henry Fowler, who had started life as an engineer on Vancouver Island, had worked for the last four years as First Writer and Clerk of the Court at Bathurst in the Gambia, the tiniest and least productive of the four West African Settlements.

Although the Gambia came under my grandfather's jurisdiction he never visited this swampy territory which he called 'that most useless & sickly of all the Queen's possessions'. More than five hundred miles distant from Sierra Leone in a north-westerly direction, the Gambia was far closer to the big French naval and military base in Senegal. The French, who bought ground-nuts from the Gambia, would have liked to acquire the settlement, and the British would have been delighted to have got rid of it. Negotiations had been started, but, owing to a sudden and inexplicable outcry in England against the transfer, they had fallen through. First founded as a slaving station in the reign of Queen Elizabeth, the Gambia had long since become a meaningless liability. Like Lagos and Cape Coast, it too lay at the mercy of ferocious inland tribes, and the handful of white traders at Bathurst were subject to overnight invasion scares and would send urgent appeals for a gunboat to Sierra Leone. Even this action was difficult to achieve, since owing to the unimportance of the Gambia few ships called there. Quite often the quickest way of communicating with the Governor-in-Chief at Sierra Leone was to send letters to Liverpool to catch the outgoing mail.

In the three autumn months of 1872 eighteen out of the thirty Europeans in Bathurst had died of yellow fever. Amongst these was the able Acting Administrator of the settlement, Mr Henry Simpson, who died at sea of remittent fever on his way to see Governor Pope Hennessy at Sierra Leone. 'In no part of Her Majesty's Empire is one brought so constantly face to face with Death as on the West Coast of Africa', Pope Hennessy wrote to his friend Lady Ely. 'Last week the mail steamer from Gambia brought me a widow—nine months married—to send home; the same steamer bringing despatches to me from her dead husband, who . . . was ill only four or five days.' It was small wonder that morale at the Gambia, even by British West African standards, was low. 'No philanthropist comes here for purposes of disinterested teaching or example,' wrote Mr Jackson, the Judicial Magistrate at Bathurst, 'no invalid comes to recruit his health —no professional man settles to practise—no emigrant brings his wife or children, and though Europeans do live and indeed do die here, not one in my experience has ever regarded these Settlements as his home. . . . The British Settlements in the Gambia are Settlements for the purposes of trade in the most exclusive sense of the word.'

Social life in the Gambia was as restricted as on the island of Labuan and certainly no less traumatic. Picnic parties exploded into scenes of drunken jealousy. English merchants threatened one another with a horsewhipping. Innocent young ladies were exposed to the leering obscenities of Captain 'Brandy' Cooper. Coloured Dr Spilsbury, the Colonial Surgeon, peddled contraceptive drugs. A Wesleyan missionary was arrested for intriguing with a hostile native King. The Matron of the gaol accused the gaoler, Mr Griffiths, of assaulting his female charges and of taking gin-sodden prisoners to dig for buried treasure in the Christian cemetery by night. Every year or two an outbreak of cholera would interrupt these antics, silencing friends and enemies, lovers and rivals alike with the indiscriminate and final silence of the tomb.

Mr Henry Fowler, my grandfather's choice for Acting Administrator of Lagos, was a fairly intelligent and energetic young man who had been praised for his behaviour in the most recent Gambia cholera epidemic, but whom the Colonial Office found 'somewhat bumptious'.

In May 1872 he had been granted six weeks' leave to go to see Governor Pope Hennessy, who was then on his way to Cape Coast and Lagos. In fact Mr Henry Fowler had had to skip from Bathurst in a hurry. His next-door neighbour in that townlet was a middle-aged English lady, Mrs Anna Evans, to whom he made an allowance of eight pounds a month, and who had unexpectedly and inconveniently become pregnant. Mrs Evans was niece by marriage to the most powerful merchant in the Gambia. This uncle, Mr Brown, insisted that Fowler marry Mrs Evans although he was already engaged to her cousin, Miss Harriet Lloyd. It came out, moreover, that Fowler had been giving Mrs Evans certain drugs obtained from Dr Spilsbury on the pretext that they were destined for a negro girl. Immediate escape from Gambia had become imperative for Mr Fowler. He applied for a transfer on the grounds of 'manifestations of difference of opinion' with some of his colleagues.

Warmed, as always, by an Irish smile, Governor Pope Hennessy detained his young countryman in Lagos and promoted him at once. Nothing if not inconsistent my grandfather was perfectly ready to excuse in Henry Fowler sexual *mores* which he fiercely condemned in hateful Governor Ussher or in his own father-in-law, Hugh Low. After he had left the coast he kept up a desultory correspondence with Mr Fowler: 'To obviate any more difficulties of the kind I got married', the latter wrote to him from Bermuda in 1874, 'and am now here with Mrs Fowler.'

The staff of the Colonial Office did not share Pope Hennessy's enthusiasm for Fowler, who soon suggested that his own brother, a London bank clerk, was the ideal candidate for a vacancy in the Treasury in Sierra Leone. Mr Wodehouse, a newcomer to Downing Street, minuted sagely: 'One Fowler is, perhaps, enough at present for the West Coast.' Lord Kimberley agreed.

IV

We may recall that John Pope Hennessy had been seconded from his new Governorship of the Bahama islands to administer the West African Settlements for the term of six months. Soon after his arrival on the Coast the Colonial Office informed him that they had offered the permanent appointment to Mr Keate, the Governor of Natal, who had accepted it. For Keate, an elderly married man with children, this was likely to be his last Governorship and also his most strenuous assignment: 'Mr Keate', a Colonial Office clerk wrote with some *Schadenfreude*, 'will not find W. Africa a bed of roses.'

To the Colonial Office, and in letters to Pope Hennessy, Governor Keate showed reluctance to assume his new responsibilities. They would involve leaving his family in England, and he feared the climate for himself. On this latter point my grandfather constantly reassured him: 'You will hear a good deal of talk about the sickness at Sierra Leone', he wrote. 'But I can assure you I have not yet had one minute's ill health in Sierra Leone. Indeed I believe that any sensible adult who avoids the sun, takes plenty of active exercise & lives temperately can enjoy the same uninterrupted good health that I do. The doctors —who seem a little puzzled that I have never consulted them about my own health—say a good deal of my immunity from sickness derives from the fact that I came here exactly at the proper season, that is when the drying up of the rains had ceased.' In the end it was agreed that Governor Keate should take over from Pope Hennessy in February 1873. Since the Ashantis were by then invading the Gold Coast Protectorate, Governor Keate, with his English manservant, his tweed and white flannel suits, and a copy of *Lorna Doone*, at once set off aboard the yacht *Sherbro* for Cape Coast Castle. He died there of African fever within the week.

Governor Keate's 'lurking horror of the African coast' had led my grandfather to suggest to the Parliamentary Under-Secretary of State a most unorthodox exchange by which he himself should remain in West Africa while Keate took over the far healthier governorship of the Bahamas. His motives for this proposal, which the Colonial Office bluntly rejected, were, as usual, a mixture of the practical with the idealistic. The West African salary was higher than that of the Bahamas. My grandfather was trying to pay off his debts and to support his mother and his three sisters at home. He was also anxious to save enough to buy a small house in County Kerry or County Clare, partly with the aim of re-entering Irish politics. At no moment of his career, nor in the midst of the most seductive tropical scenery, did Hennessy forget the sad and windswept country of his birth, its grey rivers and sombre lakes, its roofless hamlets and arrogant foreign landlords. But in wishing to remain in Africa he was equally inspired by a determination to help a people who seemed to him as downtrodden as the Irish themselves—the Africans of the British Settlements.

Although the Secretary of State for the Colonies feared that Pope

Hennessy had been 'bamboozled' by the wily Ashantis and the thoughtful Egbas, it was frankly admitted within the Colonial Office that most of his measures in Sierra Leone, and some of those at Lagos, were timely and successful. 'Mr Hennessy has acted wisely & well', was the Downing Street comment on his abolition of the crippling road tax under which the natives of Sierra Leone had suffered cruelly for years. He equally abolished the poll tax, and, as we have seen, pushed on a vast scheme of sanitary reform. His chief ally and adviser in these matters of taxation was the Reverend Percy Tregaskis, the coloured incumbent of the Wesleyan Buxton Chapel in Freetown. The Colonial Office distrusted missionaries—'missionaries', wrote Mr Herbert, 'are often the most mischievous and dangerous elements in any difficulty between our officers and native races'—and though they approved the results of Mr Tregaskis' advice, they felt that Pope Hennessy 'had put himself too much in the hands of the missionaries'.

The people of Freetown harboured no such reservations. 'Today I am the victim of popular ovations, bands, processions, religious services, public dinners & illuminations', Pope Hennessy wrote to Mr Robinson of the Colonial Office on 22 August 1872. 'But he is a wise man who does not forget the chance of a reaction, especially in Sierra Leone in such weather.' This public demonstration, during which all offices and shops were closed, and Freetown streets filled with braying bands and crowds of people 'bearing flags, banners & branches of trees' culminated in a mass movement on Fort Thornton, where Mr and Mrs Pope Hennessy stepped out to receive an ovation on the lawn. 'To the many, and the poor in all lands have that distinction', wrote a reporter in the local newspaper *Negro*, 'Governor Hennessy is heaven sent.' The writer added that the people's gratitude for the lifting of the taxes 'found expression in the shouts which echoed from Freetown to Benguema, and reverberated from Kent to Wilberforce—"God Bless Pope Hennessy!"' For many years thereafter 'Pope Hennessy Day' was annually celebrated in Sierra Leone.

Cuttings descriptive of these popular tributes were sent on by Governor Pope Hennessy to the Colonial Office, where they were acknowledged curtly. A native petition for the retention of Pope Hennessy as Governor-in-Chief was refused by Lord Kimberley in September 1872. In October Governor Hennessy, who had recently seen many of his subordinates, and even several officers of the *Sherbro*, die of fever, fell ill himself. His attack was a mild one, but his young wife contracted the fever badly. By the end of November the Governor had lost all wish to stay on the coast, blaming the climate as 'so very queer'. This switch of viewpoint coincided with increasingly disquieting reports from Cape Coast and from Lagos. In neither place were things going according to plan. Instead of releasing the Basle missionaries the Ashantis were completing their preparations for war, while the King of Elmina seemed to be planning a rebellion to assist them. The Egbas had not opened the roads to the Yoruba and in Lagos King Docemo and his bellman were behaving in a more and more extravagant manner. And then, in the second week of December, the vanguard of a great Ashanti army, at last equipped with ample arms and ammunition from the coast, left Kumasi for the front. In January they had crossed the river Pra and, after a swift series of victories over the tribes of the British Protectorate, they were in a position to threaten the destruction of Cape Coast. The Sixth Ashanti War, which aroused nation-wide excitement throughout Great Britain, was unleashed.

When first the news that the Ashantis had crossed the Pra reached him at Fort Thornton, Governor Pope Hennessy did not pay much attention. For some weeks past he had been exchanging bickering letters with Colonel Harley, the new Administrator of the Gold Coast, and it was clear to him that whatever it was that was happening on the Pra must be Colonel Harley's fault. 'Though I do not believe that this is an Ashantee invasion, or the prelude to an Ashantee war,' he asserted in a despatch to the Secretary of State on 13 February 1873, 'yet I think it quite possible that it may be converted into something of the sort by injudicious action, and even by injudicious words, uttered by the Administrator. . . . Remembering the very friendly interviews I had last year with Cotico, the highly intelligent and dignified Envoy of the King of Ashantee . . . I have instructed Colonel Harley to tell him that I do not believe that the king is, in any way, mixed up in this matter.' 'Col. Harley it seems has not got on well with the King of Elmina, and has also got into some little trouble with Ashantee traders at Cape Coast', Pope Hennessy wrote to his crony, Commodore Commerell of HMS *Rattlesnake*. '. . . The result of it all is a reported Invasion of the Ashantees—12,000 strong, 9 towns in the protectorate destroyed—fighting at Yankomassie; and of course requisitions on Sierra Leone for help.'

Simultaneously with these reports of the commencement of the

Sixth Ashanti War, Governor Pope Hennessy received urgent demands for reinforcements from Governor Berkeley at Lagos, where King Docemo and the Egbas were now convinced that they could force the British Government out, and from Captain Cooper of the Gambia, which was threatened by a local tribal war. These requests struck him as slightly comic. 'My dear Lord', he wrote to Kimberley in a private letter. 'At the same time the Administrators of the Gambia and of Lagos asking me for troops, and the Administrator of the Gold Coast reporting disturbances in his Settlements! They are all perhaps a little too much alarmed. As to the Gambia . . . Captain Cooper seems too apprehensive. I do not think there is any danger. As to Lagos, even if troops were needed, I could not send them now. But it is quite unnecessary. Anything of the kind would only be a waste of money & a display of weakness. . . . As to the Gold Coast there are rumours of disturbances, but Col. Harley gives me no information, & is I fear in the hands of the European agents as advisers.'

In the third week of February 1873 Governor Pope Hennessy, relieved by his short-lived successor, Governor Keate, sailed with his wife for Liverpool. It was a year almost to the day since he had landed at Freetown and faced up to the intractable problems of West African administration. Satisfied that he had done well, he was startled, on reaching London, to find that a sort of inquest upon the causes of the Sixth Ashanti War had been begun. To him the causes of this war were all too obvious—they lay in the blunders of stupid British subordinates like Ussher, Glover and Harley, who had totally failed to understand the African mind. The investigations dragged on. Despatches were published, and 'papers laid upon the table' in the House. Mr Pope Hennessy accused Colonel Harley, and Colonel Harley replied with vigour. Inside the Colonial Office the question, from being a major embarrassment, became a major bore: 'If all the officials with whom Mr Hennessy found fault began to justify themselves, a special department will have to be created for this business', commented Mr Hugessen. 'It is well known, I think, by Mr Herbert', Sir George Barrow wrote in February 1873, 'that one of the "pope's" failings is to endeavour to establish infallibility & at the same time to obtain supremacy—hence his liability to anathematise all around him—in order that he may have the sole *credit* of what may be done—but this is a two-edged sword, and instead of silencing others, he may be the victim of his own selfish policy.'

v

By 1 March 1873, when Governor Pope Hennessy, ensconced
in hired rooms in Savile Row, was busy making plans to cross the
Irish Channel to place his sick wife in St Amas Hydropathic Establishment, Blarney, and to receive an address from the Mayor and
Corporation of Cork, the Ashanti armies were within twelve hours
of Cape Coast Castle. In early June Colonel Harley was sending des-
perate accounts of the 'hundreds of thousands' of Fantee refugees,
starving and riddled with smallpox, who were crowding under the
Castle walls. Piecemeal reinforcements from England proving inadequate, it was decided to send out Major-General Sir Garnet Wolseley
with instructions to invade Ashanti territory, occupy Kumasi and
force a peace treaty on the Asantehene. An expeditionary force followed Sir Garnet. It was composed of battalions of the Rifle Brigade,
the Royal Welch Fusiliers and the Black Watch, with detachments of
Engineers, Artillery and auxiliary services. These men, shipped out
to rot and die in the dim rain-forests of Ashanti, were supplemented
by detachments from the West Indian Regiments. Some of these negro
soldiers came from Jamaica, others from the Bahamas.

One Saturday evening of November 1873 the new Governor of the
Bahamas, His Excellency Mr John Pope Hennessy, CMG, gave a
dinner-party in the cool, candle-lit Government House at Nassau.
This was a valedictory meal offered by His Excellency to Major
Strachan and his fellow-officers who were off to fight the foe in
Ashanti-land. At the end of dinner the Governor raised his glass and
proposed: 'Success to Sir Garnet Wolseley and the British Forces on
the Gold Coast.'

For this he was thanked, amid cheers, by Major Strachan.

BOOK IV

A TRANQUIL INTERLUDE
THE BAHAMAS 1873–1874

THAT THERE WERE people in England—people, moreover, 'in high places'—who blamed his personal administration for the outbreak of the Sixth Ashanti War was not the only shock awaiting Governor Pope Hennessy on his return from Africa. He had convinced himself that he would never now be told to take up his Bahamas appointment, but would be given Trinidad or some other superior Governorship instead. 'After all I have done and suffered I can hardly imagine that they are going to send me to the Bahamas', he wrote to Sir Charles Adderley, one of his chief admirers in the House of Commons.

Whatever their failings, the staff of the Colonial Office gave a good deal of careful thought to re-shuffles within the service, and the Secretary of State was in no way prepared to reverse a decision on an appointment once it had been made. Pope Hennessy had been offered the Bahamas, he had accepted the Bahamas, and to the Bahamas he must go. He had most probably been selected for the assignment owing to his political experience; the Bahamas Assembly, representing settlers who had been born and bred in the islands for several generations, had always proved independent-minded and obdurate. For years this legislature had been on bad terms with successive Governors and had proved impossible to manage. The Public Treasury was bankrupt: 'These returns are unsatisfactory', noted a Downing Street official on the Acting Governor's financial report for 1872: 'The expenditure continues in excess of the Revenue and the Public Debt amounts to £54,161. It will be a good thing to get Mr Hennessy at work as quickly as possible.' Further, the Acting Governor at Nassau had just been appointed to succeed Governor Berkeley at Lagos, and it was essential that he should proceed to that new trouble-spot without delay.

Faced with this disappointment, Pope Hennessy next adopted the species of evasive tactics he had used in 1866 over his original appointment to Labuan, that 'penal settlement off Borneo'. He pleaded that after four years in Labuan and one year on the Fever Coast of Africa he had the right to twelve months' leave. The Colonial Office politely demurred. As late as May of 1873 he was still lingering in Ireland with his sick wife. In a final effort to influence Lord Kimberley he telegraphed (from the post office at Blarney) that his departure might kill his wife and would destroy his own health. Lord Kimberley replied, also by telegram, that Hennessy must go at once to the Bahamas, or resign. On receiving this peremptory message my grandfather sailed next day aboard the Cunarder *Russia* from Queenstown. He was attended by an Irish aide-de-camp, Lieutenant Alfred Moloney, and he left his invalid wife to follow after him in the charge of her sister-in-law, Mary Hennessy. To Lord Kimberley, Pope Hennessy wrote a biting letter of complaint which made the Secretary of State very angry. 'When, six years ago,' this letter ended, 'I abandoned another career to enter the Colonial service, I did not anticipate that such could possibly be the reward of my official work.'

Pausing in New York to change ship, and to grant a *New York Herald* reporter a caustic interview on Home Rule for Ireland and the purblindness of all British policy there, the Queen's new representative in the Bahamas landed at Nassau, New Providence, in the morning of 27 May 1873. Partial, perhaps, to an Irish patriot, the *New York Herald* stated that 'in his previous executive positions Governor Hennessy has shown a rare degree of caution in dealing with political matters'. The Bahamians, a stubborn and out-of-touch community, took the same view: 'We hope', wrote the editor of the *Nassau Guardian and Bahama Islands' Advocate and Intelligencer*, 'His Excellency may be as successful in the Government of the Bahamas as he has been in that of the West Coast of Africa.'

From the point of view of nerves and health, at any rate, my grandfather's eight months in the Bahamas formed a respite from his experiences both on the Fever Coast and on Labuan, for the climate of the Colony was then, and still is, considered 'one of the most delightful in the world'. The administrative territory, covering four thousand square miles, consists of nearly seven hundred low islands and more than two thousand 'cays' and rocks—Crooked Island, Hog Island, Pig Rock, Bird Rock and so on—lapped by translucent shallow seas. The most westerly islets of this archipelago lie fifty miles from the coast of Florida, the most southerly, much the same distance from Cuba. The seventeenth-century capital, Nassau, is on New Providence, an island fifty-eight miles square. A vivid world of flowering trees and shrubs and creepers, in 1873 the Bahamas were still famous for their flocks of pink flamingo, which have become less and less numerous in the last fifty years.

There is no question that my grandparents were happy in Nassau and were well liked there. Instead of a handful of exhausted, bickering colonial officials, they found a large civilised community of old-established settlers, amongst whom they could and did make real friends. The negro population, on the other hand, suffered from malnutrition and a strong tendency towards pulmonary consumption. In this the Colonial Office chose to think the Bahamas a special case: 'We should not, however, generalise from the Bahamas', wrote Sir Henry Taylor, the Downing Street expert on colonial prisons and hospitals. 'They have none of the exuberent fertility of others of the W. Indian Colonies and the people of New Providence have been accustomed to live a good deal on and off the sea, wrecking, turtling and sponging and fishing.' Sir Henry likewise observed that a large part of the revenue of the Bahamas was derived from Import Taxes 'falling on the food of the people. It was at one time thought that the cheapness of food in the West Indies promoted idleness, and a policy was conceived of stimulating the negroes to industry by taxes enhancing the price of food—the proceeds of which taxes should be showered back on the negroes in the shape of public institutions for their benefit and elevation. The policy has failed because the negroes have been contented with bad food rather than increase their exertions and because there never was money enough raised to do anything in the West Indies beyond pay the salaries of Government Officials.' He added that it was the opinion of local medical authorities 'that this system of taxation is injurious and unjust. Mr Pope Hennessy whilst at S. Leone, I believe, abolished nearly all taxes on articles of general consumption.' Sir Henry Taylor hoped that Governor Hennessy would do the same in the Bahamas.

Governor Pope Hennessy set to work with characteristic speed, drawing up schemes for imposing taxes on luxuries whilst repealing those on necessities, for introducing proper sanitation into Nassau, and for reorganising the 'totally inadequate' police force of fifty-eight men whose salaries were five months in arrears, whose uniforms were in rags, their bedding falling to pieces and their Enfield rifles so old that even had the rust been chipped off them they could never have been fired. He also wooed the Assembly to some tune: 'He certainly is an effective wire-puller', Mr Meade of the Colonial Office admitted, on reading a despatch in which the Governor announced that he had persuaded the Assembly to repeal taxation on the public officers' small salaries. He likewise fought the Colonial Office on behalf of the Assembly, a typical subject being the maintenance costs of the military barracks at Nassau, which should really have been paid from London. 'Your Lordship is aware', he wrote to the Secretary of State, 'that for the last five or six years the Opposition has commanded a majority in the Assembly; and that until July this year no really good understanding existed between the Government and the Assembly on financial questions. Recently, however, I have succeeded in getting the Assembly to vote additional taxes for objects of Imperial interest (such as Telegraphic Communication with England and the Insular Mail Service) and I trust that Your Lordship will not press me to bring the question of paying for the maintenance of the Barracks before the Legislature.' He also introduced certain prison reforms, such as abolishing the shaving of women prisoners' heads since he thought it wrong for them 'to work in open fields under the sun, deprived of their natural protection'.

As soon as my grandmother reached Nassau from Ireland, an agreeable series of balls and at homes were given at Government House, which had been swiftly refurnished. This refurnishing was itself another minor triumph for the Governor's handling of the Assembly, since he got them to grant money for this purpose generously. When he first reached Nassau he had found Government House in a shocking state: 'During the few days that the Admiral of the Flying Squadron was staying with me it was impossible not to feel ashamed of the want of decent furniture and fittings. There is not a carpet, mat, floor-cloth, or curtain of any kind in the House, nor is there a single room adequately furnished.' He urged that the Crown Agents should spend three hundred pounds of the grant in purchasing a large Wilton carpet from an emporium in his home-city of Cork.

How long this peaceful state of affairs would have continued, we cannot tell; for in June 1874 Governor Pope Hennessy was called home on leave. His departure, from 'Prince Alfred's Landing' in Nassau, drew greater crowds than had 'ever been seen gathered together' in that city. The *Nassau Guardian* declared that 'no Executive Officer ever took his departure from our shores with greater and more universal respect than Governor Hennessy'. 'Since Mr Hennessy's arrival here—only about a year ago—he has been an indefatigable worker for the good of all classes in the colony', the leader writer of the same newspaper reminded its readers. '. . . It was Mr Hennessy's consummate ability and tact which cleared the political horizon from portending storms; which secured the financial credit of the colony from all detractors; which has carefully guarded and honourably maintained the well-being of the whole people without distinction; which has cultivated and cemented social amenities; while at the same time he has been a faithful exponent of science and greatly encouraged education. Men of this class are a great blessing to any colony, and more especially to one like our own, which requires from the paucity of its resources and its isolation from the rest of the world, a vigorous intellect to think for it and a wise hand to rule it.'

It stood to reason that a régime which gave such satisfaction to the inhabitants of the Bahamas, with their traditional dislike for Downing Street rule, might be liable to awake suspicions amongst the Colonial Office Staff. According to their creed Crown Colonies, if not actually profitable, should at least be able to pay for themselves and thus save the Office from Treasury carping and from questions in the House. My grandfather had given them to understand that in eleven months he had easily solved the financial problems that beset the Bahama islanders but, by now, the Downing Street experts had become sceptical of such miracles, and spoke of Hennessy's 'sanguine financial temperament'. When, later that same year, a new Governor revealed that public expenditure in the Bahamas seemed to be as much in excess of revenue as it had ever been, members of the West Indian Department waxed sarcastic. 'Singular', minuted Mr Cox, 'that when Mr Hennessy leaves a Colony the state of the Finances are not found to be in so satisfactory a state as he has led us to believe.' 'Bahamas, West Coast and Labuan have all suffered under Mr H's Financial mismanagement', added one of Cox's colleagues. 'The worst of it is that He thinks himself a great authority in such matters.'

The Permanent Under-Secretary, Mr Robert Herbert, was irritated on a different count. Before leaving Nassau Pope Hennessy, by a deft but unusual directive, had deprived his *locum tenens*, Mr Dumaresq, the Colonial Secretary, of all power to take decisions in the Governor's absence. 'This is a characteristic instance', wrote Mr Herbert, 'of Mr Hennessy's desire to manage everything according to his own personal views and with no regard to the rules of the office.'

On the face of it, it might have seemed improbable that Pope Hennessy would receive immediate promotion in the Colonial Service. Yet he had not been on leave three months before he was transferred from the Bahamas to become Governor and Commander-in-Chief of the Windward Islands, a 'first-class Governorship' with a salary of four thousand pounds a year. For Pope Hennessy was but one of many Tories to benefit materially from the 'revolution of March 1874' when the Liberal Government of Mr Gladstone was defeated after a six-year tenure, and the Conservatives once again formed a Government with Disraeli as Prime Minister for the second time.

BOOK V

THE FEDERATION RIOTS
BARBADOS 1875–1876

I

AS ENCOURAGING for John Pope Hennessy as Disraeli's return to power was the fact that Lord Carnarvon now succeeded Lord Kimberley as Secretary of State for the Colonies. At forty-two, the new Secretary of State was only three years older than Pope Hennessy himself, and in the days of my grandfather's Parliamentary career they had become well acquainted and had shared many interests—the cause of Poland and the state of English prisons amongst them. Since his extreme youth Carnarvon had felt strongly about the Colonies. During a short previous term as Secretary of State from 1866 to 1867 he had forced through the successful Federation of the British North American possessions which now form the Dominion of Canada. 'The enemy of all obvious injustice', Lord Carnarvon was a convinced Conservative of Liberal tinge. He was a very cultivated man, a distinguished archaeologist, and had translated ten books of Homer. In the past he had had long conversations with Pope Hennessy at Hatfield and elsewhere and he now wrote, in a reply to a letter of congratulation from the Governor of the Bahamas: 'You have made many steps since you first adopted a Colonial career. ... If at any time you should desire to communicate with me privately, pray do so.' This, and the fact that Carnarvon was first cousin to the Permanent Under-Secretary of State, Mr Robert Herbert, with whom he was on Christian name terms outside the Colonial Office, seemed to augur well for Pope Hennessy's future.

As Secretary of State Lord Carnarvon developed the hospitable habit of inviting Colonial Governors on leave, his office subordinates and even certain colonials themselves, down to stay at his ugly great house in Berkshire, Highclere. Amongst his guests, one September week of 1874, were Mr and Mrs Pope Hennessy. Just before the end of this visit, Carnarvon took Pope Hennessy aside and told him that he had been chosen to succeed Mr Rawson Rawson, the retiring Governor of the Windward Islands. 'Whilst fully sensible of Lord Carnarvon's personal kindness', Pope Hennessy wrote to the Prime

Minister, Mr Disraeli, 'I am also well aware of the powerful word that was spoken on my behalf.' The appointment was gazetted in February 1875.

On the strength of this new appointment, John Pope Hennessy purchased a picturesque sixteenth-century house at Youghal, on the Blackwater Estuary in his home county of Cork. Then known as Raleigh's House but now called Myrtle Grove, this building, which has panelled rooms and stands in a walled garden of old yews and myrtles, is supposed to have been the place in which Raleigh smoked the first pipe of tobacco ever seen in Ireland. My grandfather began collecting material for a book *Raleigh in Ireland*, which he published in 1883. He also installed his mother and his three sisters in the house. The ownership of an old and indeed historic property in Ireland meant a great deal to John Pope Hennessy, for it was a tangible symbol of his rise in a life which had begun in congested circumstances in Mount Verdon Terrace, Cork.

A further extension of leave was now granted to Pope Hennessy, since his wife was expecting a child. In mid-August, 1875, a son—this writer's father—was born in London. He was given a Polish godfather and the names Ladislaus Herbert Richard. Known in the family as 'Bertie' he replaced in his parents' affections the little boy they had buried in Sierra Leone. They took Bertie with them to Barbados when he was barely three months old.

Also on board the *Nile*, by which my grandparents travelled to Barbados, was Mr des Voeux, Administrator of St Lucia, and his wife. St Lucia was the only Crown Colony in the group of the five Windward islands. It thus had an Administrator rather than a legislature and a Lieutenant Governor. Like many of Pope Hennessy's subordinates, des Voeux was from the first charmed by his new chief's conversation and 'compelled to admire his moral courage and sympathy with the oppressed. These qualities,' des Voeux writes in his memoirs, *My Colonial Service*, 'together with his humorous cheeriness, prevented me from ever really disliking him, and I thus came to regard with comparative equanimity doings which, to say the least, were not worthy of commendation.' He was much startled by the 'unscrupulousness' of many of Pope Hennessy's projects and acts, and still more so by the open manner 'indicating either unconsciousness or cynicism' with which the Governor-in-Chief candidly discussed his plans. We may here once more recall, which Mr des Voeux did not, that the hero and to some extent the political mentor of my grandfather's youth had been Benjamin Disraeli, who was not famous for his scruples nor, indeed, for a love of absolute truth.

Des Voeux had first met Hennessy at a Queen's birthday dinner given by Lord Carnarvon at his house in Bruton Street in June 1875. At this meal a professional bore, Sir George Bowen,

'was talking, according to his wont, in a somewhat loud voice. After a remark had fallen rather flat to the effect that he had had an interview on the same day with the Pope, Victor Emanuel and Garibaldi, he shortly afterwards said, apropos of nothing: "Very extraordinary thing, very extraordinary; I was asked to dine the same day with the Prime Minister and with the Archbishop of Canterbury." Upon which little Pope Hennessy, who was sitting on the opposite side of the table, said even louder: "A much more extraordinary thing has happened to me, Sir George", and when asked what, replied, "*I* have been asked to dine *neither* with the Prime Minister *nor* with the Archbishop of Canterbury!" '

During the voyage to Barbados des Voeux discovered in Governor Hennessy 'that peculiarly Irish faculty for giving a humorous complexion to every ordinary incident'. However steep the sea or high the temperature Hennessy's good spirits never flagged. When a flying-fish flashed into his cabin through the port-hole he had it cooked for Mrs des Voeux, who had been unable to eat solid food for several days. 'Altogether', des Voeux concludes, 'I could not have wished a pleasanter travelling companion, and in consequence I cherished the hope that our official relations would be equally satisfactory—a hope which the sequel proved to be not altogether justified.'

Governor and Mrs Pope Hennessy, with baby Bertie, two servants and a handsome new carriage bought in London to be drawn by horses sent down from New York, reached Bridgetown, Barbados, on 1 November 1875. As the *Nile* anchored in the busy roadstead of Carlisle Bay, lively with schooners, sailing-ships and fishing-boats, they saw in the grey light of early dawn a long low shore with a lighthouse at one end. As the sun rose, the buildings of Bridgetown showed white across the water, and behind these the neat Barbadian landscape stood revealed. For while Barbados, which is shaped like a leg of mutton and is roughly the size of the Isle of Wight, has no mountains, no forests and no rivers it has also had, for many generations, no waste lands. The whole island is covered with fields of cane, yams and sweet-potatoes and with native huts and villages. Avenues leading to imposing country-houses, solid old parish churches filled with Stuart and Georgian funerary monuments, lend to the tropical countryside an irrevocably English air. Bridgetown itself, despite the warehouses reeking of rum, the coloured poui trees, the swarm of negro workers clad in stained and faded linen jackets of raspberry-red, or blue, or deep yellow, was the most trim of the colonial capitals which Governor Pope Hennessy had seen. In Nelson Square the small statue of Lord Nelson was at that time painted pea-green. On the wide savannah the red-coated soldiers of the garrison were lounging, while elegant ladies and gentlemen galloped across the dry, coarse grass, taking their morning ride.

Compared to Nassau in the Bahamas, Bridgetown was, in one sense and in one sense only, cosmopolitan, for it formed the hub of all steam navigation in West Indian waters. The Bay was constantly filled with British and foreign shipping—merchantmen, naval detachments, liners and private yachts. This perpetual coming and going of visitors—South American Presidents on their way to Europe, British, French and German naval officers, rich or distinguished English tourists—made the position of Governor in Barbados one of the most socially exacting, as well as one of the most expensive, on the Colonial Office list. It was not a Colony in which the Governor's stipend of four thousand a year would go far.

When Pope Hennessy's carriage, with its escort of mounted police, drove uphill to the circular driveway in front of Government House the Governor and his wife saw before them a large white building, Palladian in style, with deep verandahs on all sides shaded by venetian blinds. The floors were highly polished and had few carpets. Froude, who stayed in the house ten years afterwards, remarked on the pleasant darkness of the rooms: 'In the subdued green light human figures lose their solidity and look as if they were creatures of air also.' At the back of the house big bay windows looked out on a narrow walled garden, made mysterious by parasite creepers, cabbage palms, cannon-ball trees, mahogany trees, almonds and talipots. Climbing plants made a ferny grotto in which a fountain tinkled, splashing brown and white orchids hung in wire baskets from the roof. The house and garden were much to my grandmother's taste.

The Governor, with his aide-de-camp beside him, drove down to be sworn in at the Gothic Revival Assembly Rooms at one o'clock. 'Never before was there such a large and brilliant gathering of the *élite* on any similar occasion in the island', the local newspaper *The Reporter* told its readers. The rooms were so packed with spectators that many people had to stand. In a gallery used by the officials and legislators and their families a front seat had been reserved for Mrs Pope Hennessy, who held her baby in her arms.

Described by *The Reporter* as 'a gentleman of genial and plain, yet dignified, bearing' the new Governor was welcomed with notable enthusiasm. 'The entire country', we read, 'regards his advent to the Executive Office as an event which promises an administration under which we can repose in safety.' Thus auspiciously began a thirteen-month Governorship soon marked by popular disorders which seemed momentarily to threaten Barbados with a full-scale negro uprising, became a nine days' wonder in Great Britain and are still famous in Barbadian history as 'The Federation Riots'.

II

'The Queen', wrote her Private Secretary, Sir Henry Ponsonby, to Lord Carnarvon in April 1876, '. . . does not very clearly understand the origin and cause of the supposed riots, but probably you will not be able to give accurate information on this subject till you receive the written reports from Barbados.'

While it is arguable that the true 'origin and cause' of the riots of 1876 in Barbados lay in Her Majesty's own sanction of the appointment of an enterprising Irish Governor to rule over one of the most hidebound and most English of her colonial communities, this would be too facile an explanation of a brief, explosive Caribbean episode, parts of which remain murky to this day. In spite of an exhaustive thesis lately published by a Barbadian scholar,* the correct value of the highly conflicting evidence sent to Lord Carnarvon in 'written reports' from Barbados is tricky to assess. Resigned to share to some degree the Queen's bewilderment, we must, however, take a brief look at the chain of events which led to so sharp a racial outburst amidst the fields of billowing green sugar-cane and in the white streets flanked by garish bougainvilleas of the British island of Barbados that spring of 1876.

We have seen that Pope Hennessy's promotion to the Governorship of the Windward Islands was largely due to the return to power of Mr Disraeli and Lord Carnarvon. There is, however, some reason

* *Barbados and the Confederation Question 1871–1885*, by Bruce Hamilton, M.A., Ph.D. (Lond.). Published by the Crown Agents for the Government of Barbados, 1956.

to suspect that in this case, at any rate, the Colonial Office were deliberately using my grandfather as a catalyst. In Downing Street they had become thoroughly bored by the planters of Barbados and their outmoded constitution. 'At last the Barbadians have a Governor who is their match in message writing', noted the Permanent Under-Secretary of State upon one of Governor Hennessy's most crucial despatches. 'We must see that he has fair play . . . and that he plays fair himself.' 'We may leave Mr Hennessy', Mr Herbert wrote in another minute, 'to fight the battle as best he can.' To understand the tactics of this battle we ourselves may rely on what we have already gleaned of the character of John Pope Hennessy and of the characteristics of certain British colonial societies. To understand its strategy we must glance at the pattern of British Caribbean Government nearly a century ago.

In 1875, the year in which Governor Pope Hennessy took over in Barbados, the British West Indian islands were divided into five administrative units—there was Jamaica, there was Trinidad, there were the Bahamas, the Leeward Islands and the Windwards. As Governor-in-Chief of these last, Hennessy had his headquarters in Barbados and was responsible for the neighbouring islands of St Vincent, St Lucia and Grenada, and for the more distant island of Tobago. There was little logic in this administrative grouping. Each of these five colonies remained deeply individualist. They possessed no uniform system of law, of law-courts, of audit, police, prisons, lunatic asylums or lazarettos. The most westerly of them all, Barbados, had never been a Crown Colony. Its white inhabitants clung like limpets to a constitution which the Colonial Office staff categorised as 'foolish' and which indeed had not been altered since the days of the Stuarts. The tradition of life on Barbados was English, genteel and Protestant, whereas the four sister-islands in the Windward group had been so frequently occupied by the French that they hardly seemed to visitors like British colonies at all. St Vincent, Grenada and Tobago were run by Lieutenant-Governors; St Lucia alone was a Crown Colony in the hands of an Administrator. All but St Vincent were bi-cameral. Barbados had a full Treasury but an atrocious state of unemployment and of popular distress. The Treasuries of the other islands were empty, since these colonies suffered from a chronic labour shortage. Any sensible scheme by which unemployment in Barbados might have been relieved by organised emigration to these other islands which desperately needed labourers, would have encountered stultifying opposition from the planters of Barbados to whom their local unemployment situation guaranteed a reassuring and constant supply of very cheap labour. The administrative term 'the Windward Islands' was in fact a mere administrative term and did not represent reality.

The anomalies of the Windward Government had long, but not urgently, worried the Colonial Office. The obvious solution was federation, a form of unity which, under Lord Carnarvon's auspices, had been achieved in Canada and was at that very moment being canvassed for the British possessions at the Cape. The federation of Canada had been largely brought about by fear of American expansionism after the Civil War, and there was a general feeling in British Government circles that if other colonial territories could be thus consolidated the easier they would be to control in peace and the safer they would be in time of war. In the Caribbean itself the Leeward Islands had recently been federated with 'a rapid and notable success'. It was hoped that, once the Windwards had followed suit, they could soon be linked to the Leewards as a basis for one general Caribbean Confederation. This plan, which looked so rational on paper, would have been almost inconceivable in practice, owing to the peculiar and jealous character of the white Barbadian planters. These were convinced that their island's constitution was ideal, and that the slightest change made in it could only be a change for the worse. Slavery had been abolished less than fifty years ago. Since its abolition no British Governor had been able to persuade the members of the Barbados House of Assembly that any form of social legislation or of poor relief was their imperative duty or even their specific concern at all. The Assembly declared that the condition of the labouring classes was 'dependent entirely on their own energy and intelligence' and that wages 'depend upon causes and circumstances utterly beyond the control of any legislation'. What they really meant was that if the negroes could not find work then they must starve; and if they starved they could be relied upon to work for a starvation wage.

Such was the humane viewpoint of the descendants of the Stuart settlers, men who piqued themselves upon their lineage and upon their civilised mode of life. That this mode of life was already more of a dream than a fact did not disturb them. 'The days of well kept houses and stately living in Barbados have passed away for many years', Governor Pope Hennessy reported to the Colonial Office. 'Indications of penury are to be seen on all sides.' 'The well-known characteristic of Barbadians', the Acting Governor, Mr Freeling, had written shortly before Pope Hennessy's arrival, 'is . . . to consider that they and their institutions are perfect.' So far successful in repulsing all attempts at reform, intrenched behind their seventeenth-century ideas and their seventeenth-century constitution, the planters of Barbados sturdily awaited the next Colonial Office move. Yet even they did not immediately recognise in the suave, the smiling, the friendly figure of the new Governor Pope Hennessy some possible analogy with the Trojan Horse.

By 1875 the Colonial Office were not only bored by the Barbadian planters: they were becoming exasperated. Writing privately to Disraeli of the 'violence and obstinacy' of these white Barbadians, Lord Carnarvon complained that they combined 'all the vices of an ignorant middle class, absentee landlords, pettifogging attorneys and small local oligarchs'. Nor was criticism confined to London. In a public address at Codrington College, Bridgetown, not long after my grandfather's arrival, the lantern-jawed Bishop of Barbados lashed out at the 'odious self-complacency and narrow prejudice' of the European members of his flock. Bishop Mitchinson, who soon became a rather nervous ally of Governor Henessy, compared the planters to 'the white snails of Hans Andersen, who, living under burdock leaves upon which the raindrops pattered, flattered themselves that the world consisted of white snails and that they were the world'.

The Barbadian upper and middle classes did not take such comments kindly. Both by speeches in the House of Assembly—twelve of whose twenty-four members were planters—and by inspired articles in the local press they slung abuse at those whom they regarded as their natural enemies. 'An arrant hypocrite and dissembler', the influential *Agricultural Reporter* called Lord Carnarvon when Secretary of State, '. . . possesses no more power to touch or tamper with the Constitution of Barbados than the Czar of Russia or the Sultan of Turkey.' When listing the handful of Barbadian gentlemen courageous enough to advocate Federation, the same newspaper added epithets to each of their names: 'quack doctor', 'insolvent debtor', 'briefless barrister', 'bankrupt merchant', 'lately of the chain gang, St Kitts'. These were but the outward expressions of the moral tone of this ancient British colony. Corruption and jobbery were so widely accepted as endemic to the Barbadian Dream that it was no longer possible to bring peccant individuals to book. 'The whole public life of Barbados has been so rotten that I hesitate to blame anyone in particular', Governor Hennessy wrote to the Colonial Office in May 1876, after a futile investigation into a minor financial scandal connected with the Molehead Board.

Governor Pope Hennessy took up office at a moment when the Barbadian Assembly's distrust of the Colonial Office was at its height. Owing to a contested election, Acting Governor Freeling had, four days before, dissolved the Assembly. 'The sudden dissolution', Pope Hennessy reported, 'and the circumstances attending it, have caused on all sides so much distrust of the Government that I fear it will be some time before I can secure that frank communication with local gentlemen on which I counted. . . . I entertain some hope, however, that by endeavouring to gain the confidence of my Council, and by personal intercourse with individual members of the Assembly I may succeed in establishing a better feeling before I am called upon to open the next Session of the Assembly.' On the day of his arrival he announced that he would receive Heads of Departments and Members of the Legislature daily from eleven o'clock in the morning until four. By these personal interviews, and by a particularly ingratiating speech at the opening of the new Assembly, Governor Pope Hennessy did at first appear to have restored confidence in the Government. Once again, he was relying on the dangerous gift of charm to captivate his opponents. Once again it seemed to work. 'It looked to me as if he was touching us with honey', a coloured Barbadian remarked of a talk with the Governor on a subsequent occasion: 'or like the sea running round us.'

III

Governor Pope Hennessy had left London with no distinct instructions to attempt the Confederation of the Windward Islands. He had been warned above all to avoid giving the impression that the Colonial Office had a ready-made federal scheme to impose on the colonists. Downing Street had, in fact, no such scheme at all: 'It would not be convenient at the present time to *initiate here* any steps for another Confederation', Mr Herbert wrote to Lord Carnarvon, 'as our hands are full enough with the South African matter.'

Rumours that the British Government were contemplating some form of union for the five Windwards had been drifting about Barbados for several years. In June 1875, just four months before Hennessy set foot there, a great anti-Confederation meeting, attended by the members of the Legislature and by other planters and merchants, had been held in Bridgetown. Somewhat typically, this meeting was called to protest against a measure which had never been officially adumbrated, and as a warning to the Colonial Office of what they might expect should they ever propose Windward Federation. The Bishop of Barbados told Governor Hennessy that it was 'his conviction that the disturbed state of Barbados dates from the great anti-Confederation meetings of the middle of the year 1875: and that angry passion was fomented and wicked delusions industriously spread then by certain of our upper class planters'. Hennessy was, however, given to understand in Downing Street that should he be able to persuade the leaders of opinion in Barbados to agree to discuss Federation this would be most favourably regarded by the Secretary of State. The federal problem in the Windwards thus became for him yet another personal challenge; once more he would show that he could solve it in a trice. 'He is very anxious to succeed', wise Mr Herbert noted, 'but also very anxious to make out that he has achieved success even though there may be but very small results attained.'

Hennessy set to work at his customary brisk pace. Less than a month after reaching Barbados he had formulated a modest programme, later known as 'the Six Points', on which he thought agreement could be reached. He suggested that the Barbados Auditor should be made Auditor-General of the Windwards; that the Governor be given power to accept in Barbados prisoners from other islands; that the Bridgetown lunatic asylum and the lazaretto be open to candidates from St Lucia, St Vincent, Grenada and Tobago; that a Chief Justice based on Barbados be appointed for the Windwards, the whole judicial system of the five islands being remodelled; and that there should be a united police force for the Windward group. It was not a sensational programme of reform, but its very restraint aroused suspicion among some members of the Council whose advice he sought. The Speaker of the House of Assembly, Mr Grant, declared that the proposals 'would be regarded with disfavour if it were thought that he was merely introducing the thin end of the wedge which was ultimately to break up the present constitution'. To this the Governor replied that, while he would, of course, carry out any instructions that the Secretary of State might send him, it was his 'earnest personal disposition to preserve rather than to destroy the political institutions of Barbados, and to maintain, as stoutly as they themselves would wish to do, the independence of their flourishing Treasury'. This soothing answer placated the Barbadians, but it irritated Downing Street: 'Mr Hennessy still has much to learn as to the constitutional

duties of a Governor. He was gravely wrong in telling the people . . .
that whatever may be the opinion of the Secretary of State, his own
opinion is decidedly formed on the popular side.'

Hennessy at once submitted his draft scheme to the Secretary of
State, urging that in an official reply Lord Carnarvon declare that 'no
time should be lost' in putting it into effect, and that a strong Federation was necessary 'on Imperial grounds' as well as 'in relation to the
contingencies of war', but at the same time giving an absolute
assurance that 'the two main elements' of the Barbadian constitution
would not be touched. The Secretary of State complied. Meanwhile
Hennessy had been sounding out certain members of his Council, and
had arranged that one of the most influential men in Barbados, Sir
John Sealy, should propose a conference of delegates from all the
islands to discuss the plan. The Governor gained the impression—or
at any rate he gave it to the Secretary of State—that such a conference
would be a welcome move. 'Mr Hennessy is doing his work very well
and apparently with great judgement', noted Lord Carnarvon. 'There
is a fair promise of success. As regards Confederation any immediate
action is out of the question—We have as Mr Herbert says quite
enough on our hands at the Cape and a mistake or premature move
in Barbados might be not only locally but generally mischievous. But
the Conference as now proposed seems safe. . . .' To Pope Hennessy
himself Lord Carnarvon sent a private letter warning him to exercise
'every caution' and against 'the serious evil which would follow on
the miscarriage of a scheme openly proposed and attempted—Any
check in the policy in which you are now engaged would not only be
unfortunate locally, but might easily have evil effects beyond the West
Indies'.

By now the new Governor was as confident and as optimistic as
he had formerly been over the Ashanti negotiations or the finances
of Labuan. He thought that by patience, eloquence and argument he
had formed a small but strong party of prominent Barbadians to
support his federal plan. He had made himself liked by all, and was at
this moment rated one of the most popular Governors Barbados had
ever seen. Happy in the knowledge that all was going so smoothly,
Pope Hennessy set off, a few days before Christmas 1875, for a three-
weeks' visit to the islands of St Lucia, St Vincent and Grenada, aboard
HMS *Eclipse*. It was natural that he should wish to see these islands,
which had been seldom visited by a Governor-in-Chief; but his journey
took on the character of a canvassing tour for the cause of Federation.

A logical step, this expedition proved to be a tactical error. It is probable that much of the superficial agreement to his federal plans had been due to Hennessy's well-known powers of persuasion. During the short period of his absence from Bridgetown, and freed from the influence of his dominating personality, the white Barbadians began to have doubts. The opposition to Confederation hardened. By the time the Governor got back to Barbados on 10 January 1876 he was already under attack in several newspapers. The Barbadian *Times* announced that he had returned 'pregnant with schemes which are fraught with mischief', and described those who favoured the Governor's federal plans as 'toads squatting at the vice-regal feet'. On 8 February the House of Assembly rejected the proposal for a Confederation Conference as 'most objectionable', and a fortnight later Sir John Sealy withdrew his support of the Six Points.

This smart rebuff did not dismay Pope Hennessy. If he could not get Federation by one means he was prepared to get it by another. It was his open discussion of this alternative method which shocked Mr des Voeux, the Administrator of the Crown Colony of St Lucia, during my grandfather's Christmas visit to that island.

IV

Watched by the silent crowds of negroes on the quayside, their unblinking eyes like white sea-shells beneath their tattered straw hats and gaudy bandanna handkerchiefs, HMS *Eclipse* edged her way through the narrow, fortified entrance of Castries Harbour, St Lucia, on Christmas Eve, 1875. The local newspaper called the Governor-in-Chief's visit 'strangely timed' but suggested that this very fact 'would indicate him as possessing energy'. It reminded the public that Mr Pope Hennessy had 'ingratiated himself in Barbados as our readers will have seen from inter-colonial newspaper cuttings we have recently published', adding that in St Lucia his 'affability and accessibility' were winning praise for their 'perfect freedom from effort or affectation'.

During their six days in St Lucia, the Governor and his wife were the guests of Mr and Mrs des Voeux at Government House, Castries. The des Voeux who were newly married and, it will be remembered, had travelled out to the Caribbean on the same ship as the Hennessys were in the throes of domestic difficulties, since one of the two maids whom they had brought out from the household of Mrs des Voeux's mother in England had been so disturbed by her first sight of the tropics that she had taken to drink 'though for some years in a position of trust and never before having exhibited any such tendency'. The des Voeux did what they could, however, to make the Hennessys comfortable. They found that 'Hennessy showed himself in the house, as on board ship, most agreeable socially'. During his five days in St Lucia, however, Governor Pope Hennessy managed to vex the Administrator in a number of ways. He was, for instance, suspected of taking political advice from the curé of Castries and he celebrated a morning spent looking over the gaol by setting free the favourite prisoner of the Catholic turnkey without consulting Mr Gall, the Protestant Chief of Police responsible for the prison. This action, and other examples of what des Voeux called 'a careless inadvertence' were 'unfortunately ascribed by the public to a determination to snub the Protestants all round', the Administrator himself included. 'I freely confess', writes des Voeux, 'I was relieved when Hennessy left the island.'

Apart from a subordinate's natural resentment at interference from his chief, des Voeux felt a genuine disquiet over Governor Hennessy's attitude to the Confederation project, and it was their conversations on this subject which led the Administrator to suspect him of 'unscrupulousness' and 'cynicism'. Pope Hennessy spoke up with a puzzling candour: 'In fact,' des Voeux tells us, 'he evinced a somewhat rash confidence in one whom he knew so slightly. For had I been otherwise than absolutely loyal to my guest, or disclosed what was said to me on this occasion, the position which his extraordinary policy produced in the following year would have been even more critical for him.' Des Voeux explains that this policy, about which Hennessy talked with such 'singular frankness', was 'based on the principle of "*Flectere si nequeo Superos, Acheronta movebo*" '—a Virgilian quotation which he roughly translates: 'If I cannot bend the whites, I shall stir up the blacks.'

After riding through the island to see some sugar estates as well as the famous steaming sulphur-springs at Soufrière, Governor Hennessy boarded *Eclipse* at Choiseul and proceeded to St Vincent and Grenada, those mournful, dense green islands which seem to float like giant sponges on the surface of the blue Caribbean Sea. The second week of the new year, 1876, saw him back in Barbados. As Government House was being repaired, the Hennessys moved first to Long Bay Castle in the parish of St Philip and afterwards to Blackmans, St Joseph. These two removals, due exclusively to convenience, were later cited by Hennessy's enemies to prove that he had wished to withdraw from Bridgetown into the fastnesses of the little island, where, it was whispered, he could plot in secrecy and peace.

Meanwhile, the Secretary of State had sent from London a new set of Letters Patent, establishing a new Executive Council of eight members to advise the Governor in place of the old Council which, consisting of all twenty-four members of the House of Assembly, had been neither effective nor discreet. These new Royal Instructions, aimed to strengthen the Government's position and to make the eccentric constitution of Barbados conform somewhat to that of other Colonies, angered the Assembly, and influenced Sir John Sealy in his decision to withdraw his support of the Six Points. The instructions could not have reached Hennessy at a worse moment, for they did in fact materially alter the Barbadian constitution which he had sworn he would uphold.

The situation in Barbados began now to get rapidly out of hand. The Governor was being bitterly criticised in the Assembly and in the newspapers. Pope Hennessy made a last attempt to please his opponents by a charming speech drawing attention to the high proportion of university graduates in the Assembly, and even praising the vigour and independence of the press. This speech was a failure and the Governor was accused of hypocrisy and 'brazen effrontery'. Perceiving that diplomacy was useless, Pope Hennessy switched overnight to a new line: attack. He chose, as the objective for his first salvo, the state of the Barbados gaols. On the day after that on which he had made his unsuccessful public appeal to the vanity of the white Barbadians he sent to the prison authorities, through the Colonial Secretary, a minute criticising the savage floggings which took place in Glendairy Prison, calling them 'a grave scandal' which 'showed that in Barbados alone of all Her Majesty's Colonies, some of the worst practices of the days of slavery still prevailed'. If the Barbadians refused to accept flattery he would offer them an alternative—the truth.

Ever since his early career in the House of Commons, Hennessy had been particularly interested in penal reform. In an age not altogether noteworthy for its humanity, he, like Lord Shaftesbury and like Charles Dickens, was one of the enlightened few, and indeed, as we have already noted, his anxiety to render prison conditions tolerable led to his being later accused, when in Hong Kong, of 'a diseased sympathy with criminals'. On his second day in Barbados, in November 1875, he had startled the authorities by visiting the notorious

Town Hall Gaol, abolishing flogging there and introducing seven days of bread and water in solitary confinement in its stead. In December he discovered that floggings were administered in Glendairy Prison without the prior approval of the prison doctor; when he had enquired into this he was handed a punishment book in which this doctor had hurriedly signed his name retrospectively to a long list of past punishments, foolishly using the same fresh ink. The head of the prison, Mr Price, who had been a British soldier, stated that 'the Barbados floggings are more cruel than the severest floggings that he formerly saw in the army'. On asking what was the source of a shindy coming from one of the cells, the Governor was told that it was a prisoner put in irons for shamming madness; further investigation revealed that the man was, in fact, a lunatic who should never have been sent to the prison at all.

The Governor's minute accusing Barbadians of savagery created fury enough, but when he quickly followed it up by liberating thirty-nine good conduct prisoners the uproar among the planters and shop-keepers of the colony became violent. That he showed such intimate concern for the lot of the negro population of Barbados was bad enough, but that he should take pains to help and to rehabilitate criminal negroes was an insult to the whole white community. More-over, the Governor-in-Chief, accompanied by the Colonial Secretary and the Attorney-General, himself attended at the gaol on the day of this general release: 'I ... spoke to each prisoner separately, admonish-ing him, pointing out the certainty of severe punishment if again convicted, and at the same time reminding him of the advantages of good conduct and industry.' The usual custom, when a prisoner had served his sentence, had been to send him out into the world penniless, and with a patch sewn over the number of his convict suit. My grand-father ordered a cheap suit for every man released, and provided each with a few shillings from his own pocket. Not long afterwards he ordered the release of a number of piccaninnies less than seven years of age who had been sentenced to hard labour for stealing sugar cane, and had been punished while in prison for bed-wetting and for 'laughing and playing'.

Besides making it plain that he would not tolerate brutality in the prisons, Pope Hennessy had also announced that all civil service appointments would thenceforth be open to public competition, irre-spective of class, colour or creed. He let it be widely known that he was appalled by the poverty and ignorance of the Barbadian negro population, and that he was planning to demand of the Assembly a remission of certain taxes which penalised the poor, and an overhaul of the antiquated Masters and Servants Act.

In a small community like Barbados news travels swiftly, and throughout the island Hennessy had come to be regarded by the working people as their champion. At Long Bay Castle, at Blackmans, and, after the Hennessys' return to Bridgetown, at Government House, the Governor would give private audience to negro workers with police court grievances, or wanting employment. Up to forty men a day would call to see His Excellency. On one morning at Blackmans twenty-eight were found squatting beneath the trees of the avenue patiently waiting for him. 'When the planters refused them work', wrote Hennessy's private secretary, 'they involuntarily almost and instinctively came to believe that they would get justice done to them at Government House. . . . The planters would call them "Governor's men" in a taunting way, and tell them that if they wanted work to go to the Governor.' The planters alleged that the Governor would discuss questions of suffrage, increased wages, a lower duty on rum and the possibility of cheap land with these poor people. He was accused of visiting their shacks and talking to them in their yards. It was also said that he and his 'emissaries' were explaining the benefits of Confederation to the illiterate. The planters retaliated by holding anti-Confederation meetings. They told their negro workers that Confederation was simply a new-fangled word for the reintroduction of slavery. One shopkeeper was said to have summoned his black porters into the street and told them: 'If these Six Points pass today, I shall be able to buy you as slaves tomorrow at twelve o'clock.'

Nor did the planters and merchants confine their activities to the island of Barbados. Complaints about Pope Hennessy were now pouring into the Colonial Office. Some were sent direct to Lord Carnarvon at his house in Bruton Street. 'Is this statement as to Hennessy true?' the latter wrote to Mr Herbert, enclosing one such missive. 'And is he with his love of intrigue working upon the black population?' 'It looks rather like it', Mr Herbert replied, 'but those from whom such statements come are so absolutely unscrupulous that it is impossible to pay any credence to anything they report.'

Governor Pope Hennessy now convened a special meeting of the House of Assembly, to hear the Queen's new Letters Patent read and to listen to the Governor's exposition of the wishes of the Secretary of State on the Six Points. The prospect of this meeting, arranged for 3 March, caused anxiety to the opponents of Confederation. The press had already announced the setting-up of a Vigilance Committee to keep watch over the Governor's proceedings. At a great public meeting on 2 March this was converted into the Barbados Defence Association, formed with the object of preserving the Constitution, and maintaining order and 'a good understanding between the different classes of the population'. On the following day the House of Assembly met to hear the Governor speak. The events of this day, which marked the final severance of all decent or orderly relations between the Governor and the House of Assembly, proved that the plans John Pope Hennessy had casually revealed to Mr des Voeux that Christmas in St Lucia were neither academic nor idly conceived. Haughtily rejected by the planters, Confederation had suddenly and somehow become a fervent and popular negro creed. The position from which the white landlords, shopkeepers and lawyers had refused to budge at the call of reason had been quietly and skilfully undermined.

v

When the little Governor, in cocked hat and gold-braided full-dress uniform, drove down from Queen's House to the Assembly Rooms that morning of 3 March 1876, Bridgetown was bubbling with excitement. Hostile witnesses later swore that the public part of the Council Rooms was crowded with 'a most extraordinary collection of persons' armed with passes from the Colonial Secretary—'persons of the lowest class were admitted, persons with no jackets on'—all come to hear their Governor speak.

Governor Pope Hennessy opened his address by a reference to the unsatisfactory state of the sugar industry and by a bland compliment to the planters and merchants on their continued prosperity. He then abruptly contrasted this prosperity with the deplorable circumstances in which the small shopkeepers, the labourers and the masses of the people of Barbados lived, telling the Assembly that it was the Legislature's clear duty to improve these conditions and at once. He pointed out that the prisons were crowded, that a recent Royal Commission 'had developed a terrible picture of the material and moral condition of the people', and that he had been told by the Bishop of Barbados and by Free Church leaders in the colony that in no other community had they ever seen 'such intense and apparently hopeless poverty'. He urged on the Assembly the necessity of immediately organising an

improved system of instruction, increased opportunities for employment, lighter taxation and cheaper and better summary justice.

His onslaught on the smug Barbadian upper classes was followed
by a panegyric on Confederation. This would, according to the
Governor, solve all these problems for ever. By Confederation 'our
redundant population will find a natural outlet in the neighbouring
Islands when by a uniform political system, the same laws, the same
tariff, and constant means of rapid communication, the now unoccupied Crown Lands and half-tilled estates will be available for their
labour, and they can come and go from the various islands as readily
as they now pass from parish to parish in Barbados'. 'I feel sure', he
said, 'that no intelligent person who loves Barbados will take the
responsibility of standing between his poorer countrymen and the
wise policy of the British Government.' At this point the Speech from
the Throne was interrupted by ringing cheers of approval from 'the
persons with no jackets on', who were squashed in behind the
mahogany rail separating the members of the House of Assembly
from the members of the public. Such a scene had never before been
witnessed in the lofty, solemn Assembly Rooms, into which the sunlight filtered through Gothic windows filled with the stained glass
portraits of the British sovereigns since James the First.

Whatever the motives behind this speech—and it is hard to believe
that, even at his most optimistic, Pope Hennessy can have expected
the Assembly to relish his remarks—there is no doubt as to its effect.
It enraged the members of both Houses, who regarded it as demagogic
and threatening and as an attempt to appeal over their heads to the
illiterate masses. To understand the strength of this reaction we must
remember that these were men whose families for many generations
had cultivated a slave-owning mentality, and who had inherited the
traditional panic fear of a negro rebellion. It is also relevant to recall
here what had happened in Jamaica only ten years earlier, under the
rule of the notorious Governor Eyre.

With the abolition of slavery, the prosperity of Jamaica, like that
of Barbados, had declined fast. As with Barbados, Jamaica was encum-
bered with an ancient constitution enabling the House of Assembly
to block any and every attempt by the British Government to improve
conditions by edict or by legislation. Distress was so widespread that
in October 1865 a serious negro insurrection broke out in the district
of Morant Bay. The chief magistrate and eighteen other white persons
were slaughtered, and the revolt put down by Eyre with a ruthless

exercise of martial law. Eyre's cruelty, which had scandalised the British public, had been warmly applauded by the planters of Barbados and other West Indian islands. Furthermore, the Jamaican riots of 1865 had had a most significant result. The insurrection had so terrified the members of the Jamaican House of Assembly that, before he left the colony, Governor Eyre had easily persuaded them into voting for their own constitutional extinction. By an Act of Parliament of 1866 Jamaica was transformed into a Crown Colony. The new Governor, Sir John Grant, could thus introduce a sweeping series of important reforms which entirely reorganised the island, and beside which Pope Hennessy's Six Points programme looked timid and pale. The Barbados Legislature firmly believed that it was Governor Hennessy's intention to stampede them into some such constitutional suicide: *Flectere si nequeo Superos, Acheronta movebo*. They did not, and temperamentally they could not, share Pope Hennessy's earnest passion for the underdog. They were only very conscious that the underdog had teeth.

Already infuriated by a speech from the Throne which had presented them as callous, selfish and heedless of the public good, the white community in Bridgetown were shaken by its sequel. His address delivered, the Governor stepped from the beflagged peristyle of the Assembly Buildings into the glare of the street and took his place, with his wife beside him, in his bright new carriage to return to Government House. No sooner were they seated than a negro crowd surged forward, unharnessed the horses, and drew Mr and Mrs Pope Hennessy in triumph up Constitution Hill. The Governor subsequently told the Secretary of State that this demonstration was entirely unconnected with his speech on Federation, but was simply a spontaneous gesture of recognition of his attitude towards flogging, Barbados prisons and the taxing of the poor. He indicated that it merely went to show that he was popular, while the white Barbadians were not. The *Agricultural Reporter*, not the most accurate of those local newspapers which, as Bishop Minchinson said, offered nothing but 'garbage' to their readers, has another version of the incident. 'From early morn', we read, 'it had been whispered about that arrangements had been made for removing the horses and drawing the Governor's carriage by hired men, but the story was so improbable as to receive no credence.' However, the paper continues, 'about a dozen street porters and liberated convicts . . . rushed to the front, dexterously detached the horses and drew the carriage up Constitution

Hill as far as Queen's House'. The *Reporter* added that 'the entire episode was but an official arrangement. The ropes made use of were those of the late Volunteer Artillery, and were provided by the police for the occasion.'

We are now fast approaching the moment at which it becomes nearly impossible to get at the truth of what was actually happening in Barbados that unquiet spring. Charge and countercharge, rebuttal and denial were flung about. The leading newspapers shrieked about the 'dusky lickspittles, catspaws, flunkeys and other dirty emissaries' who listened to the 'oily gammon' of Pope Hennessy. Anonymous letters, many of them literate and all of them threatening, appeared on the Governor's desk. The Council Rooms were again invaded by a swarm of excited negroes (including, this time, 'negro boys without trousers'), and the Attorney-General, who had made a speech unfavourably contrasting social conditions in Barbados with those of the newly federated Leeward Islands, was kicked by a Council member on the behind. In London the Colonial Office was bombarded with private letters and official petitions. Lord Carnarvon received, and snubbed, a deputation demanding Hennessy's recall. Hostile delegates sailed from Barbados to England to repeat the same request. At this time, as we have seen, the Secretary of State could not give any coherent account of the situation to Queen Victoria herself. 'There has evidently been a panic amongst the white population', he wrote to Ponsonby, for the Queen's eye, 'and partly from real fear, partly from a dislike to the Governor (who I am afraid has not been very wise), there is a good deal of exaggeration, if not of misrepresentation. . . . I had a deputation with me this afternoon on the subject. They represented the Planter interest and though they spoke in rather an excited strain they made no specific point. Indeed, they were obliged to admit that the telegraphic information which they had sent to the newspapers and which was of so alarmist a nature was not consistent with the later telegrams which are much more reassuring and copies of which I now send. . . .'

Before we ourselves join in the Federation Riots, we must reflect a moment more upon the Governor's recent speech. By converting the cause of Federation into a popular creed he may well have hoped to get his Six Points passed. But is it certain that Confederation could possibly have proved the panacea he proclaimed it? 'The truth is', Mr Herbert of the Colonial Office commented, 'that Confederation would make extremely little difference in any way.' By proclaiming that Confederation would automatically produce a Golden Age throughout the colony of Barbados, the Governor may have misled the masses, but he may equally have been misleading himself. As we have noticed before, Pope Hennessy would snatch up a new idea with intense enthusiasm and foster it to the point of credulity. Yet on this matter of Confederation he was at first strongly supported by the Secretary of State in London, who had not only approved the Six Points programme but had been impressed by the speech of 3 March —'an able speech', was Lord Carnarvon's phrase. As a result of the riots Lord Carnarvon had serious second thoughts. Less than two months after the March speech he instructed Pope Hennessy to issue a humiliating Proclamation that 'it would be a great mistake to suppose that Confederation could either injure or benefit in any considerable degree the social condition of any class and that . . . it could do little to change the condition or prospects of the labouring class'. These instructions, due to Carnarvon's growing doubts of Hennessy's discretion and veracity, marked the final collapse of the policy of a Windward Confederation centred on Barbados. It was a policy which had alienated the white Barbadians, and had agitated the black.

Through March and April 1876 Confederation was the main topic amongst the labourers on the plantations. Negroes kept telling each other, in their sing-song drawl, that Governor Pope Hennessy was going to divide the big estates amongst them. Queen Victoria came in for her share of praise in helping to initiate this generous project. 'De Gubnor say de Queen gib de rest of Gubnor's money fou help we, but dey no gib we', one labourer was overheard explaining to another. 'He gwine gib we, and gib we land too.'

On 28 March, at a Defence Association meeting at Mount Prospect in the parish of St Peter, a negro was shot in the leg by a white man named Parris. An angry mob rushed at Parris and the other planters, who took refuge in the estate house, from which Parris escaped disguised as a negress and with blackened face. The Defence Association telegraphed to the West India Committee in London: 'Action of Governor Hennessy . . . culminated in serious riot last night at Prospect Plantation, in which a man was shot and several managers wounded and ill-treated. Repetition of Jamaica tragedy likely to follow any moment.' But it was not till three weeks later that the real rioting began:

'Riots throughout the Island, plantations and houses sacked, animals destroyed, enormous destruction property, over forty rioters shot,' [the Defence Association telegraphed on 24 April] 'troops actively employed, city threatened, business suspended, families seeking shipping, rioters repeat they have Governor's sanction. Hennessy immediate recall requisite save Colony.'

VI

Whatever the members of the Defence Association may have believed or feared, the Barbados riots of 1876 bore no visible resemblance to the riots in Jamaica in 1865. To begin with, no white man was killed nor was one injured; the only white 'casualty' was Colonel Clements, the Inspector-General of Police, who received a slight scratch on the cheek from a stone. Secondly, the rioters behaved in an oddly organised way, some one thousand persons in all moving from estate to estate in gangs of one hundred. Thirdly, they were sincerely convinced that they were acting under the Governor's orders. 'This is John Pope Hennessy's business', a ringleader at Lower Estate announced, after blowing a trumpet as a signal for the crowd to dig up all the sweet potatoes and carry them away. 'The Governor said we must not set fire nor take life, but take everything else', another leader told an underling who wanted to burn down a plundered estate-manager's house at Joe's River. An attack on the sweet-potato fields, the store rooms and the stock-yard of an estate would be heralded by a shrill blast on a conch shell, often followed by the chant: 'God Bless Pope Hennessy.' Thus, as the West India Committee complained, Barbados was given 'the strange and probably unprecedented spectacle of a large class of the population in a British colony turning out in immense gangs to plunder and riot believing that they had the sanction and were fulfilling the wishes of the representative of the Queen'.

Planned to start on Easter Monday, which, however, turned out wet, the riots began in earnest on Easter Tuesday, 18 April. They lasted just under one week. The rioters, who were led by two negro brothers named Dottin, one of whom flourished a cane with a red flag at the end of it, whilst the other waved a sword, roamed the estates, pillaging the fields, at times killing or mutilating livestock and only rarely sacking a plantation house or demanding money by threats from the planters' terrified families. Scarcely any violence was offered to white people, and rioters only put up a feeble resistance to the military and the police sent to disperse and arrest them. Eight negroes in all were killed and some thirty wounded. Noting 'the remarkable absence of injury to the whites throughout excited riots', the fair-minded Mr Robert Herbert of the Colonial Office questioned whether the West Indian negroes were really as 'easily roused' as the planters chose to make out.

Although the rioters did not approach Bridgetown—there was one minor incident a mile away—panic swept the city, driving 'hundreds of white people to take refuge in the ships in the bay, the Garrison buildings, and other places where military protection was available'. The Barbados Defence Association continued to send to London wild and inaccurate accounts of the disturbances, while the Governor, who acted, in Lord Carnarvon's words, 'boldly and vigorously', took care not to reply to telegrams from the Secretary of State until he could announce that order had been restored. By two proclamations, by a prompt use of the troops in Bridgetown and by sending to neighbouring islands for reinforcements, Governor Pope Hennessy succeeded in crushing the riots within six days. On one occasion he rode out himself to harangue the rioters at Byde Mill, telling them that their criminal actions would be severely punished, and on another he walked round the streets of Bridgetown unaccompanied and at night. He finally telegraphed to Lord Carnarvon—who had demanded exact information for a speech in the House of Lords—that ninety negroes had been arrested for plundering, and three hundred and twenty on suspicion of rioting or of receiving stolen goods. Whilst striving to minimise the extent and effects of the riots, Hennessy took pains to suggest that the outbreak was entirely due to low wages and starvation and he held up the planters to ridicule: 'I have no apprehension of renewed outbreaks' [he telegraphed] 'my only anxiety is from gentlemen threatening extreme measures such as hanging, shooting and flogging.' He stoutly refused demands 'to put up the triangles and have the ringleaders instantly flogged as they came in', and issued instead a Special Commission establishing a court to try offenders. This resistance to summary flogging he explained to his Executive Council on the grounds of its illegality, its inhumanity and the fact that it would almost certainly increase the discontent and render the situation really dangerous. He likewise refused to arm five hundred rural constables who had been hastily sworn in. 'I should be sorry to trust them with firearms' [he minuted, after inspecting this body]. 'They seemed zealous but far too nervous and excited.'

So began, and ended, the Federation Riots in Barbados. They had caused damage and terror in the Colony, a small sensation in England, and a good deal of heart-searching and uncertainty within the Colonial Office. The Secretary of State had loyally defended Governor Hennessy against the accusations of West Indian delegates, and later exonerated him, though more lukewarmly, in the House of Lords. The causes of the riots were so unclear, the versions given so varied, that at one moment it was urged that a Royal Commission should be sent out to investigate, but nothing came of this proposal. It was admitted in Downing Street that Pope Hennessy had met the crisis with courage and efficiency—but who exactly had created the crisis in the first place? 'He suppressed the riots with great judgement and coolness for which he deserves credit,' wrote Sir Julian Pauncefote, the new Legal Under-Secretary at the Colonial Office and previously Chief Justice of the Leeward Islands, '. . . but the great question is— Who set the house on fire?'

VII

Anyone who has lived for any length of time on a British West Indian island—anyone, particularly, who has had experience of old-fashioned West Indian Government House life—soon learns that, in those long-neglected colonies, rumour runs wild and truth is not merely at a discount but as rare as the mythical sea-vulture of Dominica. The most grotesque rumours gain easy currency, the most devious motives are detected behind some simple and straightforward act. At this distance of time we cannot hope to answer Sir Julian Pauncefote's question—'Who set the house on fire?' All we do know is that, though the actual rioting ended and the trials of the rioters opened, Barbados continued to smoulder throughout the summer and autumn of 1876. The House of Assembly sent a petition to London requesting Governor Pope Hennessy's immediate recall. This petition was refused, since Lord Carnarvon could not publicly condemn a Governor whom he had publicly defended. At the same time it was obvious to the authorities in Downing Street that Pope Hennessy could not be left to serve out his term in Barbados where, a hero to the negroes (who remember him with affection to this day) he was now execrated by the planters and the merchants. The situation, moreover, was beginning to fray his nerves. He sent a number of semi-hysterical despatches to the Secretary of State, blaming everyone else, including a number of his predecessors at Government House, for the Federation Riots. '*Moral*. Bring away Mr Hennessy as soon as possible', Mr Herbert minuted on one of these dated October 1876. 'I agree', Lord Carnarvon tersely jotted beneath.

In the first week of November 1876 the Secretary of State for the Colonies, with his humble duty to Her Majesty, submitted to Queen Victoria his proposal for 'the transfer of Mr Hennessy from the Government of Barbados to that of Hong Kong . . . in the belief that it has become very necessary to move Mr Hennessy from political reasons. . . . The state of the gaols, hospitals, public institutions and labouring population is really deplorable, and unless remedied may lead one day to very serious consequences: but the prejudice against Mr Hennessy is so bitter that, whilst he remains Governor, it would be vain to attempt any considerable reform.' The white Barbadians, whose resistance my grandfather had consistently underrated, had won: the first British Governor of Barbados to attempt a humanitarian reform of that ancient colony was removed by the Secretary of State because his very presence on the island had become an impediment to such reform.

There is no sign that John Pope Hennessy was aware of this sad anomaly. Leaving Bridgetown in December, after a farewell dinner at Government House, and carrying in his despatch-box a laudatory address signed by five thousand negroes, he retired briefly to Ireland, where he was given the Freedom of the City of Cork. There, in the chill little city of his birth, he pronounced his final verdict on Barbadians in an address to the Mayor and Corporation: '. . . in all my experience', he declared, 'I was never in a community where there was such deliberate oppression of the masses as in the community of Barbados, and I did feel in the struggle in which I was engaged that it was my duty to expose to the public opinion of England, Ireland and Scotland the real state of the case'. He told his 'fellow-townsmen' that his exertions had 'been productive of good result' and that the British Government, and 'all the men of weight in the House of Commons' were now convinced that 'urgently-needed reforms must be carried out in that distant colony'. In fact, he judged his administration of the Windward Islands to have been a manifest success.

John Pope Hennessy was granted three months' leave, partly to enable him to write a report on the Windward Islands and on the Federation Riots. 'No signs of any report yet from Mr Hennessy, who I think has lost all interest in Barbados affairs', Mr Wedgwood, a young clerk in the Colonial Office, noted in January 1877. Perhaps wisely, my grandfather refrained from penning this report at all. He was spending his leave more profitably—reading books upon the racial and other problems of one of Great Britain's most flourishing and apparently contented colonial communities—his new governorship of Hong Kong.

BOOK VI

HONG KONG

1877–1882

———

THE SELECTION OF John Pope Hennessy to govern Hong Kong might seem, given his colonial record to date, almost inexplicable. Yet it is likely that he had been chosen just because Hong Kong was recognised by the Colonial Office authorities as an unusually peaceful and prosperous Colony. In his previous governorships Hennessy had been given specific instructions to intro-duce change—in Labuan to try to make the colony pay; on the West Coast of Africa to take over the Dutch forts and placate the 'Dutch' tribes; in the Bahamas and Barbados to render archaic constitutions viable. In the view of the Colonial Office, and of the local merchants, Hong Kong needed few improvements and could offer small scope for Hennessy's revolutionary mind, and for his gift for stirring up a hornets' nest of opposition. 'I hope this restless spirit may quiet down', wrote someone in the Colonial Office soon after the Governor had reached his new oriental colony.

Pope Hennessy's immediate predecessor, Sir Arthur Kennedy, the only British Governor of Hong Kong to have had his statue erected by public subscription in the capital, Victoria, had won golden opinions by an inert rule. 'Sir A. Kennedy, the amiable' [we read in Dr Eitel's history of Hong Kong, *Europe in China*] 'is the model of a successful and most popular Governor who achieved local immortality by doing as little as possible whilst making himself personally pleasant to the Downing Street officials.' Apart from the hope that the thriving con-dition of Hong Kong might keep Pope Hennessy quiescent there was the further fact that the larger the colony was, the larger was the civil list, and the less was there in consequence for a Governor to do. The amply-staffed Hong Kong departments all ran fairly smoothly, and, at the apex of the administration, the Governor had little real work. 'The routine and absolutely necessary work of Hong Kong adminis-tration' [reported one of Hennessy's immediate successors] 'seemed to me from the first to be much lighter than that of any Crown Colony which I had previously governed.'

The comparative optimism of the Colonial Office staff about the new appointment was not shared by the members of the European merchant community of Hong Kong. Distressingly well-documented on the story of the Barbados riots of the year before, they awaited their new Governor with apprehension. 'There was, indeed, a presentiment that troublous times might ensue', an eye-witness of the Governor's reception has recorded in his history of Hong Kong, 'but there was also, on the part of the European community, the honest determination to judge of his administration as they might find it.'

This 'honest determination', and a natural curiosity, were responsible, one hot and misty Sunday evening of late April 1877, for the great crowd of officials and Hong Kong residents which thronged Peddar's Wharf, on the quay-side of the colony's capital, Victoria, to welcome the new Governor. The European ladies were 'accommodated in the verandah' of Messrs Melders and Company, merchants, whose offices were just opposite the wharf. They had been waiting some time when, at a quarter to five, a gun boomed out across the harbour to warn them that the P. & O. mailboat *Zambesi*, decked with flags and with the new Governor aboard, had been sighted from the Peak lookout station, moving slowly through the beautiful Lye-mun passage in the fading light.

By some error almost symbolic of a Governorship which brought turmoil to Hong Kong, the *Zambesi* perversely moored off West Point Wharf, where nobody was waiting. So soon as this mistake was realised the company at Peddar's Wharf scrambled back into their palanquins, pony-traps or carrying chairs and headed for West Point. At neither wharf was there any sign of the acting Administrator, old Mr Gardner Austin, whose duty it was to board the vessel and bring the viceregal party ashore in the Governor's official launch. Mr Austin had simply not been expecting the ship that evening, and had stayed up in the cool, damp air of Mountain Lodge, the Governor's summer eyrie on the Peak. Hearing the signal, Austin hastily mounted into his palanquin, a fine Government House chair curtained and lined with mirrors. He was borne down the steep and tortuous lane which linked the Peak with the city below. Although the eight Chinese bearers in sealing-wax red liveries with white gaiters, round mutton-pie felt hats with scarlet tassels on their shining pig-tailed heads, moved at a jog-trot, he reached West Point Wharf quite late. It was nearly seven before the Governor and Mrs Pope Hennessy landed 'amidst the cheers of those whose patience held out to the bitter end'. Only 'the outlines' of their party were visible in

the warm dusk. 'It would appear . . . looking at the matter retrospectively, and impartially,' commented the *China Mail*, 'that landing
Governors is not our "forte". To judge by the blundering haphazard
manner in which so many of these state ceremonies have been carried
out, in our experience it is somewhat astonishing that we have succeeded in getting our administrators conveyed into Government
House at all.' Governor Hennessy's short speech on landing was judged
'modest but manly, neither egotistical nor pompous'. So far so good.

Despite the British administration, the large British garrison and
the rich European traders who lived in big colonnaded houses with
flat roofs, Victoria, Hong Kong, was already in 1877 what it remains
today—predominantly and innately Chinese. There were great stone
wharfs and tall commercial buildings, two Christian Cathedrals, the
college of St Paul, the racecourse and the Hong Kong Club—yet even
so to step ashore was to be enveloped in the scurry and the scents, the
laughing excitement, the noise and the half-gay, half-melancholy
atmosphere of a Far Eastern city. Narrow streets stepped like stair-
cases ran sheer uphill, past booths where food was bubbling in iron
pots, past shops where the innumerable flattened bodies of dried ducks
formed greasy amber screens; streets in which everyone had something
to sell and most people seemed to have something of wood or tin
to make. Outside the Hong Kong hotel the cry of the chair coolies—
'Eh ché! Eh ché!'—echoed from dawn to curfew. The main streets
were blocked with jostling coolies who impeded the passage of the
British in their carrying-chairs, whilst in the Queen's Road the chair-
coolies were so aggressive that Europeans said they feared to be
impaled upon the poles. Starving beggar-children filled the streets
and clawed at the clothing of the passer-by. 'At present the state of
things is simply a disgrace; we might as well be in Malta or Cairo or
even Macao', an angry resident wrote to the local press. Along the
harbour of Victoria, and farther on round the shores of Hong Kong
island, the boat-people dwelt in their sampans, cooking, eating, sleeping and breeding in these floating hovels, polluting the sea-water with
their excrement and in perpetual danger from typhoons. Overall, the
first impression of Victoria, Hong Kong, was of a city pulsatingly and
garishly alive.

For John Pope Hennessy who had by now spent four years in negro
colonies, Hong Kong was in one way a novelty, but it was also a
resumption of the Labuan theme, with its predominantly Chinese
note. For his wife it was a return to the regions of her birth and of

her sudden early marriage. Although the Governor of Hong Kong and members of his family would generally make use of the official palanquins when moving through the city, on the actual night of their arrival they were driven by carriage up the winding streets of the city and past the open shop-houses from which lantern-light flickered over the cobblestones. Majestic Sikh policemen in crimson turbans saluted as the carriage swung by on its ascent to Government House, a plain square white building in a pleasant garden, looking blankly out to sea. The sentries at the gates presented arms. Before the open door the *compradore*,* and his Chinese boy underlings in blue gowns, stood waiting beneath the portico, a smile upon their smooth faces, curiosity in their half-closed eyes, as the new Governor handed his wife and child down from the carriage and into the hall. What did they see?

II

John Pope Hennessy was now in his forty-third year. His hair was as curling and luxuriant as ever, his eye as dartingly inquisitive, his expression as confident as before. The Roman nose, a godsend to the cartoonists of Barbados newspapers, was become more prominent, for the little Governor had grown thinner through a decade of colonial battling in tropical climates. His eye-sockets, always deep, were now cavernous. The sculptor and art historian, Lord Ronald Gower, who passed through Hong Kong on his way to Tokyo a year after my grandfather's arrival, notices in his journal that 'Pope Hennessy in looks reminds me a little of Irving, and also of what Shelley might have looked had he lived ten years longer'. Another Hong Kong visitor, the travel-writer Miss Isabella Bird, who did not like Pope Hennessy at all, described him in a letter to her sister as 'a little man much overdressed in white kid gloves and patent leather boots with a mouth which smiles perpetually and sinister eyes which never smile'. A leading member of the Hong Kong bar, the amorous Mr. Hayllar (of whom we shall hear more) once wrote in disdain of the 'unique insignificance' of the Governor's physical appearance. His diminutive size may in fact have helped to endear Hennessy to orientals, who have often found the normal scale and full-blooded appearance of British residents gross and over-bearing. But the chief impression made by Governor Hennessy on British and orientals alike was one of superlative vitality. 'He [Hennessy] would do better', wrote the

* Or major-domo.

famous China hand Sir Harry Parkes, then British Minister in Tokyo, 'if he had less life.'

Together with the Governor, there passed into the lighted hall his wife and only child. Not quite eighteen months old, Bertie Hennessy looked like any other healthy baby, save for the colour of his eyes which were of an exceptionally bright clear blue. In later life he used to say that Hong Kong was the first place that he consciously remembered, for he was nearly seven when his family left it. He led there the pampered life of a solitary Government House child, spoiled by his parents, petted by their staff, cared for by a Chinese amah, Chika, permitted to fire toy brass cannon filled with real gunpowder on the Queen's Birthday. And what of his mother who, by her wayward but thorough destruction of her private papers, leads in this book a faint and only intermittent life?

Twenty-six years old when she reached Hong Kong, Kitty Pope Hennessy was no longer the panicky obstinate girl we first encountered on Labuan. Nine years of running Government Houses had given her assurance and the habit of entertaining officially and well— 'magnificently' was the adverb used by Mr de Robeck of the Colonial Office to describe the Hennessys' reception of General Ulysses S. Grant at Government House, Hong Kong, in 1879. Movement in London society had increased her native elegance, while her somewhat eastern beauty was now at its apogee as well, it would seem, as her power to attract. For some years now, as her sparse surviving letters to him show, her attitude to her husband had been affectionate—an affection inspired no doubt by gratitude, for, but for him, she might have remained stranded on Labuan for years, her only method of escape marriage to some subaltern in an Indian Army regiment, the unexciting prospect of cantonment life stretched out before her. Hugh Low, her father, had only just been released from Labuan and appointed British Resident to the vast jungle state of Perak in Western Malaya. The Hennessys would certainly have seen him on their way to Hong Kong, when they stayed in Singapore as the guests of Mr Whampoa, a Chinese millionaire with a seat on the Singapore Legislative Council. It must have been a comfort to Kitty Hennessy to know that her father and she herself were once more in at least the same hemisphere. Later, when her relations with her husband had again deteriorated critically, she appealed to her father to come and help. For neither husband nor wife was Government House, Hong Kong, to prove congenial. 'Mrs H. sat in a dream, spoke to no one, and only roused herself to fire up fiercely at her husband who retorted with a cold sarcasm', Miss Isabella Bird wrote to her sister after a small, ungenial dinner-party there in January 1879.

However unpleasant the course of domestic events later unfurled within it, the Hong Kong Government House itself was comfortable and unpretentious and flanked by flowering trees. It possessed three turf tennis courts and two indoor asphalted ones. From its flat roof you gained a fine view over the town and the busy harbour of Victoria, whilst 'looking towards the Peak might be seen the houses of the more well-to-do inhabitants rising tier over tier amid surrounding foliage for a third of the distance up the mountain'. Beyond this inhabited belt the rest of the Peak, a mountain eighteen hundred feet high, was then still bare, a wilderness of rocks and of red-purple earth. This lack of trees was one of many aspects of Hong Kong which my grandfather immediately desired to alter. By his order nine Government nurseries were established and twenty thousand seedlings imported. Before he finally left the colony for good China firs, swamp oaks, cocoa-nut palms and young pine trees were 'dotted all over the island'. 'In this respect HE Mr Hennessy deserves well of the community', commented the editor of an habitually unfriendly newspaper, 'and he will be more likely to be remembered by posterity by means of this scheme than by any other act of his administration.'

When the British flag had first been raised on Hong Kong the whole island was as stony and as bleak as the upper slopes of its mountain remained in 1877. In the thirty-six years of British occupation a minor miracle had been performed in turning what Lord Palmerston had called 'a barren island with hardly a house upon it' into one of the greatest and most thriving trading stations in the East. Hong Kong represented a triumph for the rapacious British commercialism which Pope Hennessy, for one, so much deplored.

III

The major fact about Hong Kong in the eighteen-seventies is that it was still essentially a trading station or 'factory'—a place to which merchants came to trade but not to settle. The colony owed its existence to the British determination to make money in China, although the Imperial Chinese Government did not want foreigners in the country and did not, above all, want the opium which the British sold the Chinese people in increasing quantities. At the court of Pekin it was known that the opium habit was demoralising the nation and at the same time depleting China of silver currency.

The antagonism of the central Government to British traders inspired the Chinese provincial governors to encourage the natural xenophobia of their people. By 1839 the treatment of British merchants in Canton, the chief port at which they were then attempting to do business, had become so bad that it led to a British punitive expedition, long known in history books as the First Opium War. By the Treaty of Nanking, which ended the war and was ratified by the Pekin Government in June 1842, British consulates were established at specified Chinese ports, called in consequence 'the Treaty Ports'. But since life for the British traders in the Treaty Ports seemed likely to be as precarious as before, the local British authorities insisted on the cession in perpetuity of the bleak island of Hong Kong. In January 1841 the flag was raised on Possession Point. When the Treaty of Nanking was ratified eighteen months later Hong Kong was declared a British colony. It remains so to this day.

As was usual in these early days of empire, the British Government was reluctant to acquire yet another colony. The arguments which finally persuaded the Foreign and Colonial Offices to desire the cession of Hong Kong have been summarised by a recent historian as four in number. The island was to replace Canton as the centre of British trade. Strategically it was necessary to have a strong naval base in the area, since the Chinese Government would naturally only bow to force. It was hoped that, like Bombay and Singapore, Hong Kong might become a great emporium. It was essential that lawsuits between and against the many undesirable British merchants who were now working the China coast should be settled in British courts according to British law; and, since a British court could only legally function under the protection of the British flag, enough land must be acquired to establish a British colony. 'The colony was not thought of in terms of gain', writes Professor Endacott, 'but as the minimum required for what were thought to be the necessary institutions.' The commercial impulse which founded Hong Kong was thus analogous to that responsible for British possessions on the Gold Coast rather than to that which had led to the colonisation of the West Indies or of the hopeless island of Labuan. Also, unlike Labuan, Hong Kong had proved a marked success.

Once the colony had been officially established, building began. Industrious Chinese traders and shopkeepers, together with hordes of willing coolies, poured over from the mainland. They were followed by a wave of less desirable immigrants—pimps, thugs and drug peddlers, all anxious to find out what easy money might be made in Hong Kong. It was largely a shifting population, and British nationality was not, of course, granted to even the most respectable Chinese. By 1876, the year before Pope Hennessy's advent, it was estimated that Hong Kong island contained 130,000 Chinese out of a total population of 139,000. Partly owing to the low living standards and dishonesty of great numbers of the Chinese immigrants, partly owing to the persistent British vision of themselves as beings superior to 'John Chinaman', the strictest racial segregation was enforced. The Chinese were assigned certain areas in the city of Victoria; in other areas they were forbidden to build or to live. A nine o'clock curfew was imposed on them. No Chinese was allowed into the streets after that hour, unless he carried a permissive note from his employer and a lantern in his hand. Punitive measures were heavier for the Chinese than for any other Hong Kong criminals, flogging on the back being frequent and indignities such as cutting the queue general. Prison conditions were brutalising, and it was claimed that any improvement in them might tempt more of the denizens of Hong Kong's slums to crime. In the shoddy little Chinese houses of the city each room was ordinarily occupied by one or more families. No windows looked on to the streets, and many of the rooms were constructed inside another, like 'Chinese boxes'. There was no sanitation of any kind. Pigs were treated as members of the family and lay all day and night beneath the board beds.

Racial segregation was also forced upon the rich and educated Chinese, who had no social contacts with the British officials and merchants. These latter formed a compact but quarrelsome society of their own. They went to each others' dinner-parties, indulged in such seasonal activities as yachting, racing, shooting, tennis and croquet, took part in or patronised the performances got up by the Amateur Dramatic Club, or the Tarantula Society's fancy dress balls. Chinese servants and employees were treated without sympathy by most of the Europeans, who addressed them in that degrading nursery language, pidgin English, which the Chinese were expected to learn. Servants and coolies were too often subject to their masters' physical violence. Even Miss Isabella Bird, whose wide travels led her to survey British colonial rule with a complacent pride, was disturbed by the callousness of the Europeans in Hong Kong. 'Foreigners have misused and do misuse the Chinese', she wrote. 'You cannot be two minutes in a Hong Kong street without seeing Europeans striking coolies with their canes or umbrellas.' Lord Ronald Gower's enthusiasm for some youthful officers of the 74th Regiment whom he met at the Hong Kong Club was much diminished on finding that these young fellows treated orientals as 'if they were a very inferior kind of animal to themselves. No wonder', he concluded, 'that we English are so cordially disliked wherever we go.'

The example of the British officers was naturally followed by their men, and the police courts were filled with soldiers and sailors arrested for being brutishly drunk in a brothel, kicking and beating chair coolies or trying to rape Chinese women. The military garrison, which gave the European community some sense of security against hypothetical attack from the Chinese mainland, or by pirates from the sea, also provided public concerts on the Band Promenade on moonlit nights. It did not otherwise greatly contribute to public order. The Temperance Hall, opened in May 1876, offered soldiers and sailors fortnightly entertainments at which no alcoholic beverage was served. These were not well attended.

The Hong Kong Chinese did not take British mistreatment passively. They retaliated by swindling the Europeans at every opportunity, by staring rudely at them as though they were freaks, by banging up against them in the streets and by referring to them to their faces but in dialect as 'barbarians' and 'foreign devils'. The conviction that all Chinese were untrustworthy and deceitful had become as integral a part of the social creed of the members of the Hong Kong Club as was the fear of the negro in that of the planters of Barbados. Unquestionably there had been horrible and unsavoury elements amongst the first batches of Chinese who had flocked into the new colony in the eighteen-forties; but neglect and squalor had demoralised the thousands born and bred on the island since. Successive administrations had done remarkably little to improve the lot of the Chinese in Hong Kong. For a man with Pope Hennessy's theories of racial equality Hong Kong life provided hourly occasions for indignation. He has been described by Professor Endacott as 'the first Governor to be shocked by the unequal treatment of the Chinese'. 'He treated the Chinese as partners', the same historian explains, 'and largely because of this he was hated by the Europeans. In his enlightened policy he was in advance of his time.'

We should here remember that their contemptuous attitude towards orientals was not exclusive to the British. In 1879 General Ulysses S. Grant, in the course of the journey round the world which followed his second term as President of the United States, told the Emperor of Japan that he had 'seen things' which had made his 'blood boil, in the way the European powers attempt to degrade the Asiatic nations'. Some of the General's information must certainly have come from Governor Pope Hennessy, with whom he stayed in Hong Kong in the spring of 1879, and with whom he formed a genuine friendship. 'No man was more welcome to the General', writes the chronicler of the ex-President's world tour. 'General Grant was the guest of the Governor during his residence in Hong Kong, and formed a high opinion of his genius and character.'

IV

John Pope Hennessy's determination to treat the Chinese of Hong Kong as partners rather than as alien inferiors was perfectly predictable. By it, however, he was setting a bolder and a stormier course than any even he had yet attempted in colonial territory. It was likewise a lonelier one. He could, of course, expect neither support nor sympathy from the local Europeans, hard-headed business men who had come to Hong Kong to gain money and who regarded the Chinese merely as a convenient pool of labour for this purpose. When he made his views clear—as he swiftly and publicly did—they began by laughing at him as 'a whimsical philanthropist' with a 'namby-pamby' and 'mollycoddling' attitude to orientals. As soon as they saw that he was in earnest their protests became virulent. As passionately attached to the *status quo* as were the planters of the ancient colony of Barbados, these merchant princes of developing Hong Kong were against any form of change. On their side it must be remembered that, like the Barbadian planters, these merchants and their families were in a racial minority and suffered from the sense of insecurity which such a state engenders.

John Pope Hennessy was by now used to the almost automatic hostility of European communities in the colonies which he was sent to govern. But the real difference between his position in Hong Kong and his position as Governor of Labuan, the West Coast of Africa, the Bahamas or Barbados lay in the fact that in each of his previous administrations he could rely on the support—limited and reluctant enough at times—of the Secretary of State and the Colonial

Office staff. They might criticise him, regret his rashness and prevarication, rebuke him and even, as in the case of Barbados, remove him to another colony; but by and large they had loyally backed him up. In Hong Kong this gradually ceased to be the case. 'We must watch all his proceedings very narrowly . . .', Mr Herbert warned the Secretary of State, 'and when we see any tendency to bolt to the right or left from the path of established procedure in Hong Kong (which is an intricate one surrounded with special dangers arising from the Chinese character which he does not understand) he should be firmly and as gently as possible led back into it. He may cause not only terrible trouble but real danger by crude and thoughtless "improvements" in procedure.' Hennessy had begun his administration by minutely investigating the work and the abilities of every one of his subordinate officials, thereafter inundating the Colonial Office with analyses of their defects as well as with a myriad kaleidoscopic suggestions for improving the efficiency of each department. These self-assured comments and rather haphazard schemes disquieted Lord Carnarvon, although he had himself appointed Pope Hennessy to Hong Kong. 'It is impossible to say what Mr Hennessy may not do if time is allowed him', wrote the Secretary of State barely six months after the Governor had reached Hong Kong. 'He seems too from want perhaps of occupation to be in a dangerously restless mood.'

Lord Carnarvon resigned from the Cabinet in January 1878, on a disagreement with Disraeli about the Russo-Turkish War. He was succeeded by Sir Michael Hicks-Beach who, on taking over the Colonial Office, was briefed by his staff on the problems of each separate British overseas territory. After nine months of Pope Hennessy's rule, Hong Kong was already in a state of ferment. 'To my mind the history of all this trouble is a simple one', Mr Robert Herbert explained in a memorandum for his new chief. 'Mr Hennessy observes on arriving that long residence among Chinese, & familiarity with the Chinese character, has led the residents in Hong Kong to believe that a Chinaman is not to be dealt with as an Englishman . . . might be. He thinks this inhuman, and determines to set to work vigorously to reform what he believes to be a grave abuse. But, having no political wisdom, he proceeds in such a manner as to alienate from him all public sympathy and support, & ultimately to cause a sort of panic as to his intentions and their probable results. . . . It is very unfortunate that with ambition, ability & many good intentions, he cannot ever gain the confidence of those over whom he is placed.'

Mr Robert Herbert might have added that one of Governor
Hennessy's gravest faults—and one which was becoming exaggerated
in his middle age—was his blind conviction that he always knew best.
Eight weeks after he had reached the Colony, for instance, he rejected
the unanimous advice of his Executive Council when asked to sign a
deportation order sending back to the starving Chinese mainland a
young offender under eighteen years of age. Instead, the Governor
interviewed the prisoner personally, declared that he was quite clearly
over twenty, and must remain in the Colony. 'I fear he means to interfere freely with the administration of justice', Mr Bramston, a Colonial
Office clerk with first-hand knowledge of Hong Kong wrote of this
trivial but ominous incident. '. . . the Governor with his very slight
experience of Chinese faces, which to newcomers generally appear
to be all alike, was able to determine his age.' Again, in the year
following, he shocked his advisers and disturbed the Downing Street
staff by a lightning decision to set free forty-eight Chinese criminals
because they had helped to nurse some seamen injured in a shipboard
explosion. 'The Govr. seems to me to have been carried away by a
wave of "Gush" of w. I suspect he is a little ashamed. . . .', wrote one
Colonial Office underling. 'The whole affair has an oriental despotic
air about it which when combined with sensational elements should
not be encouraged', commented the Parliamentary Under-Secretary
of State, Mr James Lowther. 'What startling piece of legerdemain is
he next going to produce to show how ruffians may be let loose and
yet the safety of the community be preserved?' enquired, in August
1877, a correspondent of the *China Mail*.

A small illustration, or verbal vignette, of Governor Hennessy at
work on his favourite task of freeing prisoners is provided by the
lady traveller whom we have already quoted, Miss Isabella Bird.
Miss Bird, who was the guest of the Anglican Bishop of Hong Kong,
distrusted the Governor as a Roman Catholic and an Irishman and as
'the Mr Pope Hennessy who got us into, or made, such trouble in
Barbados'. 'It strikes me', she wrote to her sister after a visit to the
'simply splendid' prison in Victoria in January 1879, 'that he is *posing*
as an humanitarian. . . . The prison pleased me, but Governor Hennessy
obviously has a diseased sympathy with criminals.'

Miss Bird and Bishop Burdon had arranged to meet Governor Pope
Hennessy inside the prison, there to inspect the improvements made
on his instructions during the first twenty months of his administration. Some of these improvements seemed unnecessary to Miss Bird,

and perhaps to her companion also: 'The accommodation, food, etc., are as much superior to the houses and manner of living of the poorer Chinese as our rooms and way of living in Atholl Crescent are superior to that of the dwellers in the Cowgate', the Edinburgh lady wrote to her sister. As they were touring the prison—and learning that my grandfather had now forbidden flogging, branding behind the ear and deportation, and had ordered that brutal European warders with a long history of fines for assaulting their charges be replaced—the Governor of Hong Kong appeared himself: 'While we were in one of the yards the Governor *chasséed* in— "My dear Lord, I'm overjoyed to see you". . . . He was very voluble.' In Miss Bird's presence the Governor then began listening to prisoners' petitions through an interpreter. She observed his evident wish to remit as many of the sentences as possible, and was particularly shocked by his anxiety to pardon the mate of a ship who had beaten the ship's boy to death on the high seas. Appealed to by the Governor for her opinion on this case Miss Bird intervened forcibly against such an act of clemency and managed to dissuade the Governor from it. Hennessy spent three hours conducting Miss Bird over the prison and then, making her 'ascend his palanquin with 8 scarlet bearers' he walked beside it to the Bishop's Palace. As, a diminutive figure in white gloves, he strolled uphill beside the palanquin in which Miss Bird was swaying, the Governor spoke to her of his own convictions and his aims: 'On the way back the Governor began to defend his policy both here and in Barbados!' Neither his courtesy (which led her to suspect that he was hoping she would write about him in her new travel book) nor a visit to the Tung Wah Hospital under his auspices served to mollify Miss Isabella Bird. 'I dislike him more each time I see him', was her final verdict. Wary of charm, Miss Bird was not to be beguiled.

Miss Bird's sojourn in Hong Kong took place, as we have seen, in 1879, when Governor Pope Hennessy's unpopularity with the British in the colony was well established. But even by the autumn of the year he had arrived, 1877, the *China Mail* was writing of the 'exceedingly lavish' criticism which the new Governor had inspired. At this period the *Mail*, which came out in the evening and was one of the two influential English-language journals in the Colony, was still trying to judge the Governor impartially: 'Mr Hennessy, in our opinion, would soon make himself decidedly popular were it not for his possession of the unfortunate habit of hitting any or every head that presents itself before him, or of treading upon a continuous series of official or

communal corns.' Another day the newspaper warned its readers
against believing all the varied rumours with which the smoking-
rooms and the verandahs of Victoria's clubs were buzzing: 'There are
always a large number of "indispensable authorities" as to the intentions of His Excellency to be encountered in the Colony; in fact it is
difficult to find a resident who is not one.' The panic which had
gripped the planters of Barbados was by now beginning to be sensed
in the counting-houses and the drawing-rooms of the European
quarters of Victoria, Hong Kong.

v

The main centre of panic, and the source of most of the rumours
circulating in Victoria that summer, autumn and winter of 1877 was
the Hong Kong Club, where the bearded members sat gossiping in
leathern armchairs beneath large crystal chandeliers. The Club became
a sort of headquarters for those opposed to the Governor, and each
day brought in fresh reports of his chance remarks. He was, for
example, said to have called the night-pass-and-lantern system for
Chinese out after curfew 'a monstrous piece of class legislation'. From
this comment it was at once assumed that he meant to abolish the
system altogether. Enlightened Europeans did agree that it was absurd
that the night-pass system should apply even to such a distinguished
Chinese as Ng Choy, a wealthy agnostic barrister of Lincoln's Inn who,
on his recent return to Hong Kong, had been admitted to the local
bar, and was subsequently appointed by my grandfather the first
Chinese to serve on the Legislative Council. With some difficulty Mr
Ng Choy could indeed have got exemption from the night-pass
ordinance, but if he had done so he would only have been subject to
more annoyance from the police who had orders to stop and question
any Chinaman not carrying a lantern after nightfall. Sympathy with
his particular case was, all the same, an exception, for the European
community in general was wholly in favour of the night-pass system
—and of any other which seemed likely to keep the Chinese segre-
gated and under control. When it became known that Governor
Hennessy was not merely opposed to public floggings but had commanded that these be replaced by 'a few whippings, privately administered within the walls of the Gaol' the Europeans in Hong Kong (and
some of the rich Chinese as well) pronounced that life and property in
the Colony would never be safe again. One Englishman wrote to

the newspaper to say that the abolition of public flogging would put an end to Hong Kong's social whirl; for, flogging once abolished, the streets would become so unsafe that there could be no more dining-out.

Public flogging had been introduced into Hong Kong in May 1841, four months after the British flag had been raised on Possession Point and more than a year before the ratification of the Treaty of Nanking by which Hong Kong became irrevocably a British colony. It thus rates as one of the earliest benefits of British rule experienced by Chinese over from the mainland seeking work; a 'safeguard' stipulated that any sentence of more than one hundred lashes on the naked back must be referred to the Head of the Government for confirmation. Three years later flogging in Hong Kong had become so general that a question was tabled in the House of Commons asking why, in one day alone, fifty-four floggings had been administered to Chinese coolies merely for not having tickets of leave. In 1849 a humane Governor, Sir George Bonham, tried to mitigate these brutalities but, finding no support amongst the British business community, he let the matter drop. In 1866, when an interregnum between Governors had upset the local Europeans who found the temporary Administrator too lenient, 'the cry was for a Caesar . . . a dictator rather, with a strong mind and will, than a weak faddist'. The Secretary of State sent out an able but ruthless Irishman, Sir Richard MacDonnell. This Governor was an energetic autocrat. He did much for the Colony—he licensed gambling houses for the Chinese and encouraged them to build their own hospital—but he also enormously increased the severity of the Hong Kong penal system, extended the penalty of flogging to crimes committed inside the gaol, and instituted a system of branding and deportation. MacDonnell's supine successor, Kennedy, did little to alter these new laws, although they ran counter to the more humane views then becoming prevalent in the Colonial Office. This was the situation when Kennedy's successor, Governor Pope Hennessy, took over.

As we have seen Hennessy at once suspended public floggings. He then set up a commission to inquire into the medical effects of flogging. He improved gaol conditions and he replaced drunken turnkeys. He next tried to organise a Chinese Discharged Prisoners Aid Society, which proved a failure. By these and other measures which alienated the British community the new Governor speedily won over the Chinese, with whom he soon acquired the kind of word-of-mouth

reputation he had made for himself among the negro labourers of
Barbados. In the sordid hutments of the city, in the hongs on the
waterfront, aboard the junks and sampans word was passed on that
at length there had come to Hong Kong a Governor who intended
to be the patron and protector of the Chinese. The coolies called him
'the merciful man' and 'Number One Good Friend'. The good news
spread up the delta of the Pearl River to Canton, where it was
freely asserted that under Governor Hennessy criminals deported from
Hong Kong would now be able to return to the Colony. It has been
said that no good deed goes unpunished; by his sudden and sweeping
humanitarian reforms Pope Hennessy caused himself much future
trouble. It was his misfortune that, besides being high-minded, he was
high-handed as well.

Like all Chinese communities, that of Hong Kong was riddled with
secret societies which covertly wielded great power. The most
influential group of Hong Kong Chinese was not, however, a secret
society but the committee of the Tung Wah Hospital. This was a
large, charitable institution run in accordance with the tenets of
Chinese medicine and supported by wealthy Chinese merchants. It
had been opened in 1872, on the advice of Governor MacDonnell,
and was partly maintained by a percentage of the Government revenue
from gambling licences. Hong Kong officials had for long suspected
that the Tung Wah Hospital Committee had political aims, and the
Governors of Hong Kong had always dealt very warily with the
Committee through the office of the Registrar-General, who was
styled 'Protector of the Chinese'. Governor Pope Hennessy, however,
established direct personal relations between the Committee and
Government House through the barrister Ng Choy, a stout imposing
person in rich silk brocades who became one of the Governor's chief
counsellors. To make his friendly attitude yet clearer Hennessy was
also planning to create a new post, that of Chinese Secretary to the
Governor.

This was the pattern of Governor Hennessy's administration of
Hong Kong. Ranged on one side was the Governor, indulging with
a handful of sympathisers, in what his enemies called his 'Chinomania',
valiantly attacking the penal system and declining the advice of men
of experience. On the opposing side were most of the merchants and
many of the officials of the colony. Between these two camps the great
mass of Hong Kong orientals watched and waited, trying, not without
cynicism, to assess which side would win. One sign of the changes

operating in Hong Kong was the fact that the meetings of the Legislative Council, hitherto ignored by the man in the street, were now
thronged by the public, and 'seldom failed to draw a good house'.
'Mr Hennessy', wrote the editor of the *China Mail* in February 1878,
'has certainly so far succeeded in getting up highly interesting and
attractive meetings of the Legislative Council. Quite a number of
topics which, from a local point of view, are second to none in
importance were gaily trotted out yesterday and discussed with an
energy perfectly terrible to the scribes of the press.' 'The Legislative
Council Chamber', writes Dr Eitel more succinctly, 'was the arena of
almost perpetual strife.'

VI

Both during and after the passage through Hong Kong of 'that stormy
petrel of colonial administration' (as one of his contemporaries called
John Pope Hennessy) it was usual, in the European community, to
say that before his arrival the local Chinese had been quiet, manage-
able and obedient. In fact this had never been so. From the very
foundation of the Colony a series of violent crimes—murders, rob-
beries, kidnappings for ransom—had been almost daily—or, rather,
nightly—events. Many of these crimes were committed by Chinese
pirates or by gangs from the mainland who came down from Canton
or even from Shanghai with deliberately criminal intent. But a good
proportion of the criminals were impoverished, unemployed, resident
Chinese. Sir Richard MacDonnell's sharp legislation was said to have
checked and frightened these Chinamen; and under his successor, Sir
Arthur Kennedy, the statistics of crime, which had declined from 1872
to 1875, had begun to rise again in 1876. Further, the Kennedy régime
had to admit that they were powerless to enforce such measures as
the Servants' Registration Ordinance or to control public gambling.
When Kennedy had, for instance, tried by a modest tax on coolie
lodging-houses to bring these hovels under some kind of sanitary
control, all the carrying coolies in the Colony went on strike, trade
was paralysed and the Government gave in after three days. Crime
and disorder were as traditional in this young Crown Colony as the
opium trade which, because it was large-scale, immensely profitable,
and conducted by respected European merchants, was not considered
criminal at all.

The first year of Pope Hennessy's Governorship saw a disturbing rise in the crime-rate of 13 per cent. In the following year this increase was tripled. Now, although part of this rise could be (and by my grandfather certainly was) attributed to famine and floods in South China, causing an influx of destitute refugees into Hong Kong and a consequent rise in food prices there, it was also due to a popular misunderstanding of the Governor's aims. As it happened, although Number One Good Friend forbade flogging, disapproved of deportation and branding and was opposed to gaol sentences for small offences, he was as anxious to discourage crime as anyone else. Enunciating the principle that 'the great object of a gaol is to make it thoroughly deterrent', he introduced the treadmill, reduced the prisoners' rice ration and, on occasions, permitted deportation. He also insisted that hardened criminals should automatically go before the Supreme Court instead of being sentenced by magistrates, who could not impose heavy sentences. But by the theatrical manner in which he announced, for example, his dislike of flogging, and the very public ways in which he showed his admiration for the Chinese—sending 'a sculptured golden vase' as a gift to the Temple of Confucius at Canton, and inviting to a soirée at Government House two officers of an Imperial Chinese Naval gunboat then blockading Hong Kong harbour—he succeeded in exciting the Chinese community. From the upper classes the enthusiasm seeped downwards to the criminal ones, where wild hopes began to spawn.

Soon after New Year 1878 an armed band attacked the village of Aplichan on Hong Kong island. Then the superintendent of police and some of his constables were wounded in the streets of Victoria. In May a woman was murdered in the city; on the day after that another woman was hacked to pieces on the lovely shores of Shek-O Bay. And so it went on, at an increasing rate, into the summer. The Shek-O murder, in which a man had killed the sister of the woman with whom he lived, caused a sensation in the Colony. It was not merely the brutality of the crimes—a second woman and her child were badly injured by the murderer—that shocked European opinion: it was also the fact that, after deliberation, Governor Pope Hennessy commuted the death sentence on the culprit, Cheung Ashim. His grounds for the decision were two—that Cheung Ashim had at his trial been represented by a barrister but had had no solicitor; and that, while the prosecution had called the murder motiveless it was not so, since Cheung Ashim's woman had packed her few belongings and was setting off to live with somebody else. Protests poured into the local papers. The Governor was accused of imposing his private views on capital punishment upon a colony which did not care for them, while one of the jurors—attacked in his turn as 'a balked bloodhound' by another correspondent—wrote to announce that he would never serve on a jury again.

Impervious to all this criticism, my grandfather meanwhile was peacefully passing the hot weather up at Mountain Lodge, the Governor's summer retreat 1,700 feet above the harbour. This was a smallish and, when cloud wreathed the Peak, a damp house. Since demolished, it was then some ten years old, had narrow stone verandahs to north and south, Pompeian-red and yellow tiled floors, and commanded, from the southern verandah, an unsurpassed panoramic view across the deep blue China Sea, afloat with islets and backed by a long line of mountains. From Mountain Lodge, where Mrs Pope Hennessy received each Monday evening from five till seven o'clock, the Governor would descend in his palanquin borne by scarlet-clad bearers to the steaming, angry city below.

One night in late September of this same inauspicious year, 1878, a gang estimated at between forty and eighty armed thugs attacked a large shop in Winglok Street. They sealed the street off whilst ransacking the shop, defeated the armed police and escaped with their booty in a steam launch. When news of this latest crime broke in Victoria next morning, the European residents took counsel together and decided that they had had enough. Led by Mr Keswick, of the important firm of Jardine Matheson, they decided on a public indignation meeting 'to consider the present state of life and property in the Colony'. Mr Sangster, the Sheriff of Victoria, advertised that this meeting would be held in St George's Hall on the afternoon of 7 October. Four days before this date an European house in Seymour Terrace was broken into and burgled.

St George's Hall was part of the complex—library, museum, assembly hall, ballroom, supper-room and theatre—of the Victoria City Hall, designed by the French architect Hermitte, and opened by the Duke of Edinburgh in 1869. It was of limited seating capacity. While some of the wealthier Chinese merchants had supported the idea of a meeting, the Europeans assumed that 'the Celestials' would have the taste to recognise that this was a purely European affair and that the British merchants would have the place to themselves. In the early afternoon of 7 October Chinese residents were observed to be 'streaming down in chairs' as though on a race day. It soon appeared that they were heading for the City Hall, which they filled to such capacity that when the Sheriff, the Chairman and the Committee of the protest meeting reached it at the approved hour they could hardly get through the door. Three hundred shaven heads and smirking countenances were turned towards the sixty-odd European gentlemen at the doorway. Jokes and insults were exchanged, 'a general struggle ensued', and the Europeans 'stampeded' to the cricket ground where they formed a tight circle round the chairman. Led by the Governor's crony, Mr Ng Choy, the Chinese took up positions on the verandahs of the City Hall. A demand by Mr Ng Choy for an interpreter—since most of the Chinese could not understand what was going on—was ignored, whereupon, making a dignified gesture to his followers with his fan, the Chinese barrister led them away. They left the field in a body, cheering in a thin, unpleasant manner, laughing over their shoulders and brandishing their fans.

Whilst it did not stop the proceedings, this show of Chinese solidarity was disconcerting. Next day there were many rumours that the Tung Wah Hospital Committee had met in secret session to sabotage the meeting and protect the Governor. Coolies, boys and idle migrants, summoned or bribed by emissaries alleged to have gone about the hongs saying that the Europeans were petitioning for the recall of the Governor, were said to have packed the meeting. In a lengthy letter to the *China Mail*, Ng Choy denied that there had been any such packing, and asserted that the Tung Wah Committee had met in public not in secret. He ended by expressing disappointment that more consideration had not been shown to his fellow-countrymen attending an European public gathering in the Colony for the very first time. Yet do we not here glimpse shades of Barbados, and of those scenes in the Bridgetown House of Assembly when the public galleries were invaded by coloured 'persons with no jackets on' come to applaud Governor Pope Hennessy's speech? *'Flectere si nequeo Superos, Acheronta movebo.'*

Five resolutions were unanimously passed at the Cricket Ground Meeting, the first of which declared that 'life and property are not so unsafe in any town of the British dominions as in Victoria' and had been jeopardised by a policy of 'undue leniency towards the criminal classes', whilst the fifth asked that a Commission should be sent to the Colony to enquire into the application of the criminal law, the execution of Court sentences and the relations between Governor Pope Hennessy and his officials. A sixth resolution was added requesting the Governor to forward the other five to the Secretary of State. Within three weeks of the passing and despatch to London of these resolutions, a mammoth address signed by more than two thousand Chinese shopkeepers of the Wantshai district of Victoria was sent to the Queen. This address, soon followed by one from the Tung Wah Hospital Committee cast in similar terms, emphasised the satisfaction of the Chinese community with Governor Hennessy's methods, attitude and views. 'He embodies the mind of heaven and earth, he lives to promote life, and harsh punishment therefore is not placed in the first rank' reads one sentence of the shopkeepers' address.

The Chinese community was informed in May 1879 that Her Majesty had been 'pleased to receive their address'. The Secretary of State for the Colonies, on the other hand, continued to ignore the Cricket Ground resolutions. When a reminder was sent to him by the movers and seconders of the petition, Sir Michael Hicks-Beach declined to consent to a commission of enquiry. In November 1880 Sir Michael's successor, the Liberal Lord Kimberley, gave official approval to nearly all Pope Hennessy's plans for penal reform. Flogging in public was abolished, all Ordinances providing for the specific flogging of Chinese were repealed and flogging itself was prohibited save in the rare cases in which it would have been inflicted for a similar offence in the United Kingdom. In all cases Asiatics should be flogged 'on the breach and not on the back'. After three and a half years Hennessy's humane views had triumphed. He had got his way, but at the cost of great unpopularity. 'The Governor', [commented Mr Meade of the Colonial Office in May 1881] 'made some changes in the criminal law of Hong Kong about flogging & branding, measures which were good in themselves but which he carried out with a singular want of tact & judgement.'

In April 1880, despite his vertiginous effect upon the Colonial Office staff and upon the Europeans of his own colony, the Governor of Hong Kong was made a Knight Commander of the Order of St Michael and St George. Now Sir John Pope Hennessy, he had achieved yet another of the ambitions formed during his obscure Cork boyhood. So delighted was he with the honour that, with characteristic disregard for protocol, he had it published in the *Hong Kong Gazette* before it had been announced in London, a step which caused astonishment both in Downing Street and in the Colony itself.

THE ALLOCATION OF HONOURS has ever been one of the more mysterious aspects of British public life. Pope Hennessy's knighthood was given to him after the unexpected defeat of the Tories in the General Election of April 1880. In a long valedictory private letter—an omnibus reply to no less than nine private missives of the Governor's—Sir Michael Hicks-Beach, the retiring Secretary of State, told Hennessy that he could not recommend him for the government of Tasmania, then vacant, but that 'it seemed to me that I ought before leaving office, to mark my sense of the energy & ability you have shown at Hong Kong in some way: and therefore I have recommended you for the KCMG, which I trust will be agreeable to you'. The anomaly of a Secretary of State thus praising and rewarding a governor of whose activities the subordinate officials of the Colonial Office almost unanimously disapproved can only be explained in political terms and attributed to the loyalty felt by a Tory Minister towards a former Tory Member of Parliament.

With his knighthood, Pope Hennessy's tendency to autocratic rule increased. The staff of the Eastern Department in Downing Street began to lose all hope of being able to control him and, as they called it, 'to pin him down'. 'Before discussing these Estimates', one of them wrote in October 1881 for the benefit of Hicks-Beach's successor, Lord Kimberley, now once again in charge of Colonial affairs: 'I wish to call Lord Kimberley's attention to one point: It is absolutely useless at present to communicate with Sir J. Hennessy, because he locks up the despatch, shows it to no one, and never answers it; and if it relates to expenditure of any kind he can simply disregard the instructions and spend as much money as he likes, giving no account and never being found out.' 'I believe', Lord Kimberley replied, 'he makes no secret that he simply puts by such of our despatches as he does not like.' Already in the Hong Kong period, Pope Hennessy seems to have been subject to moods which, in after years in Mauritius, led a section of the leading colonists there to suggest that he was going off his head. Frenzied bouts of activity would be followed by days of lassitude; it was later said that no governorship in the history of Hong Kong had been distinguished by so many admirable projects initiated, discussed, partially executed, and then allowed to drop. The *China Mail* complained that the administration was 'handled in such insubstantial fashion, more like the work of a dreaming theorist than that of a practical legislator and diplomatist, that the Governor is earning himself no small amount of ill-will'. As usual, Sir John Pope Hennessy was wholly complacent over his own plans, his unorthodox methods, and their bizarre results. Replying, in what must surely be one of the most candid speeches ever made by a British Colonial Governor, to an address presented to him after his return to London by the Aborigines Protection Society which sent a deputation to wait on him at Claridge's Hotel, he was reported by *The Times* as explaining to his listeners that 'the truth of the matter as to the majority of the Crown Colonies was that the Governors strove to ascertain what Downing Street would like to hear, reporting home accordingly, rather than embroil themselves with any part of the people over whom they ruled, or get themselves voted nuisances by the red tapeists of Downing-street'. This, he most correctly added, was 'a course he had never followed'.

In Downing Street, Sir John Pope Hennessy was voted more and more of a nuisance. After he had persuaded the Admiral on the station to report secretly to himself on defence matters, thus by-passing the General Commanding with whom he was no longer on speaking terms, his friend Mr Herbert noted: 'He is making it exceedingly difficult to employ him.' His Colonial Secretary changed seven times in five years, and at least one of these, a Mr Marsh, openly applied for a transfer on the grounds that he could no longer work with the Governor. The Colonial Office were perfectly sympathetic, but they did not judge the reason valid: 'It is, however, childish of Mr Marsh to expect that he can be removed merely because he does not get on with Mr Hennessy. If this became the custom there would be hardly any colonial servants left in the various colonies from time to time administered by Mr Hennessy.' Those who did not work closely with him, or whose views were not opposed to his, succumbed to his charm as freely as ever. 'Even if I were sure of the fact stated, I should be careful not to write anything to Mr Hennessy in a tone of censure', the British Minister in Pekin, Sir Thomas Wade, wrote in November 1880: 'All other considerations apart I recd. much kindness from him in the Spring.'

II

One side of Government House life which Pope Hennessy had always enjoyed was the entertaining. In Hong Kong there was even more scope for this than there had been in Barbados; it had been reckoned that some £70,000 was annually expended in salutes fired in Victoria harbour to welcome distinguished or royal strangers. In 1879, as we have already noticed, the Governor organised a splendid reception for the former United States President and Civil War hero, General Ulysses S. Grant, with whom he made as firm friends as he did with 'Chinese' Gordon who was his guest in 1880 and with whom he afterwards kept up an interesting correspondence on Sino-British relations. In May 1880 Prince Henry of Prussia, second son of the Crown Prince and Crown Princess of Germany, and a grandson of Queen Victoria, paid a long visit to Government House. This visit became yet another occasion for a local row, and for a shock to the Colonial Office. General Donovan, who commanded the Hong Kong garrison, and who refused to speak to the Governor for allowing Chinese to buy, and build on, land near the barracks previously regarded as a European quarter, refused to lend the military band to play at the Queen's Birthday dinner at Government House, and even organised a separate dinner in the Queen's honour on that day. By telegraphing to the Secretary of State, Governor Hennessy succeeded in getting the War Office to order the General to release the band. Prince Henry (who had meanwhile offered his own German band from his ship, the *Prince Albert*) was asked by the Governor to act as co-host with him at this dinner, and to propose the Queen's health. The idea of inviting a foreign national, however closely related to Queen Victoria, to act as host in a British Government House ran contrary to protocol and caused pain in Downing Street. Like certain other physically abstemious and strict persons, Sir John Pope Hennessy freely exercised that extreme and ultimate form of self-indulgence: he did precisely and invariably what he liked.

The visit of Prince Henry gave the Hennessys a special pleasure, for, in common with the majority of their contemporaries, they dearly loved a Royalty. Sir John had kept up his tenuous connection with the Court, and a species of indirect, long-distance access to The Queen's attention, by means of his correspondence with his old and loyal Irish friend, Jane, Marchioness of Ely. In May 1880 he wrote

Lady Ely a blithe account of young Prince Henry of Prussia in Hong Kong:

'Prince Henry has been staying here for the last few days' [he told her]. 'There was no official landing, for on board the *Prince Albert* he wishes to be regarded simply as a Naval Officer, but tomorrow he will appear as a Prince when the principal people in Hong Kong will have the honour of meeting him at luncheon and H.R.H. will take part in the ceremony of unveiling the Prince Consort's picture.

'He seems to enjoy his holiday and quiet life on shore, playing lawn tennis with my wife and myself, driving her Sumatra ponies and walking about incognito with Baron Seckendorff. He gets up early and seems to have a keen appetite for breakfast at eight o'clock. He says it is the first time he has tasted fresh butter since leaving Europe. Fortunately it is the coolest month of May we have had here for years, but I have begged of him to avoid going out in the middle of the day, and never to do so, when the sun is shining, without his sun-helmet and an umbrella. Baron Seckendorff, however, is so very careful and sensible, and so devoted to the Prince, that indeed any advice on my part is quite unnecessary.

'. . . He has a healthy, fresh complexion, sun burnt a good deal but with rosy cheeks from the sea breezes. He plays lawn tennis with great vigour, in fact he strikes the ball too hard though we have a very long court. At billiards too and in driving the Deli ponies he never gets tired.

'Since you saw him at Osborne he has grown a good deal. He will be a tall man but not too tall, probably about the height of the Prince Consort—everyone speaks in admiration of his sweet expression, his bright blue eyes and pleasant voice. His upper lip is beginning to show a slight moustache. He walks very erect and with a quick step, throwing out his chest.

'For one so young he seems to take a real interest in the places he has visited. He is picking up much useful information about the East and will soon know more of the Queen's colonies than Lord Odo Russell himself.'

This letter was followed by another, assuring Lady Ely that 'everything went off yesterday perfectly', and telling her that 'Baron Seckendorff thought it better that the picture should be unveiled by the Governor as it was an act of state, and that the Prince should say a word or two: which he did in a clear voice but with evident emotion'.

Both were passed on, as was intended, by Lady Ely to the Queen, who sent them to the Crown Princess of Prussia in Berlin.

In December 1881 HMS *Bacchante*, on a world cruise with the Prince of Wales's young sons, Prince Albert Victor (afterwards Duke of Clarence) and Prince George (afterwards King George V) on board, put in at Hong Kong. The two princes were in the charge of their tutor, Mr Dalton, but they were treated in the same way as all their other fellow midshipmen. Instructions had been issued that they were to receive no special or royal welcome in any British colony in which they landed. Sir John Pope Hennessy, however, 'encouraged preparations on a large scale for their entertainment'. The harbour and town were illuminated and when the Admiral at Hong Kong remonstrated with him, the Governor replied that 'he had received the special commands of Her Majesty' which over-rode any other instructions. Mr Lucas, of the Colonial Office, suggested that the Queen's Private Secretary should be 'asked about the special instructions sent by the Queen to Sir J. Hennessy, seeing there is no record of them at this office'. 'Yes,' added one of Mr Lucas's colleagues, 'it would be curious to find out something about this connexion which exists between Sir J. P. Hennessy and great people at home.' In the event, the Governor himself was over-ridden, and merely received the princes in a private capacity, showing them the Government House gardens and his own oriental collections. 'His Excellency showed us many curious and beautiful things', the princes' published diary (which was really concocted by their tutor) notes for Christmas Eve, 1881: 'which he has collected during his residence here, amongst others a Japanese drawing on a screen representing the first Portuguese ship that came trading to Japan: the people on board have enormous baggy breeches and the friars have already landed on shore. Sir Pope Hennessy has just returned from a visit to Pekin, whence he also brought back several specimens of ancient Chinese art in roof-tiles and porcelain. He already has one of the best collections of blue china going'. On the boy princes' return from a visit to Canton a few days later they lunched quietly at Government House, the British and French Admirals being amongst the other guests. The French flagship *Thémis* was currently paying a courtesy visit to the units of the British fleet at Hong Kong. 'The French band' [the Princes' diary records] 'played during lunch in the verandah.'

In June 1882 the Eastern Department of the Colonial Office was outraged to learn of a bill for £800 for photographs taken, on the

Governor's orders, during the visit to Hong Kong of Prince Albert Victor and Prince George of Wales. Not mollified by hearing that the original bill had been £1,000 and that two hundred had been voluntarily sliced off by the photographer, the Secretary of State termed it 'a monstrous extravagance' and directed that Sir John Pope Hennessy, then in London, should be requested to explain. Writing from Claridge's Hotel, Sir John agreed that the sum was 'apparently rather large', but that 'the temporary presence in Hong Kong of so eminent a photographer as Baron Stillfried' had enabled him to have the harbour, the illuminations and the new plantations of trees photographed 'in the very best style'. 'His charges', he wrote of the most fashionable European photographer then working in the Far East, 'are, unfortunately, very high; & I take some blame to myself. ... At the same time it must be admitted that the photographs obtained by the Government are most interesting & valuable.'

III

Sir John Pope Hennessy also took advantage of the presence in Hong Kong of the famous German photographer—whose work was grandly stamped '*Baron Stillfried—China and Japan*'—to commission a portrait photograph of himself. In earlier years in the Colony he had been photographed, leaning against a carved balustrade and holding his stick and his top hat in his hands, by the Afong Studio in Victoria. The contrast between these two photographs, separated in date by some four years, is revealing. Whereas the earlier one has a certain careless, almost theatrical, atmosphere about it (one is reminded of Lord Ronald Gower's comparison of Hennessy with Irving), Baron Stillfried's, taken in the winter of 1881, shows the Governor half-length and gazing out full-face, his arms folded, his narrow shoulders drawn together, his mouth tense and defiant, his eyes fanatical, the star of a Knight Commander of St Michael and St George upon his left breast. It seems the photograph of a man suffering from severe mental strain, the photograph even of a man at bay.

After four years in Hong Kong, Pope Hennessy had good reason to feel overwrought, for he had largely defeated his own ends. In some directions he had indeed triumphed: he had forced through measures about which he felt passionately and which were admirable in themselves if not in the way in which they were brought about. As we have seen, he had improved the prisons and the penal laws. He had launched an attack on pauperism, and had tried to deal with the very complex problem of 'domestic slavery' or *mui tsai*, a questionable system by which girl children were bought 'for adoption' by better-off Chinese families. He had made proposals for altering the brothel laws, which were inhumane and had been primarily designed by one of his predecessors to provide what Pope Hennessy bluntly called 'clean women' to quench the lust of British soldiers and sailors stationed in Hong Kong. He had, against sharp opposition, ordered that land in quarters hitherto reserved for Europeans should be made available for Chinese settlement—a measure which sounded alright in itself, but which produced land-speculation on a very large scale and, after he had left the Colony, a financial collapse which ruined, amongst many others, his Chinese friend Mr Ng Choy, the barrister who had supported him at the time of the Cricket Ground meeting. He had obtained permission to appoint one Chinese—the same Ng Choy—and one Indian as members of the Legislative Council, which had never had an oriental serving on it before. The appointment of Ng Choy seemed to him a logical one, for he did not see, as did Downing Street, its implications and its potential dangers. 'I have approved Mr Ng Choy as a *provisional* appointment to the Council', Sir Michael Hicks-Beach had written to him in a private note: 'I don't doubt his personal loyalty or worth. But it seemed to me that, at any rate for the present, it would not be well to recognise Chinese representation on the Council as a regular thing. The position which Hong Kong occupies with regard to China is very peculiar, and of course very unlike that of the Straits Settlements. In the event of difficulties, actual or threatened, between England & China, a Chinese Councillor might be anything but trustworthy: and yet, if permanently appointed, it might be very impolitic to show mistrust by removing him.' This reasoning made little impression on Pope Hennessy, who had, amongst many other convictions, the firm one that the Foreign Office did not in the least know how to handle our relations with either China or Japan. On a visit to Canton he went to call upon the Chinese Provincial Governor, but ignored the Acting British Consul. In Peking he was received by the Dowager Empress (of whom he wrote a long account to Mr Gladstone) but was uncivil to the British Minister, Sir Thomas Wade. On leave in Tokyo in 1879 he had tried to avoid the British Minister, Sir Harry Parkes, but had had an audience of the Mikado and many 'valuable' discussions with the Emperor's ministers. During the same visit to Japan he had angered a British Admiral at Yokohama by refusing the offer of a British boat to go round the harbour, using instead a Japanese man-of-war's boat flying the Blue Ensign in the bows and the Japanese ensign in the stern; he had moreover been received on board American, French and Russian flagships in the harbour with ambassadorial honours and a salute of seventeen guns. 'Gov. Hennessy had no more right to a salute at Yokohama than he might have at Portsmouth', wrote Sir Michael Hicks-Beach, who as Secretary of State for the Colonies had the humiliating task of apologising to the Lords of the Admiralty over this incident.

The Colonial Office minutes on Sir John Pope Hennessy's later despatches from Hong Kong make it clear that the staff of the Eastern Department, the Permanent and Parliamentary Under-Secretaries of State, and, intermittently, the Secretary of State himself would have been glad of some miraculous means of removing Sir John Pope Hennessy from Hong Kong. But since he had done nothing which would justify Sir Michael Hicks-Beach or his successor Lord Kimberley in advising the Queen to suspend or remove him from his governorship, they could only wait patiently for the end of his six years' term of office, rebuking him meanwhile for not building a hospital when instructed to do so, or for suddenly opening a Chinese Normal School when this had been expressly forbidden. But what vexed the Colonial Office most of all was the quantity of small personal quarrels between the Governor and his subordinates which were always being referred back to Downing Street. 'Sir J. Pope Hennessy is hopelessly deficient in some of the most essential qualifications for governing a small & quarrelsome society', Mr Herbert pointed out in September 1880. 'They were a singularly quiet harmonious society before the present Gov. came there', an Assistant Under-Secretary riposted. 'Nothing', wrote Lord Kimberley wearily, 'can be more injudicious than Sir J. P. Hennessy's management of his personal relations. His defects in this respect neutralise his undoubted ability & energy.' But there was nothing the Secretary of State could do save wait for 1883, when Sir John's governorship of Hong Kong would automatically come to its end. Then, quite suddenly, there flared up in Hong Kong a scandal so public that it left Lord Kimberley with no alternative but to recall Governor Pope Hennessy, on the pretext that he was to come home on six months' leave.

One summer's morning of 1881 the Secretary of State found on his desk two copies of a letter addressed to him by a Mr Thomas Child Hayllar, QC, a member of the Hong Kong Legislative Council and the leader of the Hong Kong bar. The letter, a duplicate of which was sent privately, while the original was forwarded through the Governor with a covering despatch, must have made even the most imperturbable clerks in Downing Street gape and rub their eyes. 'My Lord', began this letter, 'I have the honour to inform you that His Excellency, Governor Hennessy, made a violent and felonious personal attack upon me in one of the public roads of this Colony, on the evening of the 27 April last. The attack, which was founded on no cause or reason, was made with an umbrella, with the sharpened ferrule of which His Excellency used repeated efforts to thrust out my eyes. . . .'

Robert Herbert, the Permanent Under-Secretary of State who submitted this letter to his chief Lord Kimberley, knew too much about human nature to believe that an outburst so uncontrolled could have been at the same time unprovoked, and 'founded on no cause or reason'. 'There must be another side to this story' [he scribbled on the document in pencil]; '?A lady in the case.' Indeed, this abrupt scene on a shadowy road near Mountain Lodge at sunset was but the explosive crisis of a story, the roots of which spread back to the early months of my grandfather's tenure of the governorship of Hong Kong. It was a tale which, with or without justification (and this we cannot know), had caused him much personal unhappiness. If the final episode lacks dignity we may recall that it was inspired by that most obsessive and distorting of all the passions—jealousy.

Who, then, was Mr Hayllar? And why was he attacked?

IV

T. C. Hayllar, QC, the 'prosperous, learned and conscientious' leader of the Hong Kong bar, had returned to the Colony from leave of absence in May 1877, just a fortnight after the arrival of the new Governor. He was a man of marked ability, a trained pleader with good general as well as local experience and he had at different times acted as Attorney-General and as Puisne Judge when the real holders of these offices were absent. Some people resented Hayllar's bland manners and his 'modest and soft demeanour', as well as his habit, when in court, of posing his 'lily-white hand so gracefully . . . or caressing his frosted, silken beard'. But on the whole he and his wife were well-liked. As prominent members of the British community in Victoria they took part in all Hong Kong society's festivities and patronised its charitable bazaars. He was also President of the Horticultural Society's Committee. Hayllar was just the sort of cultivated man of the world—with, moreover, a special interest in trees and plants—whom my grandfather would have liked. He welcomed Hayllar eagerly, asked his advice on many problems of Hong Kong administration, invited him frequently to Government House, as well as for the excursions which the Governor took to making in the official steam launch. In May 1878 Hayllar was appointed an unofficial member of the Legislative Council. After an odd delay of three months he was sworn in at the end of August, when the *China Mail* predicted that the appointment would 'for some reasons be considered a wise one', adding, however, that it was 'just possible' that it would have been more popular a few years previously—but that it was hard to explain why.

No true explanation could, as a matter of fact, have been given in the newspaper, which contented itself with pointing out that Hayllar was disliked in some quarters for his unpunctuality in court, which he always attributed to his watch being wrong, and for 'a want of courtesy' at the bar. But there was another aspect of Thomas Hayllar's character which made him unwelcome to some husbands in Hong Kong: he was thought to be unscrupulous where women were concerned. It was said that he had left Bombay (whence he had, in the first instance, come to practise in Hong Kong) 'under a cloud', and it was known that at least one husband, a Mr Alexander, had refused to let his wife sit next to Hayllar at Government House soon after the latter had reached the Colony. Civilised and insinuating, Thomas Child Hayllar emphatically did not add peace to 'the small and quarrelsome society' of Hong Kong.

The Governor liked Hayllar more and more. He also found him helpful. During the protest meeting on the Cricket Ground in Victoria in October 1878 Hayllar was one of the few Europeans of any standing to defend the Governor and to try to get the resolutions hostile to him modified. In November of the same year he was one of two Legislative Councillors chosen, without their wives, to accompany the Governor and Mrs Pope Hennessy on a nine day visit to Canton. The fifth member of this little party was Major Palmer, the Governor's aide-de-camp, an officer in the Royal Engineers who had followed him from Barbados where he had acted in the same capacity. It is not too fanciful to suppose that in Hayllar's proximity to a very pretty, elegant and perhaps unhappy young woman on a steam-launch slowly moving up the Pearl River to Canton, lay the beginning of all the trouble.

For trouble there soon was. From having praised and promoted Hayllar, consulted him and recommended him to the Colonial Office, Governor Pope Hennessy suddenly wrote to the Secretary of State in 1879 to say that Hayllar was 'unfit for any post in Government Service', and ordered the ADC to turn Hayllar and his wife out of Government House at a reception there in September of that year. 'In this as in other cases', commented Mr Lucas in Downing Street, 'the governor has first unduly lauded & then become an open enemy of one of the leading men in the Colony.' But in this particular case there was more to it than Governor Hennessy's old habit of making a favourite, leaning on him for advice and then jettisoning him after a wrangle. For some time there had been rumours in Victoria about Hayllar and the Hennessys. Hayllar was said to have 'come between husband and wife and had the worst of it'.

An old scandal is never interesting for its own sake, and in principle the dead should be protected from the living. But, in the fragmentary state in which it has survived, the story of Hayllar seems to some extent to account for John Pope Hennessy's curious moods while in Hong Kong and for his constant desire to leave it for another governorship. More important it gives us, as do the domestic troubles on Labuan, or the *mores* of Captain Glover at Lagos and of Administrator Ussher at Cape Coast, a glimpse of life as it was lived in the Victorian Colonial Empire and of the standards of personal behaviour which ruled it. Noticeable, also, is the fact that Hennessy's only peaceful governorship—his short year in the Bahamas—was one during much of which Kitty Hennessy, ill in Ireland, was only briefly with her husband. Possibly her presence in some way disturbed him, for we have already seen that in January 1879 a total stranger, Miss Bird, observed them getting on with each other extremely ill. The Governor's wife was invariably liked and even admired by the residents of the Colonies he ruled, but she may well have been the object, on her husband's part, of a jealous passion which she could not return. The admiration and sympathy of an adroit and personable man like Hayllar can hardly have been unwelcome to Kitty Hennessy, though there is no factual evidence whatever to show what her feelings were.

It soon became, at Hong Kong, my grandfather's hospitable habit to invite a party of his more intimate friends for excursions in his steam-launch along the coasts of Hong Kong island, with its long bays of white coral sand, or across to Kowloon on the mainland which, with Stonecutters Island, had been ceded by the Chinese in 1860. Mrs Pope

Hennessy did not join in these marine parties; but one of the guests was usually Thomas Hayllar. Some time in the late summer of 1879 Hayllar began to make regular last-minute excuses for not going in the launch. When this had happened several times running the Governor's suspicions were aroused. They were confirmed one September day by the covert looks exchanged between his other guests when His Excellency read aloud to them a note from Hayllar which he had sent down to the launch at the moment of its departure. The Governor in his turn asked to be excused and hurried up the Peak to his summer residence, Mountain Lodge. Bursting into his wife's boudoir, with its blue-and-white china and eastern silks, he found her in colloquy with Thomas Hayllar, who was showing her a book which, on seeing the Governor, he tried to hide. The Governor snatched it from him, glanced at it and recognised it as a volume of 'indecent prints' of classical statuary in the Museo Borbonico at Naples. Hayllar explained that he had brought the book to show to the Governor. Kitty Hennessy declared that she had not even noticed the engravings. The Governor turned Thomas Hayllar out of the house and gave orders that he was never to be admitted within its doors again.

While less bulky than any of the fourteen volumes which comprise the first catalogue of the Museo Borbonico, the volume of line illustrations of selected objects and statues in the museum, printed in Naples in 1825, is a substantial quarto difficult enough to conceal under a sofa cushion. It was a volume which many Englishmen travelling in Italy—Hennessy's hero Disraeli included—had brought back for their libraries. While it would not now be considered remotely 'obscene'—one of the words my grandfather used of it—some of the engravings of naked male and female classical figures could certainly, by rigid middle-class Victorian standards, have been considered suggestive. Two years later, when the whole episode had been brought officially before the Secretary of State, and when my grandfather had retrospectively decided that the book was in fact not obscene, he was criticised inside the Colonial Office for having failed to establish the nature of the book more precisely. Mr Courtney, a newcomer to the Office, considered it, on the other hand, unfair to assume 'that Sir John Hennessy would, under such circumstances, proceed with the deliberation of a man drawing up a *procés verbal*'. 'This is surely impossible', he wrote: 'I picture to myself the unexpected husband, the agitated wife and the wretched intruder. The first demands the book, opens it, sees Musée Borbonico on the top of the page and a filthy picture opposite, and book and man are out of the house in five minutes.' He wrote that he himself was not familiar with the catalogue of the Naples Museum 'and Sir John Hennessy may know little more', but that he thought it perfectly natural that the Governor, in his anger, should be 'somewhat hazy' as to exactly what kind of book it was. Mr Courtney was doubtless right. But the cardinal point is surely that if Hayllar—who was accused of intending to 'debauch the mind' of the Governor's wife—did not think the book improper why did he smuggle it into Government House and, when interrupted, try to hide it?

v

Not unnaturally, the Governor's first instinct was to hold his tongue about the Museo Borbonico incident. The only person to whom he would seem to have spoken freely of it, as well as of other 'private and domestic affairs', was his German protégé, Dr Ernst Johann Eitel. This scholarly man, who subsequently wrote a long history of Hong Kong, was a native of Esslingen in Württemberg, had taken a degree in philosophy at Tübingen University, and had settled in Hong Kong as a missionary. He had an English wife. In 1875 he had been appointed by Governor Kennedy as Director of Chinese Studies (a purely honorary post as examiner of English students of Chinese) and two years later he had published *A Chinese Dictionary in the Cantonese Dialect*. His thorough knowledge of Chinese and his teutonic loyalty to his superiors had attracted my grandfather's attention. He was first made Inspector of Schools and Acting Chinese Secretary to the Governor, posts which brought him a thousand pounds a year; in 1879 the Governor created for him the new position of Head of the Interpretation Department, with another thousand pounds salary annually; in September 1880 Dr Eitel was made a naturalised British subject by the Governor's special ordinance; and in October of the same year he became the Governor's private secretary. An attempt by Governor Hennessy to make Eitel Registrar-General had been defeated by a telegram from the Secretary of State. Inside the Eastern Department of the Colonial Office Eitel was distrusted. At the Governor's request he had drawn up a report on pauperism in Hong Kong, in which he had severely criticised the Poor Law of the United Kingdom, and had referred to Great Britain's 'barbaric policy of brute repression', to 'pieces of class legislation' and to the injustice of British treatment of the Chinese. This report he had translated into Chinese, and it had been widely published in Hong Kong by the Governor's order. 'If the Chinese are not already convinced that they are a downtrodden ill-used race, they will speedily learn it with these Chinese proclamations of the Govr.' commented someone in Downing Street. The rise to place and power of this forty-year old foreigner naturally exacerbated the British officials of the Hong Kong Government, one of whom described it as 'terribly galling'. The *China Mail* referred to Dr Eitel as 'His Excellency's Private Secretary, whose unfortunate position, as a kind of ever-present mouthpiece of the Governor, seems lately to have given him a dash of overbearing bluntness that leads to an excess of friction whenever it becomes apparent'. Rightly or wrongly, within the Colony Dr Ernst Johann Eitel was very much disliked.

When assuming the duties of Private Secretary Eitel had at least had the sense to stipulate that he did not want the Governor to confide in him about his domestic troubles; but this did not prevent his chief from constantly referring to them—it was, perhaps, a necessary outlet—and even before the appointment Governor Pope Hennessy had told him of the scene in Lady Hennessy's boudoir at Mountain Lodge. The Governor hedged a little about the actual obscenity of the book but so described a picture he had seen in it that, wrote Eitel, he 'clearly impressed upon me the idea that the picture in question was not a work of art but a bawdy picture'. The Governor also told him that Hayllar had been causing him much annoyance for many months.

In April 1881 the King of Hawaii visited Hong Kong on his way to Europe. 'I hope', wrote Lord Kimberley in one of his cheerful private letters to Sir John Pope Hennessy, 'that you found H.My. of the "Sandwich Islands" an agreeable potentate.' As it happened, the King's visit had been far from agreeable, for it had triggered off yet another quarrel between the Governor and a leading Hong Kong resident, Mr William Keswick of Jardine Matheson. Mr Keswick, an unofficial member of the Legislative Council, acted as Consul for Hawaii in Hong Kong. As such he had arranged to meet the King when his ship came in to Victoria Harbour and to take the monarch and his suite to stay in his own house above Victoria. When this plan reached the ear of the Governor he despatched Dr Eitel to meet the boat likewise, and to persuade the King to stay at Government House. This 'miserable squabble'—as Lord Kimberley, when he heard of it, termed it—ended in a triumph for the Governor which

Mr Keswick did not forgive. A further episode personally annoying to Sir John occurred during the Hawaiian visit, when another leading resident, Mr Johnson, gave a garden party for the King. Lady Hennessy attended this entertainment, but the Governor did not. A Chinese photographer took a group picture of the chief guests, which included Lady Hennessy and Mr Hayllar. Johnson later received a private message from Lady Hennessy asking him to have the photograph suppressed, and saying that she knew that the Governor would be upset if he saw a copy of it. Johnson instructed the photographer accordingly; later finding that the Chinaman was still selling copies, he threatened him with prosecution if the plate were not destroyed. It was a few days after this garden party that the Governor set about Mr Hayllar with his umbrella, on a quiet road near Mountain Lodge.

The fact that Hayllar had allowed three months to elapse before complaining to the Secretary of State—he said that he was awaiting legal advice from England—and the excited and vindictive tone of his letter when he did write it, made 'a very bad impression' on Herbert, the Permanent Under-Secretary. 'Yes. The Govr. was ill-advised and hasty: Mr Hayllar may have been something much worse', commented Lord Kimberley, 'but of course I have not the means of knowing the real facts.' 'I imagine report bears out Mr Hayllar's statement rather than Sir J. Hennessy's, but it is no use to repeat the scandal which is abroad on the subject', wrote another member of the Downing Street staff, who had private contacts with Hong Kong: 'I hope for the sake of Hong Kong the governor will be removed, in which case the colonists would gladly replace the umbrella with a stronger one to be used with similar effect on future occasions. The handle of the late one is I am told mounted & placed over Mr Hayllar's mantelpiece.' This souvenir is said to have had a silver plaque attached to it, reading: 'A Memento of the Battle of Mountain Lodge.'

As might have been expected, the two versions of this basically sad affair—that of the victim and of his attacker—differ materially. Hayllar declared that the Governor had tried to blind him, 'lunging the weapon into my face with all his strength and with a fury quite inconceivable'; that he had received a cut close to his left eye and one on the chin, both of which drew blood; that the Governor's demeanour had been 'insane and violent', his language and insinuations horrible and degrading, and that had he not, owing to 'the unique insignificance' of the Governor's physique, been able 'rapidly to disarm him and break his weapon', he would 'now be suffering from a permanent injury'. In the despatch which he sent to the Secretary of State enclosing Hayllar's letter, Sir John Pope Hennessy declared this to be a complete misstatement, and wrote: 'he omits the material fact that, at the moment, in question, he had insulted in my presence a lady of my family, who had previously told me that this gentleman had been in the habit of following her into shops and annoying her on the public roads. As the insult on that occasion occurred under my own eyes, the chastisement instantly followed. I was holding my little boy with my left hand, and with the right, in which I had an umbrella, I at once struck the assailant, when he called out "Forgive me, Sir, I was mad: forgive me". The umbrella, which was a slight one, broke by the blow. The whole affair—the insult to the lady and the prompt but not excessive chastisement that followed—did not occupy many seconds. Fully conscious of his own misconduct he never asked me for any explanation directly or indirectly from that day to this. . . . What I did on the 27th April was what your Lordship or any other gentleman would have done under the circumstances.'

Somewhere between these two versions of the same event the truth must lie. Once again we resemble the Colonal Office clerks at the time of the scandals in Labuan and the riots in Barbados: we have insufficient information. The choice of the word 'assailant' for Mr Hayllar in the Governor's report seems an interesting one. And whatever can the nature of the 'insult' have been? It might have been Hayllar's failure to lift his hat or it might have been his attempt to speak to the Governor's wife, or it might even have been a certain smile which the Governor would have taken as an insult to himself. Two aspects of the matter alone seem certain: that so violent a physical reaction on the Governor's part can only have been actuated by the tension of tormenting jealousy; and that the incident played straight into the hands of his many enemies in the Colony who must have persuaded Hayllar to send in his complaint to Downing Street after he had remained silent for three months. If this was the object of the letter, it soon began to have the desired effect: 'If it were practicable to transfer Sir J. Hennessy to another Government the knot would be best cut in that manner', suggested Mr Herbert, on 8 September 1881 when Hayllar's letter had reached the Office. Two days later a telegram from Hong Kong, followed in eight weeks by another letter from Hayllar, announced that he had withdrawn his complaint. The Colonial Office, in reply, telegraphed that Lord Kimberley was relieved that he did not need to consider the matter. Peace seemed restored, but not for long.

VI

Thomas Hayllar's letter to the Secretary of State withdrawing his previous complaint against Governor Pope Hennessy was couched in terms which, even for a lawyer, were arcane. Its gist was that, having heard that garbled versions of the true story were going round Hong Kong, he had originally written to Lord Kimberley 'with a view to putting a stop to most injurious statements, and of courting an enquiry into my conduct'. He wrote now to say that he realised that he had been suffering under a misconception, but that he was 'anxious to place on record, and to have it most distinctly understood, that to the act of no person other than myself, can that misconception be in any way, or to any degree, traced'. This covert reference to the Governor's wife can only be attributed, like the second letter itself, to the timely intervention of a figure from the earlier pages of this book—Kitty Hennessy's father, Hugh Low, between whom and his son-in-law John Pope Hennessy we may recall that there reigned a most cordial dislike.

We have incidentally noticed that in 1877 Hugh Low had at long last escaped from the living death of existence on the swampy island of Labuan, and been chosen for a job after his own heart—that of British Resident at the court of the Sultan of Perak, a vast forest kingdom in western Malaya. In Perak the Colonial Office left him free to define his own duties and to assume any responsibilities he felt necessary for his task of influencing, and restraining, the Sultan, his family and his subjects; for by now the development foreseen and feared by the Colonial Office forty years earlier had become a fact—the British Government found that it could no longer control its peripheral possessions on the Malay Peninsula without exerting some form of authority in the turbulent native states of the interior.

Living at Kuala Kangsar in a spacious verandah'd bungalow perched high above an elbow of the great yellow Perak river, Hugh Low was the only white man in that part of the huge jungle state. He had a small native bodyguard, from which sentries for his house were drawn; but he had really to rely on his personality alone to keep the Sultan and his subjects in check. The first British Resident, Mr Birch, had been brutally slaughtered by the Malays in 1874, so the position could hardly have been called a sinecure. Low was an excellent Malay linguist, and through this gift, and his own very human attitude to native races, he soon made himself respected and furthermore much loved by the people of Perak, over whom he came to wield an immense influence for peace and progress. For companionship in his bungalow he kept an ape and a small gibbon named Eblis. These were intelligent creatures, who learned to open letters and pretend to read them, were mutually jealous of one another, and ate sitting up in chairs at Low's own well-kept dining-table, being solemnly served by the Malay 'boy' at every meal. As in Labuan, Low was busily occupied in the study of plants and fruit-trees, and of the birds, the animals, the butterflies and the snakes of the forest. He also planted just behind his bungalow the first rubber-trees to be reared in Malaya, from Brazilian seed sent out from the Royal Horticultural Gardens at Kew.

This useful, solitary, tranquil existence had evidently been interrupted by an appeal for help from his only daughter Kitty. No longer, as in earlier marital quarrels on Labuan, could she flee her husband's house to take refuge in her father's; but she could at least write and beg him to take a ship at Fort Butterworth or Penang and hasten to Hong Kong. Hugh Low had already been there once on a family visit when, under a species of truce with his son-in-law, he had stayed as a guest at Government House. This second time—and the fact is indicative of the state of tension between the Governor and his young wife—Low elected to take rooms in the Hong Kong Hotel, opposite the Hong Kong Club. It is likely that he had met Thomas Hayllar on his previous visit, which fell in the period of Hayllar's ascendancy at Government House; in any case he now made friends with him, and they were to be seen in the streets of Victoria, 'riding in chairs side by side jocularly talking together'. It was clearly Low who persuaded Hayllar that to sustain his accusations to the Secretary of State or—an alternative Hayllar had also considered—to bring a case for assault against the Governor of Hong Kong in a British court of law could only damage the reputation of Lady Hennessy. So far as Hayllar was concerned, Low's mission of mediation was a success.

Low was, however, counting without his son-in-law. Never of a noticeably forgiving nature, Sir John for once had a good deal to forgive. Of the two copies of his letter of complaint to Downing Street Hayllar had despatched one, as we have seen, directly to Lord Kimberley. The other copy, to be submitted in the normal manner through the Governor, he deliberately sent to the Colonial Secretary's office, where it was opened and docketed by gossiping Portuguese clerks. The contents of the letter were therefore known all over the Colony before the Governor himself had so much as heard of it. Moreover, the Governor, whatever he wrote to Lord Kimberley, must by now have been thoroughly ashamed of the umbrella outburst. To regain face, and to get even with Thomas Hayllar, he decided, in a moment of profound unwisdom, to give the widest possible publicity in his turn to the story of the Museo Borbonico catalogue. The particular scandal, already two years old, had long been decently buried. Without a thought of the consequences and blinded by his desire to damage Hayllar, the Governor set about disseminating within the British community the details of his own correspondence on the subject with the Secretary of State. He did not do this personally or overtly. He selected for it a moment when he himself would be out of the Colony paying his respects to the Empress Dowager and her Ministers in Pekin, and as his instrument he chose his devoted, loyal and literal-minded German Private Secretary, Dr Ernst Johann Eitel.

This ill-conceived intrigue resulted in the near ruin of Dr Eitel, and the removal from Hong Kong of the Governor himself.

VII

On 11 September 1881 Sir John and Lady Pope Hennessy left Hong Kong for six weeks on a visit to Pekin. The day before leaving, the Governor had telegraphed to the Secretary of State that Mr Thomas Hayllar wished to withdraw his charges. The matter seemed comfortably settled. On the eve of his departure, however, the Governor had a long talk with his private secretary, Dr Eitel, reiterating instructions he had already given him: that any members of Council who wished were to be shown his despatches about the umbrella incident, and that the references in these to the Museo Borbonico catalogue should be fully explained by Eitel to prove just how abominably Hayllar had behaved. The despatches had so far been seen only by Justice Russell and a Colonel Hall. Eitel, who was an almost alarmingly truthful man, afterwards swore that the Governor had repeatedly told him that he must even create opportunities to show the documents and to put forward the Governor's case. Eitel further said that he himself saw the necessity for spreading the information widely since 'rumours were in circulation which ascribed the treatment the Governor had accorded to Mr Hayllar to causes & motives injurious to the Governor's reputation and interests'. 'At the same time', wrote

Eitel after his disgrace, 'the view I took of the duties of a Private Secretary and which I now think was a wrong one, though the Governor had often confirmed my conception of it, was such as implied absolute subordination and absolute identification of interests. I felt grateful for the gentle and trustful treatment His Excellency had at all times accorded to me and altogether I knew myself under great obligations for his unwearying kindness towards me. His wishes were therefore commands to me.' '. . . I have learned to take a different view of my duties', the disillusioned private secretary added. 'I see now that my German conception of the duties of a Private Secretary was indeed a wrong one.' What combination could be more disastrous than that of a literal-minded German secretary and a volatile, inaccurate Irish chief?

So Dr Eitel began to talk, to show despatches and to condemn Hayllar right and left. In after years Sir John Pope Hennessy was fond of talking about the 'cabals' formed against him in Hong Kong, and it is true that he had made many enemies who longed to see him leave the Colony in the way that Hayllar was said to have arrived in it—'under a cloud'. By authorising his Private Secretary to speak freely against Hayllar, the Governor now played straight into his enemies' hands. Nine days after the Hennessys had left for Pekin, Dr Eitel received a letter from a friend of Hayllar's, a Mr Johnson who was likewise a member of the Legislative Council. He wrote that dreadful rumours about Hayllar were circulating in Victoria, and that these were being attributed to Eitel. Eitel injudiciously replied that the Governor had authorised him to show certain documents and that if Johnson could call on him next day he would do so. Johnson called, had a lengthy interview and was told 'in confidence' about all Hayllar's misdemeanours. On leaving the Secretary's office he went straight to Hayllar (who had obviously sent him in the first place), and then made a sworn statement before Hayllar's lawyer. Hayllar issued a writ for slander against the Governor's Private Secretary, claiming twenty-five thousand Hong Kong dollars damages. The wretched Eitel telegraphed the substance of the writ to the Governor in Pekin and sent him a detailed, panicky letter on the same subject. In October Hayllar left for Shanghai on Jardine Matheson business, and no action on the writ was taken until his return in the first week of November.

Sir John Pope Hennessy, in the interim, was thoroughly enjoying Pekin and Tientsin. In the course of his journey he was able to confirm all that General Gordon had told him when staying as his guest at Government House the year before. He satisfied himself that British policy *vis-à-vis* China was hopelessly mistaken and that British diplomatic and consular representatives in the Chinese Empire could hardly have been more misguided. On his return to Hong Kong he sent his conclusions in a private letter to Lord Kimberley who stiffly replied: 'I am sorry to hear that you have formed so poor an opinion of our diplomatic and consular services in China. When I was at the FO, which of course is a long time ago (1861), the Consular Service was singularly efficient, and Sir T. Wade [the British Minister to China at the time of Hennessy's visit] is certainly a man of remarkable knowledge and ability. I think you must make allowance for Hong Kong opinion which was always at variance with our Consuls and diplomatists: at least it used to be in my time.'

On his return to Hong Kong at the end of October, the Governor told Eitel that he would 'make the lawsuit his own' and 'take the conduct of it into his own hands'. He would also pay Eitel's costs to the lawyer whom the latter had consulted. In the meantime Sir John's father-in-law, Hugh Low, had himself engaged a counsel, Mr Drummond, presumably to look after the interests of Lady Hennessy who would have been as publicly compromised as the Governor should Hayllar have pursued his case. Drummond and Low together concocted a letter of retractation for the Governor to sign. To force him to do this they used a promise and a threat: the promise being that if Pope Hennessy signed Hayllar would withdraw the writ, the threat being that if he refused to sign Hayllar would press the case 'for the purpose of creating scandal and annoyance during the visit of the Queen's Grandsons' to Government House. Under this double pressure the Governor gave way: 'In the face of that threat, and of Mr Low's conduct,' Sir John wrote to Lord Kimberley, 'it was clearly my duty to make any personal sacrifice, consistent with the preservation of my honour, to get the action withdrawn.' Eitel was made to sign two letters of apology taking the blame on himself, the Governor wrote a letter of apology to Thomas Hayllar, and telegraphed to the Secretary of State in London asking for authority to cancel the whole correspondence. This request was refused.

Governor Pope Hennessy's attitude to his protégé and Private Secretary now underwent one of those swift revolutions for which he was well known. At first he said, as we have noticed, that he would make the case his own. He refused Eitel's repeated offers to resign, made on the grounds that Lady Hennessy had now taken an intense dislike to Eitel herself: 'I should not remain there [i.e. at Government House]', wrote Eitel in one of these offers, 'when my presence there appears to be as disagreeable to her as it is repugnant to my own feelings under the circumstances.' But in the end the Governor did accept Eitel's resignation, and appointed a new Private Secretary, Mr Northcote. Eitel began to write to the Colonial Secretary's Office to complain that the Governor's papers of retractation, which reflected on Eitel, were being 'shown in a quasi public manner to leading residents in the Colony and at the Hong Kong Club'. He emphasised that 'His Excellency allowed the case to be carried on up to, and then withdrew at, a point disastrous to my interests'. In January 1882 the new Private Secretary, Northcote, wrote to his predecessor to say that Governor Pope Hennessy refused to grant Eitel an interview: '. . . I am directed to point out to you that your memory has betrayed you into so many inaccuracies respecting your oral communications with His Excellency that he finds himself compelled, with extreme regret, to avoid any further oral communications with you.' It might be thought that, abandoned by his patron and hated in Hong Kong as a jumped-up foreigner, Eitel would have sunk beneath the waves of public disapproval. In fact he survived Sir John Pope Hennessy by many years, living to write a charitable and just account of Hennessy's Governorship in his rather pedestrian history of Hong Kong, which was published in 1895. It was Eitel who used of his old chief the striking words quoted at the beginning of this book about 'all the crowd of dark and bright powers that were wrestling within' John Pope Hennessy's soul.

However deserted Dr Eitel and his English wife may have felt immediately after their betrayal, they were not in fact without powerful supporters, though these were individuals whom they did not personally know. In quiet and distant Downing Street Eitel's plight aroused the sympathy of the staff of the Colonial Office who thought him 'very much to be pitied for being left to bear alone the open discredit of an untruth which was not really his. In serving his chief' [wrote Mr Ebden in a minute] 'Dr Eitel may not have been troubled with considerations of delicacy or chivalry. It is true that he was engaged in dirty work. But it has yet to be proved that dirty work was not given to him to do, or that he did not act throughout in perfect good faith and in strict obedience and grovelling loyalty to his master.' The attitude of the Office towards Dr Eitel was humane, compassionate, and shocked. The influential Permanent Under-Secretary, Robert Herbert, concluded that both Hayllar and Pope

Hennessy had lied, but that it was difficult 'to be very severe upon a man who has erred when discovering that attempts were made upon his wife, or when endeavouring to avert further disclosures. And I am inclined to think that Mr Hayllar did attempt to be too intimate with Lady H. If so, Sir J. H. was probably ill-advised, under whatever pressure from his father-in-law, in endeavouring to hush the matter up.' There was general agreement in Downing Street that, after the Hayllar-Eitel scandal, there was but one solution open to the Secretary of State: that the Governor should be instructed to 'leave and quit Hong Kong as soon as possible'. Lord Kimberley himself wrote the appropriate three-word epitaph to this sorry tale of passion and intrigue in the South China Sea. It was, the Secretary of State reminded his subordinates, 'a pitiful business'.

His luggage filled with silken banners, embroidered addresses and other tributes from the Chinese community of Hong Kong, Sir John Pope Hennessy departed from the Colony, ostensibly on leave but actually for good, on 9 March 1882. Travelling via Ceylon—where he succeeded in exasperating the Acting Governor, Mr Arthur Birch, by calling on the Roman Catholic Bishop before signing the book at Government House—and India, he reached London in a few weeks. Taking up his residence at Claridge's Hotel, he was soon once more exerting his charm and his polemical skill upon Lord Kimberley and Sir Robert Herbert.* The Secretary of State directed that no more time be wasted over inquests into Sir John's five years' achievement in Hong Kong. '. . . Lord Kimberley has desired that a sponge should be wiped over Sir J. P. Hennessy's record at H. Kong', an Assistant-Secretary of State noted for the benefit of his colleagues, 'as it is unprofitable to go into all reasons and justifications for his various failures in attempts at making accurate statements & in substantiating wild charges agst his principal officers.'

Instead, the Secretary of State and his advisers set about finding a fresh British colonial territory to be committed to Sir John Pope Hennessy's care.

* Mr Herbert had recently received a knighthood.

BOOK VII

MAURITIUS

1883–1889

CHAPTER ONE

———

WHILE IN HONG KONG, Sir John Pope Hennessy
had several times applied to the Secretary of State for the
Colonies for promotion to an Australian Governorship—
either New South Wales, Queensland or Tasmania. These applica-
tions had been refused by Lord Carnarvon and by his successor at the
Colonial Office, Sir Michael Hicks-Beach. But on his return to the
United Kingdom 'on leave' from Hong Kong in 1882, he was offered
by Lord Kimberley the Governorship of Queensland. He accepted
with alacrity. No sooner was the appointment made than the Queens-
landers raised objections to being administered by a Roman Catholic.
Lord Kimberley had the unenviable task of telling Pope Hennessy
this riling news in a private interview in Downing Street. Hennessy
afterwards wrote the Secretary of State a confidential note of protest,
saying that he was now compelled to consider whether he 'ought to
remain in the Colonial Service, or change to a career where no religious disability exists', and asking Lord Kimberley's permission to
speak privately 'to two members of the Cabinet'. Kimberley hedged.
He replied that he would be 'sorry to think that any "religious
disability" existed in the colonial service' and that he had 'alluded,
no doubt, to a feeling said to prevail in a particular colony'. Instead
he offered John Pope Hennessy the Governorship of the island of
Mauritius, which, though only seven hundred square miles in area, was
a 'first-class' Governorship and regarded, inside the Colonial Office,
as of 'great importance'. Pope Hennessy declined.

The arguments by which Lord Kimberley persuaded Hennessy to
change his mind included one which influenced him strongly. If, the
Secretary of State deftly explained, Hennessy could not go to Queensland because he was a Roman Catholic, his selection for Mauritius was
precisely due to the fact that he was one. The French Mauritian créoles
and their coloured compatriots* were fervent Catholics, and Pope

———

* In the nineteenth-century Mauritius the word 'créole' was still used in its
original sense of any European born in the island. Today the meaning of the
noun has changed and denotes Mauritians of mixed or 'coloured' blood.

Hennessy, as the first Catholic Governor to be appointed by the British, would be in an unique position to enlighten the Colonial Office on the religious and educational problems of the Colony. The Queen approved the appointment on 8 December 1882. It was also during this first week of December that Lord Kimberley relinquished the Colonial Office and was succeeded there by the Earl of Derby, a long-standing personal friend of John Pope Hennessy, for whose judgement he showed considerable respect. Mr Lucas, one of the two private secretaries to the Secretary of State, briefing Lord Derby on the reasons for Hennessy's appointment, explained that the current problems of Mauritius—prisons, education, and the relations between employers and Asiatic labour—were very much the same as those which Sir John had faced in Hong Kong. 'But whereas in Hong Kong it is difficult to go wrong' [wrote Mr Lucas] 'in Mauritius it takes a governor all his time to persuade people what is right.'

After an extension of leave, during which he completed and published his book *Raleigh in Ireland*, Sir John Pope Hennessy sailed with his wife and child on a Messageries Maritimes steamer from Marseilles in May 1883, stopping on the way at the islands of the Seychelles in the middle of the Indian Ocean, since these were then a dependency of Mauritius. They reached Mauritius on 18 June. As the ship *Calédonien* dropped anchor in the shining natural harbour of Port Louis, small launches filled with officials took off like water-beetles from the landing-stage to welcome the Governor. 'The door of the spacious deck cabin opened' [runs a retrospective newspaper report] 'whence stepped forth the newly arrived Governor of Mauritius, faultlessly uniformed, hastening to receive those who pressed forward to welcome him, with that genial kindly smile, which never forsook him, even in the severest crisis of his administration.' Rowed ashore in his official barge, the new Governor was received by the Mayor of Port Louis, inspected a guard of honour drawn from the three Companies of British troops then in the Colony and proceeded across the Place d'Armes to the old Hôtel du Gouvernement, which, like most of the public buildings of Port Louis, dated from the days of the French. Here he was received in the Throne Room by the Council, who welcomed him in an address read out by an eminent public man of mixed descent, Sir Virgile Naz. Before the new Governor's arrival certain of the local newspapers had questioned the wisdom of sending out to Mauritius, a colony in which five separate racial communities co-existed but did not coalesce, a man so notorious for his theories

of racial equality. But once there Sir John Pope Hennessy was welcomed gracefully and with a typically Mauritian warmth and courtesy.
This was a mode of behaviour to which he responded well: '. . . allow
me to thank Your Excellency for the very kind manner in which you
spoke to me yesterday concerning my services', the retiring Procureur-
Général Pellereau wrote to the Governor a few months later. 'It was
the expression of your generous and warm-hearted disposition, and
this mode of dealing with men is not wasted on me or on this community which is kind-hearted.'

In Downing Street, his enthusiastic welcome aroused interest and
renewed hopes: 'Sir J. P. Hennessy has received a very warm and
friendly reception', Sir Robert Herbert noted. The new Governor had
sent back to the Colonial Office copies of seven Addresses presented
to him on his arrival in Port Louis. One of these came from the
horticultural *Société d'Acclimatation*, a name which caught Sir Robert
Herbert's eye. '(We shall see how they succeed', he parenthetically
suggested to Lord Derby, 'in "acclimatising" His Excellency.)'

II

Whatever the true reasons for Lord Kimberley's selection of John
Pope Hennessy to govern Mauritius, no choice, as it turned out, could
have suited the major part of the population of the island better.
The people and the problems of this French-speaking Crown Colony
reminded him of those of his native Ireland and went straight to his
heart. The islanders returned his affection with gratitude. Known
to this day in Mauritius as 'le Gouverneur des pauvres'—the first
British Governor to take a positive interest in the plight of poor
Mauritians of African or Euro-African or Asiatic stock—he is also
remembered by the French Mauritians as the Governor who persuaded
the Secretary of State to grant an elective franchise to the Colony,
and who jeopardised his whole career for the principles in which
he believed. As elsewhere, his rule in Mauritius was marred by sharp
disputes and acrid enmities; but these are now forgotten—or, rather,
recollected only by the lineal descendants of those who, eighty years
ago, opposed him. He made the very genuine grievances of Mauritians
his own, and is still looked upon by most of the islanders as a symbol
and a saviour. His statue stands in the Place d'Armes. The chief street
in Port Louis, and others in the small towns of the island, are called
after him. Anecdotes of the stirring period of his Governorship have

been handed down in the families of his friends. In Mauritius he at length achieved a local immortality.

The stage of his greatest humiliation and then of his greatest triumph, Mauritius was the last colony Pope Hennessy was put to govern, and will therefore be the last colony we shall examine in this book. It was an island about which singularly little was known—and, perhaps, still is known—in the United Kingdom, always careless of the smaller components of that Empire on which the sun was once alleged never to set. In Port Louis they have framed an envelope in which Queen Alexandra (ever an absent-minded Consort) had despatched her reply to an address sent her from the Colony. Upon this envelope, the Queen had scrawled in her large looped hand: 'Port Louis, Mauritius, British West Indies.'

Far from being in the Caribbean, Mauritius is in fact at the other side of the world, and lies some six hundred miles east of Madagascar. It ranks visually amongst the most exquisite and romantic-looking islands of the world. After fifteen years in the Colonial Service, John Pope Hennessy was well accustomed to exotic scenery. He had endured the vagaries of many climates, most of them unhealthy. Yet nothing in all his previous experience can have surpassed in beauty that first morning vision of Mauritius, seen from the deck of the mail-boat *Calédonien* as she steamed lazily between the twin forts—Fort William and Fort George—which flank the entrance to the harbour of Port Louis. Later that same morning, his oaths of office taken, the Council's address accepted and answered, the new Governor drove off with his wife and child in an open landau on the road leading up through Coromandel and Beau Bassin to Réduit, the secluded eighteenth-century French château which serves Mauritius as a Government House on the high lands behind Port Louis. As the landau passed through the rolling cane-fields—for sugar then formed the mystique, the only purpose, we might fairly say the fetish of Mauritian life—Governor Hennessy may have been reminded of Barbados; but, sugar fields apart, the two colonies had nothing in common. Barbados is a flat and unromantic island, as resolutely British as Guildford or Southsea. The countryside of Mauritius, the former Île de France idealised by Bernardin de St Pierre in *Paul et Virginie*, is as idyllic as the book which it inspired. From district to district the scenery changes; there are deep shadowy ravines through which bright rivers flow, there are streams and waterfalls and torrents, there are silent beaches lined by palms and casuarina trees, there are old

French planters' houses, there are wooded plains and forests filled with Javanese deer. But the most singular feature of the landscape of Mauritius is a cluster of steep little veridian mountains, their outlines like the fretwork of some wayward but imaginative child. All of these mountains—Le Pouce, Les Deux Mamelles, La Tourelle du Tamarin, Le Morne Brabant and the rest—possess the trick of looking both larger and nearer to you than they are, for the shattering harsh sunlight of the Tropic of Capricorn (just north of which Mauritius lies) eliminates all sense of perspective, making the distant seem close, in the way an object brought under a magnifying glass almost appears to jump at the observer.

The most eccentric in shape of these Mauritian mountains is Pieter Both, called after a Dutch naval commander drowned in 1615 when his ship, returning westwards with a flotilla from the Dutch East Indies, was smashed upon the reefs between Flic-en-Flac and Tamarin Bay. An irregular conical mountain, Pieter Both carries balanced on its narrow, neck-like summit a huge boulder which from certain vantage-points resembles a human head; Sir John Pope Hennessy used irreverently to refer to Pieter Both as 'the Queen in her coronation robes'. Be that as it may, a local legend murmurs that the day the head rolls off from Pieter Both into the valley below will be the last day, for Mauritius, of British rule.

British rule in Mauritius began in December 1810 when it was captured from the French during the wars against Napoleon. The island's fine harbours, both at Port Louis and at Grand Port near the former capital, Mahébourg, in the south, together with its strategic position in the Indian Ocean made it, in these pre-Suez Canal days, of great consequence. From the shelter of its harbours French privateers could and did freely harry and capture British merchantmen on the route to and from India round the Cape. Thus it was for strategic reasons that, in the peace settlement of 1814, Mauritius was retained by the British although they handed back the volcanic and less valuable neighbouring island of Réunion-Bourbon to the French. With the development of steam Mauritius became a major coaling-station on the way from Australia to the Cape, and although by the opening of the Suez Canal in 1869 the tonnage of shipping annually using Port Louis harbour steadily decreased, the Colony was, as we have seen, still rated a first-class British possession. Occasionally it had been suggested that Mauritius should be exchanged with the French for Pondicherry and their other Indian stations; but no one in Downing

Street really took this scheme very seriously. And so it came about that an island whose upper and middle classes spoke and thought in French, whose laws, ideas and way of life were irrevocably Gallic, remained subject to the British Crown. Under British rule the colony's French name, l'Île de France, was changed back to that which its Dutch colonisers had given it in honour of Prince Maurice of Nassau. 'Mauritius' it became once more. Mauritius it remains today.

III

One of the peculiarities of the history of Mauritius is that there never have been any indigenous Mauritians. For countless centuries the lonely haunt of the dodo, the giant tortoise and the fruit-eating bat, Mauritius was apparently known to the Phoenicians and almost certainly visited by the barques of the Arabs and the Malays. But it was not until the late fifteenth century that one of Vasco da Gama's captains landed on the island from his ship *The Swan*. He christened his discovery the Island of the Swan and, since he himself was named Mascarenhas he called the whole scattered group of islands which he came upon in the Indian Ocean the Mascareignes. The Portuguese seem to have found no particular use for the Island of the Swan and made no serious efforts at colonisation.

The dodos and their companions were left once more undisturbed until the arrival of the Dutch in 1598, who re-named it Mauritius and claimed it in the name of their Statholder, Prince Maurice of Nassau. For the next forty years the Dutch seamen merely made use of Mauritius as a larder, where they could stock their ships with live animals or fresh meat, and could also take on water. In 1638 they built a fort in the south of the island near Grand Port; from this small settlement Tasman set out on his voyage of discovery to Australia and Tasmania. Dutch sailors returning from Java brought to Mauritius deer and sugarcane. During the period of the Dutch occupation (which ended in 1710, when they withdrew) the dodo, an artless bird which could not fly and did not understand the carnivorous nature of human beings, became extinct, the Dutch eating all the birds and the little pigs the Dutch brought into the island eating all the dodos' eggs. In 1715 the French East India Company took over the island, naming it l'Île de France; in 1767 the French Government forced the Company to surrender its title; and from then until the British invasion of 1810

l'Île de France, 'Star and Key of the Indian Ocean', remained a prosperous colony of the French crown.

When the British came they found in Port Louis and on the estates
of the planters a highly civilised and sophisticated aristocratic society.
Port Louis was a fine town, well paved and drained, its great harbour
filled with shipping, its little play-house crowded by opera-goers.
By the terms of the capitulation, the British authorities guaranteed
that the French-speaking population would preserve their language
and their laws, their religion and their customs. This was a generous
gesture but not perhaps a wise one, since it gave British Governors a
rational excuse for ignoring the claims of French Mauritians to take
part in an administration carried on in English. By an unpopular
ordinance of 1847 English replaced French in the Supreme Court. As
the century advanced young Mauritians found that they had to become
bi-lingual, although the wives and daughters of the planting aristocracy
seldom learned English at all. In 1881 Mr Napier Broome, who
administered Mauritius just before Pope Hennessy's arrival, supported
his own policy of staffing the Colonial Secretary's office with English
clerks from Great Britain by explaining that 'from the local circumstances of the country, the power of writing a good plain straightforward letter or despatch in the English language is not often to be
met with'. Socially the English and the French did not mingle. There
was a general sense of frustration and grievance; scholarships for study
in England won by clever boys at the Royal College were sometimes
rejected by their families, who sent their sons to Paris instead. A
good many French Mauritian families withdrew from the Colony
entirely, either returning to France or settling near Durban in Natal.

This emigration and repatriation of French families was slightly,
but only slightly, counterbalanced by the arrival in the island of
British and other European traders, attracted by the immense prosperity of Mauritius in the nineteenth century. These were the kind of
persons we have observed in Colonies already mentioned in this book
—persons who were commercially but not intellectually minded.
That deterioration of intellectual standards which seems too often to
have marked British rule in a former French colony—we find a
parallel in St Lucia and Dominica under French, and then British,
control—gradually began. When Charles Darwin visited Port Louis
in 1839 he was astonished to find in that city 'large booksellers' shops
with well-stocked shelves', one of them containing forty thousand
volumes; it is impossible to find one good bookshop in Port Louis

today. The French tradition of education was continued at the Collège Royal, now rechristened the Royal College. Individual French families maintained their contacts with Parisian life. But commercial standards were replacing cultivated ones; and only amongst the old French families, and then only by intermarriage and by social exclusiveness, did the old *douceur de vivre* survive the impact of British rule.

Charles Darwin's visit to the colony fell just six years after an event which had permanently and radically altered the social and economic structure of Mauritian life—the abolition of slavery in 1833. Like all the sugar islands under British rule, Mauritius had of course depended on slave labour. Once liberated, the former slaves refused to work in the cane-fields, asserting that manual labour was degrading. To save the sugar industry from complete ruin, the British Government devised a scheme—also applied in Trinidad and other Caribbean colonies—for importing Indian labour, chiefly from Calcutta, Bombay and Madras. The first coolies, seventy in number, reached the island in 1834; the census of 1881, less than half a century later, shows that they were then coming in at the rate of 2,000 a year. The Indian community was in that year assessed at nearly 250,000 men, women and children, or 69 per cent of the total population of the island. This grave imbalance provided the rich sugar-planters, of whom there were some 300 in the colony, with a constant supply of cheap labour; but, as a few of the more perspicacious planters foresaw, it could lead in the future to the Indianisation of the whole island, should there one day be an elective system of government in Mauritius. The planters' solution was to keep the Indians down. In this they were supported by the Mauritians of African blood—reckoned in 1881 at 28,000 males, not counting their numerous dependants—between whom and the Indians a mortal antipathy arose.

Divided amongst themselves—Hindu-Muslim riots were frequent occurrences in Port Louis—the Indians were kept down with a vengeance. They were not well paid. Heavy penalties were imposed on them for trifling offences. Educational facilities for Indians were limited. Until forbidden, by an ordinance of my grandfather's in January 1884, most of the Indian carters, gardeners, milk-sellers and hawkers were dressed in the rotting, cast-off red coats of the British Army, which Indian traders imported by the thousand, unpacked from stinking bales, and sold. The Indians, for their part, did not do much to ingratiate themselves with the other communities in Mauritius. On Pope Hennessy's arrival in 1883 he found that 'the little that was left in Mauritius of primeval forest is being steadily destroyed by Indians who have leased the land as speculators in timber. Everyone remarks that the daily process of destruction exceeds the comparatively feeble attempt at tree planting.' The rapid and alarming spread of the 'cuscuta' creeper, which was killing tens of thousands of trees in Mauritius—an ordinance for its destruction was passed in 1884—was attributed to its deliberate dissemination by the poorer Indians, who fed their lean cattle on the parasite. A report from a Committee appointed to enquire into pure water supplies found that the streams of the colony were being polluted by Indians washing their dirty clothes, thus filling them with soap-suds and indigo dye; coolies working on the sugar estates 'and who were more or less encrusted with syrup and sugar' washed themselves in the streams at the end of the day, whilst their womenfolk rinsed dirty crocks and scrubbed their animals in the running water. Hard-worked, ignorant and treated with hostility, the vast Indian community was by no means a carefree section of the island's multi-racial population.

As we might expect, Sir John Pope Hennessy did his best to alleviate the lot of the poorest Indians; and after the passing of the new constitution in 1885 he 'took steps towards getting the intelligent and responsible members of the Indian community to enter into the political system of Mauritius' by appointing a Mr Gnanadicarayan Arlanda for a seat in the Council of Government as a nominated member, as well as by ensuring that the Indian population were properly informed of their voting rights under the new dispensation. By these actions he risked, and incurred, the hostility of certain distinguished French Mauritians such as M. Célicourt Antelme, a testy elder statesmen of whom we shall hear more. The arguments which the Governor used to combat what he termed his opponents' 'dread of the Indian population' and their 'fear that the Indians would swamp the true Mauritians' was, however, a curious one. He pointed out that although the schools of Mauritius were technically open to Indian boys, only 19 per cent of all the students were Hindu or Moslem. This suggested to his mind that there was no danger of 'any invasion into our political life of the Indian population'. He said that he had seen Indians in other Colonies and during his travels in their own country; and he was convinced that they were not politically minded. 'Perhaps', he said in the course of this speech in the Council Chamber, 'they are too sensible to be politicians; . . . you may rest assured that neither the Indian community, nor the Chinese for whom I have also a great regard, will ever trouble your political life. I like both the Indians and the Chinese' [he continued] 'but they are foreign to our style of politics; they have certain customs and usages of their own, in some respects perhaps more rational than ours; but, at all events, they are not in our political system.' He believed, he said, that 'in future this Island will be governed by the Créoles of Mauritius'.

It seems strange that a political theorist as advanced as Governor Pope Hennessy can have so misinterpreted statistics and so misread the future. History has disproved his words, as the briefest visit to contemporary Mauritius, with its massive preponderance of Indian politicians, goes to show. The development of rule by a créole oligarchy may or may not have been desirable for Mauritius, but once the Indian majority were given democratic rights it became a forlorn hope. What Sir John Pope Hennessy achieved in liberalising the constitution of Mauritius did indeed give immediate power and scope to the French families; but it could not and it did not protect them from 'Indianisation' in the long run.

In the discontent of the Mauritians, Pope Hennessy found a ready-made cause well suited to his talents as a dedicated disturber of the *status quo*. In Barbados he had had to persuade the negro labourers that they were ill-treated; in Hong Kong he had done the same for the Chinese. But here in the Mauritians he found a people who were only too vocally aware of their own grievances and who were longing for a Governor to set these right. Moreover, the state of political impotence in which the French Mauritians had been kept by the British administration was all the more exacerbating to them because they knew themselves to be able and intelligent, superior to and better-bred than many of the coarse-grained minor British officials sent out to control the colony's affairs. 'It must be remembered that the cultivated and educated class in this island is numerous, considering the smallness of the community', the Lieutenant-Governor wrote to Downing Street shortly before Pope Hennessy's appointment. 'The extraordinary richness and prosperity of Mauritius, and its long settled law and civilisation, have nourished an island aristocracy, which is, perhaps, without example in any country of similar extent, for its numbers, its social refinement, and its intelligence and activity of mind. Our planters . . . live on their estates, and many of them belong to families of old date, amongst whom the soil of the island has for generations been held and passed under the French Code. Our merchants . . . are men of high commercial ability and standing. Our Bar is equalled in few English Colonies. . . . The medical profession here is similarly well manned, not by practitioners who have emigrated because they have failed to make their way in England, but by gentlemen of island families, who have been sent to Europe in their youth to be educated in the schools of London, Paris, or Edinburgh. As for the local press, it is enough to say that Port Louis boasts seven daily morning journals, a number . . . not equalled I believe in any Colonial town.'

This was the state of the thriving, civilised but inevitably disgruntled French Mauritian community when Sir John Pope Hennessy reached the island. 'This is an agreeable Colony' [he wrote to a friend, Sir C. Strahan, then governing Tasmania]. 'The people of all classes are most kind: something like our old friends at Nassau, but on a larger and higher scale.'

IV

Although he could not speak French, the fact that their new Governor was not English but Irish and, to them most significant of all, a Roman Catholic, delighted the Mauritian créoles of French descent. Naturally pious, they had, further, learned to look on their religion as a bulwark against the Protestant British administration, or, as the most intelligent of Pope Hennessy's predecessors put it, as 'a badge of nationality'. This phrase was used by Sir Arthur Gordon (later Lord Stanmore) in a despatch of April 1874, in which he frankly told the then Secretary of State that, despite the guarantee given by the British Government after the conquest of the island in 1810, the local administration had for long thought it 'expedient to attempt to anglicise and Protestantise the island' and that the Roman Catholic Church 'instead of being recognised as the prevailing religion of the country, was treated as a tolerated sect, to be repressed and checked'. The Government schools, Gordon (himself a Protestant) explained, had become 'engines of proselytism, and converts to Protestantism attained a favour which those who adhered to their religion looked for in vain'. Gordon added that 'almost all the natives of the island who hold any considerable office under Government are Protestants, members of Roman Catholic families. . . . I do not hesitate to say' [he concluded] 'they would not have attained them, had they retained their original faith.'

Besides this much-resented effort to convert young Catholics to the Established Church, the British Government had so contrived it that the Roman Catholic Bishops of Port Louis were always Englishmen; one of these, Bishop Collier, had embarked in the 'forties on a deliberate policy of weeding out the remaining French priests in the island and replacing them by recruits from home. Sir John Pope Hennessy, who soon quarrelled with Bishop Scarisbrick (a difficult sixty-year-old prelate from Lancashire who was Bishop of Port Louis at the beginning of Hennessy's administration) contested both this policy, and the Secretary of State's support of it, strenuously. Still smarting from his rejection by Queensland on religious grounds, he told Downing Street, as usual, exactly what he thought: 'If in laying down that policy', he wrote to the Colonial Office in 1885, 'Her Majesty's Government hoped to use the Roman Catholic Establishment as an engine for making the population more loyal to England, a mistake has been committed. Such a policy is regarded by the Mauritian community as a sort of penal law that has not received the sanction of the local legislature. It is a policy that injures the Roman Catholic Religion in Mauritius and does no good to the State.' Since he never took pains to conceal his views, the new Governor's championship of this, as of other specific Mauritian causes, was quickly known throughout the island. The mailboat called at Mauritius only once a month, so the seven lively newspapers daily published in Port Louis had to content themselves with local news, and with keeping a suspicious lynx-like watch on all the doings of the Government. During his first months these journals—ranging from the diehard *Cernéen* to the radical *Sentinelle de Maurice*—were unanimous in praising the new Governor. Even his personal appearance, and what they called his dignified but genial manner, and his open smile won him a startlingly good press. 'Il nous semble que l'arrivée à Maurice de Sir John Pope Hennessy doit commencer pour le pays l'ére du bien-être de tous', one newspaper concluded, in an article in which Mauritius was referred to as 'La Petite Irlande'.

Nor was it only newspaper editors who voiced their hopes. At a banquet offered at the charming old Port Louis restaurant, La Flore Mauricienne, to Monsieur Eugéne Leclézio to celebrate his appointment, in November 1883, as the first Chief Justice of Mauritian blood —an appointment, needless to say, due to Pope Hennessy's urgent advice to the Secretary of State—the Chairman of the gathering, Monsieur Victor Delafaye, made a very gratifying speech. Owing to some illness of Lady Hennessy, the Governor could not be present and had telegraphed his apologies from Le Réduit. In a loudly applauded panegyric proposing Sir John's health, Monsieur Delafaye reminded his audience that for the first time in British Mauritian history this traditional toast could be made with sincerity and applauded with real enthusiasm. In earlier days, he remarked, the company at such a banquet would listen to this official toast with indifference, and clap their hands 'par simple politesse'. But now all was changed: '*Tempora mutantur*' [quoted Monsieur Delefaye] '*et nos mutamur in illis!*' Sir John Pope Hennessy, he reminded his audience, had demolished that 'wall of ice' which had separated previous British Governors from the people of the Colony. Cold and haughty, these pro-consuls had known nothing about the Mauritians, content to see and hear only what their little court of prejudiced alien officials wished them to know. Sir John, from the moment of his arrival, had shown that he intended to discover Mauritius for himself, to listen with his own ears and to judge with impartiality. Monsieur Delafaye's speech was constantly interrupted by violent applause.

During this early honeymoon period of his rule in Mauritius— before the rows over the new Constitution had swept across this tropical island with all the force of one of its own destructive hurri- canes—the new Governor's popularity was aided and enhanced by that of his wife. A recent article in the most animated of contemporary Mauritian newspapers, *Action*, reminds modern Mauritian readers that no Governor's wife has ever been 'autant aimée par les Mauriciens que Lady Hennessy'. After her first reception for the ladies of the island at Le Réduit in June 1883, a guest predicted in *La Sentinelle de Maurice* that Lady Hennessy would be the most sympathetic and the best loved of any Governor's wife, for she combined the distin- guished qualities 'de la Lady anglaise' with 'le charme simple et incom- parable de la Créole de race'. Her manners were described as natural and fresh, with the added grace of a slight shyness. Her figure was 'svelte' and elegant, her fine large eyes seductive. Later, at a great ball (which we shall attend) at Le Réduit, Kitty Hennessy, in a dress of old-gold satin embroidered with huge bouquets of roses, cut with a high corsage and half-length sleeves, pink flowers in her raven hair, won further praise for her manner of greeting her guests, making each one feel that he or she was an old friend. It was known, and liked, that the Governor's wife was a thoroughly religious woman, who had gone to pray in the Roman Catholic cathedral in Port Louis on the morning of her arrival in the island, and before she had even seen the Govern- ment House at Le Réduit. Moreover, in Mauritius, she soon devoted herself to good works, organising meals for the afflicted during outbreaks of smallpox and of cholera, sending, and often taking herself, food cooked in the Réduit kitchens to starving families in village hutments, organising paid sewing-workrooms for penniless girls. When Sir John and Lady Pope Hennessy finally left Mauritius in 1889, 'une députation de pauvres' presented her with a letter of heartfelt thanks, part of which ran: 'Partout nous porterons le souvenir des bontés dont vous nous avez comblés, cela avec une bonne grace, une simplicité, une passion du bien à faire qui ravissait: vous apparteniez aux pauvres et les pauvres vous appartenaient.' Like her husband, Kitty Hennessy found in Mauritius an ideal field for her activities. Unlike him, she spoke perfect French and she formed close and loyal friendships with the ladies of the Leclézio and other families, intelligent and highly cultivated women very different from the colonial officials' wives with whom she had had to consort for so much of her married life. Up at Le Réduit, which is probably the most pleasant colonial Government House of the old British Empire, she could be happy again and forget the horrors of Hong Kong. Here in 1885 she gave birth to a second son, Hugh, welcomed throughout the Colony as 'un petit Mauricien' and a 'living souvenir' of the Star and Key of the Indian Ocean.

We must now look over the grounds and the rooms of Le Réduit, a secret and secluded old house lurking at the end of a long winding avenue of ancient camphor trees.

v

Le Réduit owes both its name—'The Retreat'—and its origin to a half-hearted British attempt to invade the then French island in 1748, at the time of the War of the Austrian Succession. Admiral Boscawen, who had been ordered to sail from England with a large fleet to attack Pondicherry in French India, tested out the defences of Mauritius on his way. L'Île de France was then governed by the able and famous Mahé de Labourdonnais. Not realising that the Colony's defences were in fact weak, the British Admiral called off the projected invasion and continued on his way to India.

The successor of Labourdonnais, a French Governor named David, decided, however, that the British threat had been serious and could easily recur. He therefore arranged for the construction of a roomy wooden stronghold, protected by ditches and gun emplacements, on a spur of the Moka range, fifteen miles above Port Louis. Thither the women and children, and perhaps even the Government itself, could retire if the enemy raided Port Louis in force. The site, on a V-shaped promontory high above the two ravines in which the Rivière Profonde and Rivière Cascade join, was dramatic, and more or less defensible. From its northern verandah, Le Réduit commanded a wide view out across the Indian Ocean; the house and gardens were cooled by the scented wind from the sea. Then as now, Port Louis—backed by mountains which seem as if they wish to crowd the hot old paved city into the harbour—was suffocating from November until April. All those who could retired to their houses in the uplands of Mauritius; and in this way the French Governors began to use Le Réduit first as an occasional and then as a permanent residence. One of them, de Souillac, declared that it was only at Le Réduit that he 'found the peace of mind and energy to devote himself to the affairs of the island'. In 1778 rot and white ants having rendered the wooden building uninhabitable it was reconstructed in stone—a low, two-storeyed central block with a tiled roof, and with eastern and western wings.

On the French capitulation the building was taken over by the British Government, and continued in use as the Government House. In 1868 one of the worst of those hurricanes which form the scourge of Mauritian life—demolishing houses, uprooting avenues of giant trees, destroying sugar-crops, wrecking gardens, killing animals and sometimes people as well—shattered Le Réduit, tore the roof off the east wing and almost killed the Governor, Sir Henry Barkley, and his wife. After this disaster the house was patched up; but in 1880 on the advice of Pope Hennessy's predecessor, Sir George Bowen, a listless administrator who spent much of his term of office outside the Colony, and was notorious for his love of food, his passion for the chase and for his clownish vanity the house at Réduit underwent a thorough reconstruction. This work, which took two years to complete and cost some £9,000, included the removal of a staircase in the western wing. This added three hundred and ninety superficial feet to the central hall, which, equipped with a new wooden floor, was converted into an impressive ballroom. Lieutenant-Governor Broome, acting for his chief Sir George Bowen (as usual away from his post) informed the Council of Government in Port Louis in November 1882 that 'the task of reconstructing the house built by the Chevalier de la Brillane for the Governor of Mauritius more than a century ago has been solidly executed. The residence is now in every way worthy of the Colony, and allows the Head of the Government to offer proper accommodation to those who are his guests.' When the Hennessys entered into possession, in June 1883, the house was therefore in an excellent state of repair. As with other Government Houses he had from time to time inhabited, Governor Pope Hennessy felt that the furniture and decorations needed renewing. He put in a request to the Crown Agents, through the Secretary of State, for a full-sized grand piano, a dining-table specially designed to seat forty persons, fourteen long wall mirrors for the ballroom, thirty-six cut glass wall brackets, 'an expensive hall clock', electro-plate, lamps, china and glass. The Secretary of State considered this proposed outlay 'excessive'; but the Governor persuaded the Council in Mauritius to sanction the full expenditure, amounting to more than £1,250.

In the later nineteenth century, the most usual approach to Le Réduit from Port Louis was by the odd little railway which wound over deep ravines and through sunlit cane-fields to Curepipe. Ever since the great malaria epidemic* of 1867, the aristocracy and the richer merchants of Port Louis had definitively moved up into the hinterland, creating at Curepipe a new residential town. The old eighteenth- and early nineteenth-century houses of Port Louis, mostly built of painted wood, with spacious verandahs, mysterious high-walled gardens, and trellis screens were abandoned, although some of their owners had them dismantled and transported bodily to the heights of Curepipe, a town remarkable for its ten-foot high hedges of clipped green bamboo, over which morning-glory flowers profusely trail; as well as for its rainfall, one of the heaviest on record, which sheathes books, shoes and clothes in several pervasive forms of mildew. The morning descent, the evening ascent of business men between Port Louis and Curepipe soon became almost a ritual, each gentleman having his own recognised seat in the little double-decker railway carriages—the lower deck, comfortably upholstered, for the first-class, the upper deck, with wooden benches, for the *hoi polloi*. The Governor had his own ornate small railway carriage which would take him from his private station at Le Réduit to the terminal at Port Louis or to Beau Bassin or some other station along the line. Free travel by rail when on public business was a Governor's perquisite; but Sir John Pope Hennessy seldom used the railway, pre-

---

* The epidemic of 1867, which occurred before the true cause of malaria was known, killed one-third of the population of the capital, Port Louis, and one-ninth of the total population of the island.

ferring a smart horse-drawn victoria, with lacquered door-panels and shining harness.

The approach to Le Réduit by the carriage drive is one of a singular and mysterious charm. At a certain point along the roadside near Moka, two tall stone gate-posts, each surmounted by a royal crown, stand sentinel in the shade. Passing between these, you turn into a long winding tropical avenue, flanked by the uneven shapes of great camphor trees, their tangled roots hanging from their contorted branches in the warm, still air. At the bottom of this avenue there crouches an old colonial country house, a deep double-storied verandah the length of its friendly, unpretentious façade; its roof tiled; wings jutting forward to east and west. The fat pilasters of this southern verandah are wreathed in magenta bougainvilleas, and there is a general impression of ferns in tubs, of old mounted cannon, of a luxuriance of exotic greenery. In front of the house, in the centre of a circular grass lawn, is a sundial. White-uniformed Colonial police, and a fluttering Union Jack, are the only indications that this is a British official residence and not the quiet, deserted haven of some long-forgotten contemporary of the author of *Paul et Virginie*.

The front doors of Le Réduit open straight into the ballroom, which is embellished by ten huge gilt-framed wall-mirrors. Crossing the polished floor you emerge on the wide and lofty north verandah at the back of the house. This verandah, again, is supported by pillars, and it is paved in black and white stone. A broad lawn extends to the wooded ravines at the end of the garden; the view is completed, in the distance, by the deep blue of the Indian Ocean. Owing to the destruction of the 1960 hurricane, this great expanse of lawn looks at present very empty; yet previously it was carefully landscaped, and dotted with ancient mango trees, with clumps of Chinese pines (planted by my grandfather from Hong Kong seed) and with flowering shrubs. At the far, far end of the lawn some grass steps lead down to a look-out point, with a seat and an iron railing that is clamped into the rock. From this vantage place, known as the 'Bout du Monde', you may peer dizzily down past the heavily wooded sides of the ravines to the frothing red waters of the Rivière Cascade and the Rivière Profonde. The water swirls and rushes about great flat boulders, and as often as not the diminutive, doll-like figure of a wading fisherman searching the rock-pools for that delicious Mauritian species of langouste, the *camaron*, may be seen. If you follow the ravine-side westwards a path leads you into Réduit woods, where the ebony trees grow. Elsewhere is a large flower-garden, a plantation of royal palms, and an enclosure in which a pair of giant tortoises doze or roam. It is hard to imagine a more ideally peaceful setting for the closing years of an exacting and tempestuous colonial career.

Although, as we shall shortly see, Sir John Pope Hennessy found Mauritius anything but restful, he vastly appreciated Le Réduit, where he planted trees, irrigated the lawns and, with an eye to the island's future economy, started experimental tea and tobacco plantations. His own letters describe how he liked to sit and brood on the bench at the Bout du Monde, how he would take his son Bertie fishing and swimming in the rockpools of the gorge, how he would watch the mangoes ripen on the aged trees and try to guess which day each fruit would fall. He also, more oddly, liked to climb the trees. He was a fond if energetic parent, and his elder son always looked back on Réduit days with nostalgia.

A vivid picture of Governor Hennessy at Le Réduit is to be found in a rare book, *From Journalist to Judge*, published in 1910 by Frederick Condé Williams, formerly a Judge of the Supreme Court of Mauritius. Williams and his wife lived in 'a retired and picturesque villa', The Nook, almost at Réduit gates. They became familiar with the 'grassy glades' and 'picturesque *points de vue*' of the grounds, and with the rustic seats on which Pope Hennessy's predecessor, Sir George Bowen, had whimsically had lines from Virgil, which he thought applicable to the sad tale of *Paul et Virginie*, inscribed. 'Through these woodland walks' [Williams relates] 'I constantly strolled with the dapper little governor Hennessy, who, politics apart, was the most untiring conversationalist and interesting companion.' My grandfather would regale the Judge with the story of his own life, in episodic form: 'In this anecdotal flow alone it was that the humour of the true Hibernian asserted itself: for, under ordinary circumstances, Hennessy was by no means a festive Irishman; rather, a small statuesque person, of uplifted head, piercing eye, and aspect somewhat grave and pre-occupied. He spoke no French, strange to say; was far from going down to Port Louis with the regularity of his successors, and generally held meetings of his Executive Council at home. . . . An indefatigable wanderer about the grounds of Réduit, I never could induce him to stroll beyond their outer gates unless he was conscious of being perfectly and scrupulously well dressed. His pockets were often filled with seeds, brought from Hong Kong, of some Chinese variety of conifer—the *pinus sinesis*, or some such name—and these he would constantly stop to sprinkle about the Réduit grounds, which should afford a plentiful crop of resulting pines by now.' One of the Governor's favourite topics, based on his youthful medical training in Cork, was that the time could not be far off when life would be prolonged and the tissue of 'adult prime' preserved indefinitely by 'a process of admixture by injection'. And so they would potter on, speculating on this and that as they threaded their way between talipot palms and beneath the overhanging banyan trees. The rainbow colours of the Mauritian sunset turned and changed on the horizon, above the nearby tropical sea.

My grandmother, too, was contented at Le Réduit, arranging flowers on the verandah for some musical evening, or tending the chapel, which, complete with almoner and angelus bell, the Hennessys had installed in the west wing; or simply sitting gossiping in the shade with neighbours who had driven over from Moka for an informal call. House guests of the Governor and his wife at Le Réduit found the same warm hospitality which had touched Sir Thomas Wade and other of their visitors in Hong Kong. 'I assure you I have never met with such kindness from any Government House as I have here in Mauritius', Sir William Hewett, admiral commanding the East India station, wrote to Lady Hennessy, after she had returned a necklace he had bought her in Bombay, and which as Governor's wife she was not permitted to accept.

On 8 August 1883, when the new Governor and his wife had been in the colony only a few weeks, Kitty Hennessy, aided by the Colonial Secretary, the Private Secretary and the ADCs, planned a ball at Le Réduit to celebrate her husband's forty-ninth birthday—an anniversary kept secret until half-way through the entertainment. This ball was much more than an ordinary official reception, and was described by one of the guests as 'une vraie fête nationale'. The disparate members of the Mauritian community met on neutral ground and, for once, some of them said, 'all barriers were down'. The ball had been organised with particular care. A special shuttle train service to and from Le Réduit station operated until half past two in the morning. The little station itself was carefully decorated with Venetian lanterns; a fleet of carriages waited to take the guests up to the house, and both avenues were gay with Venetian and Chinese lanterns dancing merrily in a slight wind. The band of HMS *Euryalus* was playing in the front verandah which was brightly lit with lamps arranged to give the impression of a night of full-moon. The ballroom and the back verandah were turned into a veritable flower garden. The host and hostess stood receiving at the door, and later joined indefatigably in the dancing. At midnight *God Save the Queen* was played, the dining room doors swung open, and the banquet—which an aspiring Port Louis *littérateur* described as combining the tastes of Pantagruel with those of Brillat-Savarin—began. After this came the Royal Toast; then Admiral Hewett proposed the Governor's health in glowing terms to 'delirious' applause. Inquests during the week pronounced it to be the most successful ball ever given by any British Governor; although some people complained that an equerry system to introduce the guests to one another should have been operating, since as a result of the rigid stratification of Mauritian society, many of them were mutually strangers—the barriers, it seems, had not been altogether down. But on the whole the atmosphere of the birthday ball was praised on every side. The hyperbolic author of one article in a Port Louis newspaper went so far as to see the 'harmony' of the evening as symbolic of a new relation between Mauritians and their Governor. He hoped that this harmony and this understanding would spread out across the whole island, and that a Governor whom they felt they could recognise as a friend would love the Mauritians as they wanted to be loved, and would let them love him in return.

The ball at Le Réduit—which had even rated that enthusiastic speech from a British Admiral amongst its several surprises—marked the high tide of the first phase of Governor Pope Hennessy's popularity in Mauritius. With Englishmen like the Colonial Secretary, Mr Charles Bruce, the Admiral, the Colonel commanding the troops, and the English Bishop Scarisbrick in full support, he seemed to have achieved the impossible and unattractive political aim of pleasing all men.

It was a phase that did not last. As a leader in the *Pall Mall Gazette* explained in July 1887, when Pope Hennessy's Mauritian troubles were arousing some attention in the London press: "You might as well pour acid into a solution of soda and marvel at the effervescence as be amazed at the commotion that follows Sir John's advent in a Crown Colony. The work that he does is necessary and in the main excellent. But it outrages every arbitrary tradition of the Service, and is based upon principles and points to ideals utterly at variance with the principles and ideals on which Crown Colonies have been founded and are still administered.' A strong partisan of what it called 'the Home Ruler of the Colonial Service', the *Gazette* described Governor

Hennessy as 'a man of intense, almost feverish, intellectual activity, whose presence acts as yeast in every society into which he is thrust, and he has been interned time after time in communities where the number of educated men can almost be counted upon the fingers. Hence wherever he goes he generates unrest. It is the unrest of growth, the mobility of life. But it is naturally a phenomenon that is regarded with profound alarm by all who desire to see things remain as they are.'

VI

In the halcyon opening months of his rule in Mauritius, Governor Pope Hennessy relied on the advice and close co-operation of five men. The first was his Colonial Secretary, Mr. Charles Bruce. The second was Admiral Sir William Hewett, Commander-in-Chief of the East India Squadron, then, owing to the outbreak of war between France and Madagascar, stationed in Port Louis. The third was the commander of the small British garrison in the Colony, Colonel William Hanbury Hawley. The fourth was the Roman Catholic Bishop of Port Louis, the Right Reverend William Benoît Scarisbrick. The fifth was an elder statesman of Mauritius, 'the Nestor of the Council', Monsieur Célicourt Antelme. This promising alliance did not endure. The earliest to defect were the Colonel and the Admiral, who severed all relations with the Governor. The next was Monsieur Antelme, who became Pope Hennessy's bitterest enemy and began industriously to canvass his recall. The Bishop then fell foul of the Governor, who accused him of having 'little sympathy' for the Mauritians, of being pro-English and, in fine, 'a traitor'. This left Mr. Charles Bruce who, after trying manfully to accommodate his conscience to the Governor's policies, applied to the Secretary of State for a transfer and in 1885 was given the Lieutenant-Governorship of British Guiana. A short look at the characters and attitudes of these five men will help us to understand the mounting drama which turned Sir John Pope Hennessy's Governorship into the most memorable episode in the history of Mauritius since the capitulation of 1810.

Charles Bruce, afterwards knighted and now remembered as the author of the big two-volume work, *The Broadstone of Empire*, had arrived in Mauritius as its new Colonial Secretary four weeks before Governor Pope Hennessy. For that brief period he had administered the Colony with marked success. He was an erudite and cosmopolitan man of forty-six, who had been educated at Harrow, at Yale University, and in Germany. An excellent linguist, he had worked as an assistant librarian at the British Museum, and had then been made Professor of Sanskrit at King's College, London. In 1868 he had been sent to Mauritius as Rector of the Royal College; his passion was public education and, after Mauritius, he had gone on to Ceylon as Director of Public Instruction in that Colony. In 1883 he had been offered, and had accepted, the Colonial Secretaryship of Mauritius. In later years Bruce was himself appointed Governor of Mauritius. He was a man of wisdom and of experience. In the personal recollections with which his book is leavened, he gives a singularly coherent account of his difficulties with my grandfather. He remarks that when he accepted the Mauritius appointment he did not know that Hennessy was to be his Governor: 'From public sources of information' [he writes] 'I knew something of Sir John's adventurous and turbulent career, that he had appeared as an angry boil on more than one part of the body of the Empire. . . . By personal friends and governors who had preceded or succeeded him, and colleagues who had served under him, I was warned that my berth was not likely to be a bed of roses. But I was not dismayed. . . .' In a further passage he points out that, whatever their political disagreement, his 'social relations with Sir John and his family were of the happiest, and I may say here, once for all, that they were never severed'.

Of Admiral Hewett we know little, save that he was an officer in the best traditions of the Royal Navy, loyal, and certainly not gifted with a political turn of mind. By long tradition a suite of rooms, both in the unfurnished, disused old Government House in Port Louis, and at Le Réduit, were reserved for the use of the Admiral-on-the-Station and were known as 'the Admiral's Rooms'. Those at Le Réduit were in the western wing. Apart from installing a Roman Catholic chapel in one of them, Governor Pope Hennessy at first respected this tradition. It was Admiral Hewett who had written so warmly to Lady Hennessy in gratitude for Réduit hospitality, and had bought her the necklace she could not wear. After the Admiral's secession, however, 'the Admiral's Rooms' were given to Bishop Scarisbrick, and re-named 'the Bishop's Rooms'. When Bishop Scarisbrick fell into disgrace, they were simply called 'the rooms in the western wing'.

Colonel William Hanbury Hawley, who ended his career as a Major-General, was a close ally of Admiral Hewett. He was in his fifties, was an active Protestant and had served gallantly in the Crimean War for which he was decorated. His regiment was the

14th Foot. As we have seen, the Mauritius garrison amounted to the derisory total of three companies of troops, and during the Anglo-Russian war scare of 1885 Colonel Hawley openly declared in Executive Council that the Colony was completely defenceless in the face of the threat offered by three Russian frigates then near the Cape. An honourable, conventional and patriotic officer, he did not sympathise with Governor Pope Hennessy's later policy, and fought his wish to raise a local créole militia to permit of British troops being removed from Mauritian soil. Subsequently Colonel Hawley developed a positive hatred for Pope Hennessy reminiscent of that of Colonel Glover in Lagos, or Mr Ussher at Cape Coast; or, for that matter, of the General commanding the British contingent in Hong Kong.

The fourth member of this group of the Governor's original advisers, William Benoît Scarisbrick, DD, OSB, was born at Liverpool in 1828, educated at Douai, joined the Benedictines and was ordained priest in 1852. Before the announcement of his selection for the Bishopric of Port Louis in 1871, Cardinal Manning, already aware of the choice, is said to have replied to someone who asked him if the next Bishop of Mauritius would be English: 'An Englishman, yes; but a gentleman probably no, for he will be a Benedictine.' When Sir John Pope Hennessy arrived, Bishop Scarisbrick had been in his diocese for eleven years and was galled, as he wrote to Hennessy in a singularly acrimonious exchange of private letters in January 1884, to be 'told by the Governor after a six months residence in the Diocese that I have really little or no sympathy for the Mauritians. I have never courted popularity for that is ephemeral and soon fades away,' [the wretched prelate continued] 'but by the humble and quiet discharge of my pastoral duties I have won, I make bold to say, the esteem of the large majority of my flock.' A cyclone-damaged oil painting in the large, airy Bishop's Palace in Port Louis shows Bishop Scarisbrick to have been a smooth-looking, fair-skinned man with pale blue eyes, a fine-drawn face, and an astute expression, bald at the front of his head, but with long silver locks flowing to his shoulders. In Mauritius he has left behind him a reputation for being quick to take offence, to administer reprimands and to suspect slights. Like many before him, Bishop Scarisbrick was no match for Pope Hennessy in polemics or in the art of quibbling. Defeated, he retired to England in 1886 suffering from impaired health and a pronounced form of persecution mania. Rewarded by being made a Count of the Holy Roman Empire and titular Archbishop of Cyzicus, he was succeeded, as the Governor and the Mauritians desired, by a French prelate of German extraction, the Jesuit Archbishop Meurin.

The fifth collaborator turned opponent, Monsieur Célicourt Antelme, was made of sterner stuff. Of all the many, many enemies Sir John Pope Hennessy had made in his colonial career, Antelme alone was capable of massive retaliation. The *Pall Mall Gazette*, in a phrase intended as a compliment, declared Pope Hennessy to be 'as tough as gutta-percha, and as wily and as wary as a weasel'. Monsieur Alphonse Gaud, a literary youth who combined the function of being Sir John's confidential private secretary with the somewhat incompatible one of sending anonymous but very well-informed newsletters on Mauritian affairs to *Le Créole*, a journal published in the neighbouring French island of La Réunion, used the words 'old lion' to describe Monsieur Célicourt Antelme to his readers: 'an old lion of the forest, still trying to sharpen his blunted claws'. The trouble with the claws of Monsieur Antelme *père* (like many conservatives he had a very radical and noisy politician as a son) was that they were not as blunt as might have been supposed. Like some fable which La Fontaine did not write, the lion seemed for one heady moment to have got the better of the weasel.

As the most dangerous threat Governor Pope Hennessy had encountered in any of his colonies, Monsieur Célicourt Antelme deserves a more detailed portrait than our sketches of his former colleagues—the wise Colonial Secretary, the upright Admiral, the stolid Colonel and the touchy Bishop of Port Louis.

VII

Auguste Célicourt Antelme had been born on New Year's Day, 1818, less than eight years after the British conquest of the Île de France. He was thus sixty-five years old when Governor Pope Hennessy first appeared in the colony. By then Antelme was an imposing old man. He had a head of receding white hair, and his square, somewhat forbidding face, with its high, frowning forehead and searching eyes, and its deep furrows running from nostrils to trap-like mouth was bordered by bushy white whiskers. He wore the dark suits and lapelled waistcoats then usual amongst the Mauritian upper and middle classes; the ends of his broad bow tie were tucked beneath his low shirt collar. He looked, as indeed he was, a distinguished and strong-minded old gentleman, with whom few people would have chosen to cross swords. He had great wealth, great ability, and the habit of command.

At the age of eleven, the little Célicourt had been sent home by his French parents to the *Métropole*, there to be educated at the Collège de Sorrèze in the Tarn. He next read law in Paris, and, having gained his diploma as a barrister, he had returned in 1840 to Mauritius, where he immediately won for himself a name at the bar. His outstanding success at this time was a long speech he made in the *Parquet* on 14 July 1847, the eve of that day fixed by ordinance for the compulsory introduction of English as the sole language to be used in the Supreme Court. This speech, a moving farewell to the French language, was breathlessly received by his audience, which on its completion gave vent to 'an almost religious woe'. Thereafter the young man put himself at the head of a movement for the reinstatement of French—after all, the true language of the island—in the Supreme Court; but the most he could achieve over many years were two minor if positive concessions—that judges should no longer demand the translation of French documents; and that witnesses could, at the judge's discretion, be cross-examined in French. In 1858, Célicourt Antelme retired from the bar, to devote himself both to the public affairs of the colony, and to his private business interests. The owner of the important sugar estate of 'Stanley', near Rose-Hill, where he lived, he also had a fine hunting domain at Plaine Sophie. He founded the *Crédit Foncier* in Port Louis, and twice saved the sugar industry by journeys to London where he raised capital in the City for the creation of two big credit concerns: The Mauritius Sugar Estates and The Agricultural Bank. He was a religious and a charitable man, with high principles; and had at one time faced violent criticism from the other 'sugar barons' of the colony for seconding the efforts of the then Governor, his friend Sir Arthur Gordon, to ameliorate the dreadful conditions and cruel exploitation of the immigrant Indian labourers and their families.

It might be thought that, with his French upbringing and his French sympathies, Célicourt Antelme would be intensely hostile to the British administration and to the Governors who personified it. The reverse was the case. Over thirty years, Monsieur Antelme had added to his many other activities that of being the personal, almost the professional, friend of Governor after Governor. They turned to him for advice, listened with deference to his views, and regarded him as the spokesman of the French Mauritian community. He had become, in the words of young Monsieur Alphonse Gaud, 'maire du palais'—Mayor of the Palace of Le Réduit. His power had been almost unlimited, likewise his vanity. Deeply conservative—he had supported Sir Arthur Gordon over the Indian labourers on humane and Christian, not on liberal, grounds—he was almost alone amongst the French Mauritian planters and men of standing to oppose any attempt at giving the Colony a freer constitution. Memorialising the Secretary of State against making concessions to those who had in 1882 begun agitating for an elective element in Mauritian public life, he wrote (before Pope Hennessy's arrival) that the absolute power of British Governors to nominate all the members of the Council of Government was a safeguard for the future, and went out of his way to praise these Governors for their intelligence, their learning, their experience of public affairs, their self-respect and their sense of responsibility to the Government of Her Majesty—few of these being qualities for which Pope Hennessy's predecessors had been judged notable by the French colonists themselves. It was no wonder that Antelme was cherished in Downing Street, where he had made a great impression on the Secretary of State and his staff during those two emergency visits to London to raise money for the sugar industry. The gist of the advice finally given to each new Governor of Mauritius setting forth to take up his duties in that remote island had long been: 'When in doubt, consult Monsieur Célicourt Antelme.'

This recommendation had, as a routine matter, been given to Sir John Pope Hennessy by Sir Robert Herbert at the Colonial Office. Upon reaching the Colony, Sir John accordingly made much of Monsieur Antelme. He visited him privately at Rose-Hill, he asked him to come to Le Réduit; he listened gravely to what he said in Council, and he consulted him and other Mauritian gentlemen upon the delicate question of who should be appointed the Governor's official Private Secretary. Should he be an Englishman or should he be a Frenchman? With Antelme's help, the Governor hit upon an excellent compromise in young Mr. Arthur Johnson who read Dickens, and was a bit of both. 'I am glad to learn that you have taken young Johnson for your private Secretary.' [Célicourt Antelme wrote to the Governor in July 1883, in a note accompanied by five partridges shot that morning at Plaine Sophie] 'His appointment will be agreeable to the Community. The pure english section appearing not to like you on account of your religion and your Irish origin, would have considered the appointment of a créole of french origin as a kind of menace to them. Johnson belonging by his grand mother to a respectable and old family of french origin and by his father and grandfather to the english nationality his appointment will give satisfaction to all. It is an act of good policy.'

Six weeks after his arrival Monsieur Antelme invited the Governor and the Admiral to stay the night and shoot next morning at his estate of Plaine Sophie. This was John Pope Hennessy's first experience of the Mauritian *chasse*, an entertainment in which droves of deer are rounded up by beaters and frightened out of their woodland refuges to face the guns in the scrub-covered plain. On this August day the phenomenal number of forty stags were killed—'Un vrai carnage!' [a report ran]. 'Et peu ou pas de biches ni de daguets, s'il vous plaît; rien que des bois et des plus beaux'—but the Governor and the Admiral shot only one apiece. Group photographs, with the dead animals piled at the huntsmen's feet, were taken, and Sir John enlivened 'le tiffin' which followed by a merry anecdote about the solitary snipe which several officers of the Hong Kong garrison once claimed to have shot upon the Peak.

Early in 1884, Governor Pope Hennessy recommended Monsieur Antelme for a knighthood (which he did not then obtain). 'Mr. Antelme' [the Governor wrote to the Secretary of State] 'though, on some public questions, not in entire accord with the local community, is one of the most eminent and estimable Mauritians.' For some time there was nothing in the Governor's manner to lead Monsieur Célicourt Antelme to suppose that his days as the Government House oracle were numbered.

VIII

'These influences' [Sir Charles Bruce writes of the short-lived collaboration of the Governor and his five advisers], 'working in perfect harmony, seemed likely to produce in the European community of Mauritius a little Canada. Never, in the history of any British colony acquired by cession from France, has there been an opportunity of brighter promise. But it was not for long. It soon began to be felt that Sir John Pope Hennessy was not concerned to produce a little Canada but a little Ireland, and that he designed to use the Roman Catholic Church as an instrument to effect his purpose.' Bruce recalls that, before the secession of the American colonies, Benjamin Franklin suggested that the easiest way of destroying a great empire, or a great

cake, was by cutting slices off the circumference. He adds that Sir
John's policy seemed to him to be 'to dig a knife into the centre'.

A casual visitor at Le Réduit has recorded that the tables were
littered with books and pamphlets on Irish Home Rule. The Governor
himself 'seemed never tired of expounding to all and sundry his
opinions on the question of Home Rule for Ireland', and he was seen
to be constantly drawing covert analogies between Home Rule there
and in Mauritius. Inspired no doubt by youthful memories of British
troops in Cork City, Pope Hennessy strove, as we have noticed, to
get the British garrison withdrawn from Mauritius and replaced by a
locally raised volunteer force—which, as Colonel Hawley sharply
pointed out, would not necessarily prove loyal in the event of war
with France. Discussing Bishop Scarisbrick with the Colonial Secretary
the Governor one day declared that he 'had found the Bishop out'
and that his sympathies 'were entirely with the English'. After a
dinner given by the Mauritian Club, at which Admiral Hewett was a
fellow-guest, Sir John replied to a toast by reminding his hearers that
'the Mauritians, like the Irish, had felt the heavy hand of the English'.

Many of the analogies which Pope Hennessy drew between Ireland
and Mauritius were, of course, perfectly true. Like the Irish, the
Mauritians were alien to the English in race, culture and religion.
Like the Irish, they had been conquered, occupied and integrated
into the British Empire at gun-point and against their will. We have
seen that their religion was practically penalised, and that a campaign
to anglicise and protestantise them had been under way. Barbados
and Hong Kong—even, for what it was worth, the islet colony of
Labuan—had at least been British creations. Mauritius was a foreign
country captured in a war.

The new Governor thought he found other similarities between
the Mauritian and the Irish character, for he detected in Mauritius
that general atmosphere of kindliness and gaiety which makes life in
Ireland so easy and so pleasant. He wrote to the Secretary of State
of 'the humane and paternal character' of Mauritian jurors, and of
the general wish of Mauritian magistrates to be lenient, even when
reluctantly enforcing English laws such as that by which poor Indian
labourers were fined or imprisoned for picking twigs from trees, or
for peddling their wares without a licence. His inevitable campaign
against flogging had met (he said) with the universal approval of the
Council of Government and of the press, which had long denounced
the flogging system as inhuman, demoralising and un-Mauritian. In

the West Indies, in West Africa, and in Hong Kong, he had found that 'the so-called upper classes were earnest advocates for flogging the natives. In those Colonies the "authorities" also favoured flogging, though not perhaps with such zeal as leading gentlemen of the European community. Here I find the reverse.' Except for the language and the climate, and the continued existence of an old, indigenous Catholic aristocracy, living in Mauritius almost seemed like living at home in the South of Ireland.

Sir John Pope Hennessy's open, and at times extravagant, condemnation of English rule in Mauritius was well calculated to alienate the British officials of the Colony, and we can readily gather why Bruce, Hewett, Hawley and Scarisbrick fell away. To understand the position of Monsieur Célicourt Antelme, that eminent French Mauritian so strangely addicted to the British Raj, we must now examine the movement for constitutional reform which had been unleashed in the Colony just before Pope Hennessy's arrival there. The origin of the movement had been fortuitous, and under what the Colonial Office now frankly called 'an ordinary Governor' it might have subsided, or been delayed for decades. Pope Hennessy, however, gave it his full and public support, investing it with an aura of personal drama which appealed to the Latin, histrionic element in the Mauritian character. Encouraged by the Governor's announced intention of recommending Mauritians for important government posts, and of throwing open every branch of the Colony's Civil Service to educated Mauritian youths, the Reformists were swept by patriotic fervour. The Colonial Secretary, Mr Charles Bruce, who went to London at the height of the turmoil, ostensibly on leave, but really to warn the Secretary of State about the Governor's political activities, admitted to the Colonial Office in January 1884 that, owing to Sir John Pope Hennessy's support of the reform movement, 'it would now be impossible for Lord Derby not to give way to some extent without risking serious discontent'. 'Mauritius for the Mauritians!' was the current slogan in Port Louis. Originally provided by the Governor, it had become a war-cry overnight.

THE CONSTITUTION of Mauritius which Pope Hennessy had found when he got there was based on the rigid, Crown Colony formula by which the inhabitants themselves had some apparent say, but no real power, in the running of the country. The Legislative Council, or Council of Government, in which the Governor had a casting vote, and which assembled in the long narrow Chamber behind the Throne Room in the old Port Louis Government House, consisted of fourteen members. Of these seven were 'official members'—persons, that is to say, whose position (Colonial Secretary, Officer Commanding the Troops and so on) automatically brought them a seat on the Council and who were pledged by their very offices to support all government proposals. There were also seven 'unofficial members', arbitrarily selected by the Governor, with the Secretary of State's approval, from amongst such leading men of the Colony as were deemed suitable. These unofficial members, hand-picked as they were, could hardly have been called representative of the colonists. Unofficial members could protest against unpopular Ordinances, but they had no means of preventing these becoming law. The Constitution of Mauritius was as despotic and out of date as that of Jamaica, which the Colonial Office were then trying to make more representative and to modernise.

It was to the forced passage of one unpopular Ordinance in 1882 that the Reform Movement owed its origin. For years the deteriorating state of the rivers and forests of the island had been a cause of anxiety. A British engineer had been sent out from London to draw up a report. In this report Mr Thompson—such was his name—asserted that the cultivation of the rivers' banks was undesirable, and that the rivers required more shade. These findings were incorporated in an Ordinance making it illegal to cultivate a belt of land two hundred and fifty feet broad on either bank of any river. Since Mauritius is a small island seamed with rivers and rivulets, the new regulations meant that landowners would lose a high percentage of their cultivable property without any corresponding compensation. Protesting vigorously, but vainly, against the passing of this Ordinance, an unofficial member had suddenly yelled out in the midst of the Council Session: 'Si ce pays avait içi des représentants élus par lui, de pareils abus seraient impossibles!' His words resounded through the Colony. A Reform Committee was created, a great meeting in the Hôtel de Ville organised for 5 July 1882, and a petition to Queen Victoria was drafted, asking for an elective element in the constitution of Mauritius. This was the birth of the Reform Movement.

It was well known in Downing Street that the existing Mauritian constitution was as stagnant as Jamaica's; but whereas the Colonial Office were prepared to modify that of the latter, which was considered a loyal British colony, they were chary of allowing the French Mauritians to have any solid power. This was not only from the fear of an anti-British bias in a reformed Council, but also, in the words of Sir Robert Herbert, 'because of the ignorant and helpless Indian population which must be protected by the Crown as in every other Eastern Colony'. The Secretary of State, Lord Derby, was therefore recommended by his advisers in the Office to refuse the petitioners' request, but to suggest some slight adjustments, such as increasing the number of the unofficial members of the Council. A long and not unpersuasive letter to Lord Derby from the oracular Monsieur Célicourt Antelme helped to influence this decision. The Governor was instructed to lay the Secretary of State's proposals before the Council, and report their views.

When the petition had been sent from Mauritius the Governor had been the absentee Sir George Bowen, for whom his second-in-command Lieutenant-Governor Broome was then acting. But when Lord Derby's reply reached the island, the Governor was Sir John Pope Hennessy. In direct contravention of Lord Derby's despatch, the Governor submitted to the Council not Lord Derby's mild programme, but that of the active Reform Committee. After an animated debate, from which, owing to illness, Monsieur Antelme was absent, the Council requested the Governor to send to the Secretary of State what amounted to a second and even more strongly-worded petition for complete constitutional reform. Meanwhile, dexterously guided by the Governor, who had thrown all the weight of his office behind the Reform Movement, this had become the major popular issue in the island. The denizens of Downing Street found their hands forced, and began to speak of 'the very serious position in which we are now placed'. Sir Robert Herbert even stooped to suggesting as a solution

that the Secretary of State should reply to the petition by agreeing to
elections on the widest possible basis in the hope that, thus threatened
by a torrent of potential Indian voters, the Reformists would take fright
and abandon their reform project altogether. In the end the wisdom
of the liberal-minded Lord Derby prevailed. He sent Governor Pope
Hennessy a despatch broadly agreeing, with certain reservations, to
the Reformers' manifesto; and making the capital concession that
elected and also unofficial members should be given absolute control
over the local and financial affairs of the Colony.

Sent off from London in early April 1884, Lord Derby's despatch
reached Mauritius in May. With a few notable exceptions such as
Monsieur Célicourt Antelme, the news was received in the colony
with unbounded joy. A huge banquet of six hundred and fifty guests
was organised in the Governor's honour. This meal, elaborately
staged in a tent pitched in the courtyard of the Royal College, and
attended by rich Chinese and Indians as well as by the Europeans and
créoles of the island, was the occasion for many laudatory speeches,
and was the first Mauritian gathering at which the health of a British
Secretary of State had ever been drunk. In the following September a
thirty-two man Commission settled down to the work of drafting
definite proposals for the new constitution. Beginning in amicable
fashion, it was soon split into two antagonistic wrangling groups,
involving a number of prominent Mauritian personalities whom we
have not yet met.

II

One of the social events of life in Port Louis was the Governor's
annual distribution of prizes to successful students at the Royal
College, an educational establishment with a fine tradition, founded
by the French Mauritians in 1791. From the very start of his tenure of
office, Sir John Pope Hennessy had turned this usually innocuous
occasion into a political one. At his first prize-giving, that of 1883, he
had drawn attention to 'the lamentable fact' that of twenty Heads of
Departments in his administration, only one or two were of Mauritian
birth. This speech, of which several versions are extant, was cheered
by the parents and other relatives of the schoolchildren, and seems to
have been the genesis of the 'Mauritius for the Mauritians' movement.
In his speech in the following year, 1884, he went further and declared,
in the presence of Mr Messervy, the much-badgered Channel Islander
who was then Rector of the College, that it was a pity that the College

had not a Mauritian Rector, and that in his opinion Mr Messervy was wrong to try to make English a compulsory language for the girls as well as the boys of the Colony. In the same speech he congratulated the colonists on at last having a Chief Justice, Monsieur Eugène Leclézio, who was of Mauritian birth, as well as on the capitulation of Lord Derby over the constitutional question.

'To whom' [he asked] 'are you indebted for the fact that Lord Derby has consented to introduce an elective element in the Legislature? Let me tell you, not to the Governor of the Island, except indeed in a very humble and subsidiary way; you are indebted for it to men who were born in the Island . . . the leading gentlemen in every walk of life—they have been the politicians who have accomplished this achievement—such men as the President of the Council of Education, Sir Virgile Naz (cheers), who, though born in Seychelles was educated at a school in Port Louis; such men as Mr Loïs Raoul, as Mr Louis Rouillard, as Dr Edwards (cheers), Mr Henri Adam, Mr Ambrose, Mr Guibert, Dr Beaugeard, Mr Delafaye, Mr Henri Leclézio (cheers) and the inspiring genius of all, Mr William Newton. (Loud and prolonged cheering which was again and again renewed.)' Dismissed by the Colonial Office and by M. Célicourt Antelme as 'a noisy clique of lawyers and others who desire to obtain the control of the administration and legislation' of the Colony, these Mauritian gentlemen, some of pure French descent, some coloured, were indeed, as my grandfather said, the founders and supporters of the Reform Movement. Looking briefly at a few of the outstanding personalities in his list we may begin with one of Sir John's closest friends and greatest admirers, Sir Virgile Naz, KCMG, the first Mauritian to be knighted by Queen Victoria.

Sir Virgile, who was not of pure European stock, had been born at Mahé, the little capital of the Seychelles islands, in 1825. The son and grandson of boat-builders, he had been educated at the Institution Faraquet and at the Royal College in Port Louis, had worked as a barrister's clerk, and had then gone to London to read law. On his return to Mauritius he had had a successful practice at the bar, become a rich landed proprietor and sugar planter, and was closely involved with the high finance of the island. At the age of forty-one he had been nominated an unofficial member of the Council of Government, where he was given to making long and ornamental speeches, which even by Mauritian oratorical standards seemed verbose. He and his wife, born a Mademoiselle Constantin and sister-in-law of another leading Liberal politician, Dr W. T. A. Edwards, lived in a large house, Bélvèdere, up in Curepipe. Naz also owned the thriving old French sugar-estate of Bénarès, which is situated near the coast in the district of Savanne in the south of the island, where the breakers crash against the black sea-rocks at high tide. Sir Virgile likewise owned a hunting estate at Plaine Raoul, where he and his two brothers-in-law, Dr Edwards and Monsieur Ange Constantin, would entertain the Governor and as many as sixty guests for shoots which began at sunrise. The gossip columnists of the Port Louis newspapers considered that the luxury of the hunts at Plaine Raoul had begun to rival those of Monsieur Antelme at Plaine Sophie; ever ready with a classical reference they compared the two estates to Rome and Carthage. The political rivalry of Naz and Antelme was notorious, for while Antelme supported the English party and stood out against Reform, Sir Virgile, for all his wealth, had flung himself into the Reform Movement and would write to Sir John Pope Hennessy of 'your enlightened, liberal, farsighted and truly Mauritian policy'. In appearance Sir Virgile was rather dark-skinned, with a shrewd steady eye, a grey moustache, a high forehead and hair cut so that it curled upon his ears. He was a man of varied gifts: when the architect who was building the church of Sainte Thérèse at Curepipe walked out on the job taking his plans with him, Sir Virgile personally superintended the completion of the church from memory. Where Pope Hennessy was concerned he was an enthusiast; during the crisis of the Governor's career, for instance, Naz bought the hostile newspaper, *Sentinelle de Maurice*, and made it into 'un journal Hennessyen'.

The second Mauritian gentleman mentioned by Sir John in his Royal College speech, Monsieur Laurent Loïs Raoul, was really the father of the Reform Movement. He was a créole of Port Louïs, the son of Ussiliéde Raoul and his wife Laurencia Trublet de la Flaudaye. On leaving the Royal College he had worked for a time on the newspaper, *Le Cernéen*, but had left this to become a notary. In 1868 he had been appointed to the Legislative Council, where he distinguished himself by championing the cause of the poor and the oppressed. A member of the Council of Education, Raoul was also President of the Chamber of Notaries. It was he who had felt so strongly the injustice of the Rivers and Forests Ordinance of 1882; together with Henri Adam, Povah Ambrose, Georges Guibert, Louis Rouillard and William Newton he had set up the pioneer Reform Committee, with Naz, Bazire and Hewetson forming a sub-committee to study the technical side of constitutional reform. He was an exceedingly popular man, who held the confidence of the Governor and of the Reform Party and, at fifty-four, should have had before him a valuable political career. In July 1885, however, Monsieur Loïs Raoul and his agent were out shooting partridges at St Aubin down in the Savanne. Separating from his companion, who owing to the height of the sugar-cane lost him to view, Raoul let off his gun, gave a low cry, and fell dead amongst the cane. Writing to Sir John Pope Hennessy that same evening, William Newton told him that it had transpired that Raoul's affairs as a notary were in 'a most sad state' and that the cause of his death at St Aubin was suicide. This fact was officially suppressed; the death was called a shooting accident. Three days of public mourning were declared, offices and shops put up their shutters, the body, transported from Curepipe, lay in state at the Hôtel du Gouvernement in Port Louis, and the Governor himself acted as a pall-bearer.

Of the other prominent Mauritians whom my grandfather held up as models to the boys in his speech at the distribution of prizes in 1884 two, Mr Povah Ambrose and Dr Wilbraham Tollemache Edwards (who was brother-in-law to Lady Naz), were Mauritians of English stock. Monsieur Louis Rouillard, a barrister and later, as Procureur-Général, noted for his beautiful speaking voice, Monsieur Henri Adam (whose father had emigrated from Rouen just after the British conquest of Mauritius), Monsieur Henri Leclézio, a scion of one of the most distinguished families in the island, and Monsieur Victor Delafaye, represented all that was best in the pure-French elements of the Colony's society.

They remained loyal to the Reform Movement and to the Governor, as did Monsieur Georges Guibert. Dr Onésipho Beaugeard, a coloured laureate of the Royal College, had completed his medical studies at Edinburgh University in the place of Eugène Leclézio, senior laureate in that year and later first Mauritian Chief Justice of the Colony, whose parents did not wish their son to be educated at the expense of the British Government. Dr Beaugeard was one of those most responsible for the cleavage inside the Reform Movement as well as for the campaign, led by what William Newton called 'that old ruffian' Monsieur Célicourt Antelme, to depose and disgrace the Governor.

There remains 'the inspiring genius of us all'—one of the grandest men of coloured blood in the history of Mauritius: William Newton, whose statue forms a pendant to that of his firm and grateful friend

John Pope Hennessy beneath the royal palms of the Place d'Armes in
Port Louis today.

III

Writing to the Secretary of State in June 1884 to justify his recommendation of William Newton as a temporary unofficial member of
the Council of Government to fill the place of Sir Virgile Naz (who,
in bad health, had, like most sick Mauritians of means, withdrawn to
the glens of Cilaos, an airy resort in the mountains of La Réunion,
for a few months) Governor Pope Hennessy described Newton as
'Chairman of the Chamber of Agriculture, an eminent member of the
local bar, possessing high character, ability and the esteem of the
community'. This was all perfectly true, but William Newton was a
figure on a larger scale than this. He was a remarkably intelligent
barrister, with a passionate manner, a biting wit which could turn a
hostile witness to ridicule in a few minutes, great tact and experience
and a flaming honesty. He had once tried to be a planter, but had, as
he termed it, burned his fingers 'as many others did'. He certainly had
not burned his fingers at the bar, where, much feared as an interro-
gator, he was greatly in demand, and where he was making a good
deal of money. A thickset, powerful man of forty, with a noble,
aggressive, negroid face, he was popular throughout the island, for the
coloured people recognised him as one of themselves.

William Newton and his brothers George, who had a post in the
Seychelles, and Charles, a vivacious young barrister turned journalist
who revolutionised the techniques of journalism in the Colony, were
the grandsons of a British Sergeant in the Twenty-Second Foot,
Sergeant John Newton, who died in India, but had formed part of the
army of occupation of Réunion, when that island, like Mauritius, was
captured from the French in 1810. While there he had married a
coloured girl named Marie Boyer. She afterwards moved to Mauritius
with her son, who ended up as Inspector of Public Works in the
Colony. This son, the father of William, George and Charles, had in
his turn married a wife of mixed blood. The boys had been educated
at the Royal College and, first, William (who was born in 1842) and
then his younger brother Charles, had gone to read for the bar in
London. William Newton, like John Pope Hennessy, was a bencher of
the Middle Temple. He had begun to practise before the Supreme
Court in 1861. In 1884 he published a pamphlet on the legal position
of a Frenchman who took out British nationality in Mauritius—did

he or did he not lose his French nationality by doing so? For this treatise he was awarded the Legion of Honour. He also published a brochure on the sugar crisis of 1885 and was greatly interested in agriculture.

Newton was soon established as the intimate friend and constant adviser of Pope Hennessy: unlike Antelme and the English contingent he never quarrelled with the Governor, who often consulted him privately on administrative matters and on how to deal with the personalities of the Colony. 'It seems as if I had not seen you for an age' [he wrote to Sir John in a note of November 1883] 'and I would have gone up myself today if I had not to finish my Report. When I have written the French text, I shall translate it into English, in order to facilitate your perusal of it.' He was always 'running up to Réduit' for a talk: 'Nothing so freshes my mind more [sic] than a conversation with you', he wrote; or (when he had had a touch of the fever): '. . . I am sure that an hour or two spent at Réduit will do more than anything else to restore my health.' 'I think that between you and me, there should be no secret' [he wrote to the Governor on the evening of Raoul's suicide] 'and, besides, I know how kind, generous and noble-hearted you are.' 'I make bold to say' [Newton wrote one day to Lady Hennessy] 'that you and Sir John have not a more devoted friend than I am.' Nor was this merely the flattery of an ambitious politician anxious to stand well with authority. Newton, as he soon showed, was no fair-weather friend and he did not hesitate to say if he thought that Governor Pope Hennessy had made one of his not infrequent, impulsive mistakes. It was an affectionate and worthy friendship and, in its effects, it did the colony much good.

Newton had been among the instigators of the great public banquet offered to Sir John in September 1884. Rising with tears in his eyes in response to shouts of 'Newton! Newton!' he made an impromptu speech only slightly shorter than the complex harangue of Sir Virgile Naz who had preceded him. In it he asked his audience to cast their minds back to the state of the colony just fourteen months before. What had they been before the new Governor's arrival? Captives— 'captives we were, gentlemen—and what made our fate still more cruel—captives in our own native country!' Cries of 'oui! oui! certainement!' and prolonged applause greeted this sally. Newton then declared that he would always feel proud to have been the first to broach the Reform question with the Governor, who, he said, 'had just made known the principles which were to guide him in nominations to public appointments, and very quickly putting these principles in action, he had already merited the title of the "Mauritians' Friend" which he will always keep'. During the earlier stages of the Reform Movement, Newton stumped the island addressing 'very good, well behaved' popular audiences. Of one such speech, at Mahébourg by Grand Port, Loïs Raoul wrote to the Governor to report 'the great success of our friend Newton. . . . When he had to allude to the support which you have given to the cause of the Reform, and said that you were not only a man of superior intellect, but *un grand cœur*, there was a tremendous cheering, in which all partook.' By such means it became known in every hamlet in the Colony that the Governor of Mauritius had placed himself at the head of a national patriotic movement and was at virtual war with the Colonial Office at home. In Downing Street this subtle form of blackmail caused jitters: 'Having regard to the persons with whom we have to deal, and to the agitation which the Governor is leading against the constitution of the Colony, I think it is not expedient to do what it would be right to do. . . .' Sir Robert Herbert was forced to admit in a minute of January 1884. One of the Assistant Under-Secretaries, Edward Wingfield, was even franker: 'We are dealing' [he wrote in March of the same year] 'with an astute Governor who is only too willing to trip us up.' Mr Wingfield also suspected Pope Hennessy of 'doctoring' the official reports of his speeches, since 'more highly coloured' versions of them kept simultaneously arriving in the office, thoughtfully posted by old Monsieur Célicourt Antelme. 'Sir J. Hennessy's strong anti-English bias must also be borne in mind' [another Downing Street official wrote helplessly at this time]; 'his policy is Mauritius for the Mauritians (i.e. the créoles), and he has already, from what I gather, incidentally, made the Colony exceedingly unpleasant for the English members of the Civil Service.'

Sir John Pope Hennessy derived much private satisfaction (and, certainly, amusement) from emphasising in despatch after despatch his own popularity in Mauritius. '. . . It is my official duty' [he wrote to the Secretary of State in August 1885] 'to report that the Mayor and Corporation of Port Louis have been good enough to go to the trouble and expense of getting a full length and life-size portrait of me painted by Monsieur Avice du Buisson, and to do me the great honour of placing it in their Council Chamber where the portraits of two of my predecessors, Mahé de la Bourdonnais and Sir George

Anderson already stand. I enclose the local papers giving an account of the inauguration of the Portrait on St Louis Day.'

Some exasperated member of the Downing Street staff destroyed these newspapers, but copies of the *Cernéen* and the *Progrés Colonial* have survived elsewhere. These give detailed accounts of yet another banquet, given this time by Monsieur Lavoquer, the Mayor of Port Louis, in the Hôtel de Ville, an old two-storey building with a wide staircase and lofty rooms which stands well back behind iron railings in what was then the Rue du Gouvernement, but is now Pope Hennessy Street. The portrait, which hangs in its original position in a reception room on the upper floor of the Hôtel de Ville, shows Sir John standing in full uniform, wearing the Order of St Michael and St George, beside a table covered with a gold-fringed green velvet cloth. His left hand, resting on a book lying on the table, holds a copy of the new constitution of Mauritius. Behind him is the chair of Mahé de Labourdonnais, upon which the Governor's cloak is lightly thrown. A statuette of 'Meditation', a bookcase, a dark red drapery, and a window-frame through which is seen a landscape with the Corps de Garde mountain as its main feature, completes the picture, which was considered an excellent likeness, except that the eyesockets were not thought to have been painted deeply enough. The painter, Monsieur Avice du Buisson, was an underpaid drawing-master at the Royal College, whose son had died in Madagascar three years before, and whom Sir John had helped by commissioning him to copy a picture shown in one of the Port Louis Art Exhibitions and by trying to get someone in England to buy Monsieur Avice's stone bust of Lord Moira.

The Mayor made, in French, a speech which must have formed peculiarly unwelcome reading in the restrained atmosphere of Downing Street. 'The name' [he said] 'of Sir John Pope Hennessy will never fade from our hearts, and our children will remember that it was you, Excellency, who was the first of our Governors to say: "Mauritius for the Mauritians".' When the Governor had replied, Sir Virgile Naz contributed to the proceedings with one of his longer speeches. He was followed by several other distinguished members of the community. The healths of the Queen, the Prince of Wales, the Royal Family, Sir John and Lady Hennessy and Her Britannic Majesty's Consul in Réunion were then drunk. It was observed that Her Britannic Majesty's Consul made an extremely brief reply.

IV

Banquets, portraits, panegyrics, ardent new friends, a beautiful house to live in—can it be that John Pope Hennessy's days of trouble were over? Had he, at the close of his colonial career, found a haven as peaceful as one of the shining blue bays of his tropical island, where the waves lap over the white sand and the casuarina trees rustle in a warm sweet-scented wind? He had not; for the worst was still to come. To revert to our simile, we must not forget that those shining blue bays can suddenly become lashing cauldrons of sand and rock and sea-water, those casuarina trees be snapped, stripped, uprooted, borne bodily away by the dreaded cyclones of this part of the Indian Ocean. Years before, a British Governor and his wife had been almost swept out of Le Réduit by such a cyclone. This time it was a political hurricane that threatened the tenancy of Sir John and Lady Pope Hennessy at Moka. There were portents in the sky, but he disregarded them. He thought he could ride out the storm.

It can come as no surprise to anyone who has accompanied my grandfather thus far upon his thorny pilgrimage from Colony to Colony to learn that while he had acquired allies and admirers in Mauritius, he had acquired enemies as well—and not amongst his English subordinates alone. The very warmth of the enthusiasm he was arousing in large sections of the island community was bound to provoke in others criticism, envy and a specifically Mauritian type of ridicule.

Leading an aloof existence in the cool, flower-filled rooms of Government House at Le Réduit, Sir John seldom descended to the Government Offices in Port Louis, where his rooms were hot and under-furnished, and his luncheon had to be sent over on a covered tray from the restaurant La Flore Mauricienne. Since 1883 these Government Offices had been connected to Le Réduit by the first telephone line yet installed in the Colony and by this, and frequent telegrams sent to town by his Private Secretaries, Governor Pope Hennessy sought to administer the island. The system he had perfected in Hong Kong, by which important papers were abstracted from the files in the Colonial Secretary's office, and sent to the Governor personally at Government House where he would lock them away for months on end, was now in full operation in Mauritius. Draft despatches and relevant minutes would be hurried up to Le Réduit by 'carriole', the little government messengers' cart which would go jolting along between the cane-fields. These papers would then disappear so effectively that the Governor could not always find them himself: 'Let me see the draft of the despatch alluded to' [he minuted, for instance, in December 1883 to his Colonial Secretary, Mr Charles Bruce]. 'The draft of the despatch alluded to is at Réduit. C.B.' was the reply. For the Governor's subordinates, it was an exasperating system, but it helped him to thwart the Secretary of State. 'It is further somewhat useless to analyse and criticise cases and measures, where Sir John Hennessy is concerned' [one of the Secretary of State's personal staff reminded his chief in March 1884] 'for it is perfectly well known that as long as he is governing a colony, any instructions of the Secretary of State are treated with contempt.' 'Yes, possibly' [Lord Derby noted in the margin] 'but we must not assume this as a reason for giving none.'

While Sir John was working at his big polished desk at Réduit, or brooding over Home Rule for Ireland on a rustic seat above the Rivière Cascade, or scattering the cones of *pinus sinensis* upon the soft, receptive earth in Moka woods, Port Louis had become a seething hive of political gossip, for Mauritians have a sharp wit and love to talk. Desperately hot, Port Louis was not, however, a town with a sleepy tempo. In its own tropical way it was alert and alive; from the top of each busy street you could glimpse the masts of ships in the great harbour, reminders of reality and of the world of international trade. It was a small and personal place, where friends, enemies and acquaintances were forever brushing against one another in the old paved streets, and there was much touching and tipping of silk or panama hats as bewhiskered portly figures bustled by. Privacy was not easy to maintain in Port Louis, where everyone knew everyone else's business. African and Indian and Chinese and Arab boys, with ragged trousers and shining torsos, lounged against the yawning doorways of warehouses, registering with a furtive roll of the eyeball anything new or unusual that was going on. Sweating barristers ate their luncheon beneath the swaying punkahs of small restaurants, their shoulders hunched forward over the tables as news and scandal was exchanged. In the dark teak-panelled counting-houses and shipping offices of the city, where the smell of sugar-bags, of rum, of sun, of sailcloth and sea-water drifted in through the lowered green jalousies, businessmen were talking politics and talking money. All were trying to assess what benefits and what disadvantages the new elective constitution would bring the Colony. Argument was rife.

We have seen that in April 1884 Lord Derby, then Secretary of State for the Colonies, had acceded to the Mauritian Reform Party's plea for an elective element in the Council of Government; that Governor Pope Hennessy had been publicly thanked for his part in this decision at a large banquet in Port Louis that May; and that a thirty-two man commission had settled down in the following September to draft proposals for submission to Downing Street. We have also seen that this assembly of distinguished Mauritians, whose whole interest should have lain in preserving a united front, had soon split into two bitter factions. This was a clash of principles and personalities. The subject was the franchise.

Guided and supported by the Governor, the Reform Party of Naz, Newton, Adam and the rest were demanding a high qualification franchise—that is to say they wanted the right to vote to be limited to persons of a certain educational standard and of a certain degree of property. Their insistence on this narrow franchise aroused suspicions both in the Colony itself and in Downing Street, where it was believed that Sir John Pope Hennessy had let himself be trapped by an ambitious group of 'sugar barons' and lawyers who wished to draft a constitution ensuring that they would gain and keep power at the expense of the Asiatic and other racial minorities. 'It is of course not possible to doubt that the object of the commission is to *disfranchise* largely' [wrote Sir Robert Herbert] 'so that the small and to a great extent unpatriotic clique of professionals and small traders and planters may control matters in their own interests.' Herbert predicted an 'ingeniously gerrymandered misrepresentation of the people', while the Parliamentary Under-Secretary of State suspected that the Reformists did not 'want the people to have the power; but themselves'. At this time Herbert wrote as though the electoral commission would be unanimous in demanding a high franchise. In fact a strong opposition, hostile alike to the Reformists and to the Governor, began to make itself felt. This opposition formed a rallying point for those colonists who accused the Governor of meddling and partisanship, of leniency towards criminals and of prevarication and untruth. The leader of this hostile group was the Governor's erstwhile friend, Monsieur Célicourt Antelme.

We may remember that Antelme had become the most potent, because the most influential and intelligent, of the enemies of Pope Hennessy and of the movement for Constitutional Reform. Nobody likes to be ignored, particularly in a small tropical island community

where he has been reverently consulted by Authority for two generations. Old Antelme was actuated by pique and jealousy, but it is only
just to recall that he honestly believed that the Governor's policy
would ultimately lead to the Indianisation of Mauritius and to the
submersion of the way of life which Antelme loved. 'Mr Antelme'
[the Governor wrote to the Secretary of State] 'has so often charged
me with what he calls a fanaticism for the Asiatics, he has so frequently
expressed his horror at seeing an Indian element in the Council
Chamber . . . that I was not surprised at [his] chagrin . . . when it
became known that Mr Gnanadicarayan Arlanda, was to be appointed.'
Up to this stage Antelme's attitude was consistent and logical. His
behaviour on the constitutional commission was, however, another
matter.

   Having failed in his second attempt to put a stop to any constitutional reform, Célicourt Antelme suddenly did a total *volte-face*.
He said that, as was known, he had always been opposed to the idea of
elective government for Mauritius, but that now that the Secretary of
State had agreed to elections they should be held on the widest possible
basis. Although a conservative, Antelme thus came out strongly in
favour of a low qualification franchise, which would in fact give
to those very Asiatics whom he hated a large vote. Antelme's declaration placed him in the curious position of allying himself with such
coloured radicals as Doctor Onésipho Beaugeard, who was a genuine
democrat with a hatred of the sugar planters. After furious scenes at
the committee table, two alternative proposals were sent up to the
Governor for submission to the Secretary of State. The high franchise
scheme, called *le cens Guibert*, was that of the Reformists; the low
franchise scheme, *le cens Beaugeard*, was supported by Antelme, its
namesake and their party. After much discussion in Downing Street
the high franchise scheme was rejected in favour of *le cens Beaugeard*.
This snub to the Governor—whom one Downing Street official was
then calling 'the mouthpiece and the accomplice of an anti-English
clique in every way opposed to the policy of Her Majesty's Government'—was a great encouragement to Antelme's followers, who
began to prepare for the first election campaign in British Mauritian
history. They had recently been provided with a slogan of their own
to counter the Reformists's war-cry of 'Mauritius for the Mauritians'.
This new slogan, thought out by a hefty young atheist demagogue,
Gustave de Coriolis, was a very simple one—'Mauritian Democracy'—
'*la Démocratie Mauricienne*'. Its real meaning, in the actual context,

was obscure; but as a slogan it proved exhilarating and sounded vigorous and up to date.

v

Although the Secretary of State, Lord Derby, had opted for the wider franchise, Mauritians had good grounds for being pleased with the general prospect of their new constitution. Briefly, this provided for a Council of Government consisting of ten members elected by suffrage, nine members nominated by the Governor, and eight office-holders whose positions automatically gave them a seat on the Council. The Governor held the casting vote.

The most important concession which Lord Derby made to the Mauritians was the same as that which he had yielded to the Jamaicans under that Colony's new constitution—that 'a relative majority' of the unofficial members should have control of the island's finances and of matters of purely local interest. 'In a word' [William Newton wrote to the Governor] 'the policy of distrust towards the Mauritian community which had been persevered in for years, in spite of its baneful results has been—thanks mainly to your generous and courageous efforts—replaced by a totally different policy . . . not only more just and liberal, but at the same time more rational and enlightened.' For the first time under British rule, Mauritians were to have a real say in their own affairs.

Lord Derby's decision ran counter to the general feeling inside the Eastern Department of the Colonial Office, where Mauritian loyalty was still in doubt. It was due to Derby's own liberalism, which had drawn him away from the Conservative Party and led him to serve in the cabinet of Mr Gladstone. Derby was a cool, just, critical and open-minded statesman who declared himself against further annexation of tropical territory—a policy he would frequently sum up in the terse but not complimentary phrase: 'We want no more black men.' So long as Derby was head of the Colonial Office, Pope Hennessy could count on his sympathy and his support. In the summer of 1885, however, Gladstone's cabinet fell. Lord Derby went out of office and was succeeded as Secretary of State by his brother, Colonel Stanley, an arch-Tory. Stanley's spell at the Colonial Office was short, for the new Conservative Government, under the Premiership of Lord Salisbury, collapsed in February 1886; but, for Mauritians, it came at a moment fatal to their interests. New Letters Patent for the reformed constitution of Mauritius were issued under the Queen's sign manual in September 1885. When these reached the island by the mail-boat in October it was found that Stanley had omitted the clause guaranteeing local power to the unofficial members of the Council. He had, in effect, repudiated Derby's policy. The new constitution was, in Newton's words, 'essentially different from what we had been led to expect' and caused bitter disappointment to the colonists, who found themselves saddled with all the inconveniences of an elective system without any of its advantages. The Governor telegraphed a protest to the Secretary of State, but in Downing Street this message caused jubilation rather than dismay, 'Sir J. Hennessy is not so popular as he was' [a Mr Pearson noted] 'he has taught the Mauritians to believe in his own omnipotence and the subservience of this Office . . . '. Another Downing Street official suggested that Pope Hennessy should be summoned home for consultation. Sir Robert Herbert turned down this project as 'a difficult question to decide. . . . If the Governor were not directly hostile to HM Government and to the principle of Crown Colony Government' [wrote Herbert], it might have been a good idea, but, under the circumstances, he feared that they 'could not safely do this'. Some elucidation of Herbert's remark may be found in the fact that English politics were then inflamed by Gladstone's Irish Home Rule Policy, that Irish Members of Parliament were obstructing at every turn the business of the House of Commons, and that Sir John Pope Hennessy was in constant communication with the Parnellite leaders and might prove even more troublesome in London than in distant Mauritius. An animated House of Commons debate upon the new Mauritian constitution was the very last thing the Colonial Office wished to see.

Unable to alter the mind of the Secretary of State, Sir John fell back upon one of his usual expedients—sending anodyne reports to Downing Street and pretending that all was well. 'At length I think I may congratulate you on the termination of the long pending constitutional question in Mauritius' [he wrote in January 1886 in a private letter to Sir Robert Herbert] '. . . Constitutional agitation or agitation for political changes will not trouble you again—at least for many years to come. The elections are nearly over: no tumult, everything quiet, nearly all the electors voting (a much smaller proportion of abstentions than in England) and, above all, a representation of all classes secured.' This calming note, penned in the seclusion of Le Réduit, is dated the penultimate day of the Mauritian elections. But when the final results were in the Governor and his Reformist friends received a very nasty shock. Their candidates were almost all defeated at the polls, and the Democrats led by Antelme, Coriolis and Beaugeard received the unequivocal support of the electorate. The Governor's party accused the electors of 'base ingratitude', of apathy and of indifference. Epithets could not alter facts. The Radicals had won.

The only means by which the Governor could attempt to redress this situation was by nominating nine of his friends to the unofficial seats on the Council. One of these supporters, his crony William Newton, declined such a nomination, on the plea that as he had been rejected by the electors he did not wish to have a seat at all. Meanwhile the triumphant leaders of the Radical (or Mauritian Democratic) Party told the Governor that he must nominate members selected by themselves. This unconstitutional request Pope Hennessy refused. They then informed him that they were declaring open war upon his administration and himself.

Some three weeks after the elections there landed in Mauritius the new Colonial Secretary chosen in Downing Street to serve as chief-of-staff to Sir John Pope Hennessy. This was a blue-eyed, slightly hunch-backed Anglo-Irishman already notorious for the severe measures he had taken against the members of the Land League when a Special Resident Magistrate in Ireland, and for the brutal methods by which he had carried out British policy in evicting Irish farmers and peasants for non-payment of their rents. This individual of ill-omen was named Charles Dalton Clifford LLoyd. He spelled the second portion of his surname with two capital LLs.

VI

The appointment as Colonial Secretary in Mauritius of a rabid Protestant Orangeman—an appointment regarded locally as a deliberate and studied insult to Governor Pope Hennessy, by now well known for the violence of his Parnellite views—was a result of the resignation of Mr. Charles Bruce, the Colonial Secretary whom, we may remember, Hennessy had found in the island on his arrival, and who had been the last of his five original advisers to defect. Although personally on most amicable terms with the Hennessy family, Bruce, not unnaturally, had felt himself unable to go along with the Governor in his 'Mauritius for the Mauritians' venture. He therefore applied for six weeks' leave in July 1885, resigned when he reached London and was appointed to a position in British Guiana. With his usual courtesy he gave ill-health as the grounds for his retreat from Mauritius, telling the Governor that he was suffering from pains in the head owing to the climate and from deafness owing to having taken large doses of quinine against malaria. His farewell interview at Le Réduit terminated with a heartfelt statement by the Governor which perhaps gives us the key to Pope Hennessy's whole colonial career. 'You cannot know, Mr. Bruce' [Sir John said 'with evident emotion'] 'what it is to live and, if necessary, to die for Ireland!' How could a man with such convictions be expected to personify and complacently to carry on British imperial rule?

The withdrawal of Bruce had appeared to Governor Pope Hennessy to offer an ideal opportunity for executing another of his cherished plans—that of arranging for the appointment of a Colonial Secretary of local origin. His candidate was once again a favourite of his own—the Acting Colonial Secretary, Mr. H. N. D. Beyts, whom he recommended to Sir Robert Herbert as a man with a 'fine official record ... capacity, character and popularity'. Nicolas Beyts, CMG, was a man approaching fifty years of age, who seems to have had Asian blood, and was said to have been born on shipboard in the Indian Ocean when his mother was travelling to Mauritius from India. He had risen slowly from being a district clerk at Flacq, and later a magistrate in the Rivière Noire, to become Protector of Immigrants. Beyts, his wife and daughters had been passengers on the ship which had brought Sir John Pope Hennessy to Mauritius in 1883 and he had made friends with the new Governor during this voyage. Pope Hennessy, finding Beyts malleable and compliant, even left him in charge of the Government during a short spell of leave which he and Lady Hennessy took at Cilaos in the island of Réunion in 1886. Apart from being firmly opposed to having a local man in Bruce's place, the Colonial Office staff did not care for Beyts. On leave in London he had struck them as 'obsequious' and 'deficient in those moral qualities so necessary to the head of a great Dept. in which the Eurasian Civil Servant so often fails'. They were puzzled, too, by his origins, finding him 'very dark'; Sir Robert Herbert judged him to be 'half French and half negro'. In any case Beyts' candidature for the Colonial Secretaryship was ruled out.

In the first weeks of October 1885 the Mauritian vacancy troubled the Eastern Department of the Colonial Office. Candidates were proposed, and rejected. Offers were telegraphed to colonial officials in such disparate places as Gibraltar, Western Australia and Ceylon.

Each offer met with a polite refusal. 'Perhaps he funks it', a Downing Street clerk suggested after one of these. 'Sir H. Beresford Hancock wishes for a Colonial Secretaryship but I am afraid Sir J. Pope Hennessy would soon trip him up', Mr. Wingfield noted on a minute-sheet. 'Anyhow he would make a fight for his life', a colleague added. Lord Gifford, Colonial Secretary in Gibraltar, telegraphed that he was 'unable to accept valuable offer', and explained that he was sending his reasons privately by mail. Each candidate expressed 'cordial thanks' for the offer, but one and all they cordially declined. At last the Colonial Office found a man who was prepared to tackle the job: 'As you know, Mr. Clifford Lloyd has been offered, and has accepted, the appointment of Colonial Secretary and Lt. Governor of Mauritius', one of the Secretary of State's two private secretaries told Sir Robert Herbert in November 1885. The Lieutenant-Governorship, then in abeyance, had been revived and linked to that of Colonial Secretary to make the position more palatable to Clifford Lloyd, a man much given to fussing about his rank and his emoluments. And so, in January 1886, Mr. and Mrs. Clifford Lloyd set sail. Governor Pope Hennessy was later reported to have said, on learning of the appointment, that he would 'smash Clifford Lloyd and have him out of the Colony in three months'—an expression with an authentic ring about it, for he had used the self-same words when speaking of his father-in-law, Hugh Low, in Labuan many, many years before, and had been inspired by similarly pugnacious sentiments when dealing with unco-operative subordinates in West Africa, Barbados and Hong Kong. We must now quickly consider Clifford Lloyd's personality and his previous career.

Charles Dalton Clifford Lloyd had been born at Portsmouth in 1844; when he landed in Mauritius he had just celebrated his forty-second birthday. He came of a well-known Anglo-Irish family, his grandfather having been provost of Trinity College, Dublin. His father was the Colonel of the Durham Light Infantry Regiment. Educated at Sandhurst, Clifford Lloyd did not in fact enter the army, but joined the Burma Police Force, since his father's regiment was then stationed at Rangoon. Leaving the police, he became a Deputy Commissioner in Burma, returned to England, was called to the English Bar and was soon appointed a Resident Magistrate in Ireland, with the task of combating the spread of the Land League, that famous body pledged to prevent the collection of rents by English and Anglo-Irish landlords. His success in evicting tenants and arresting the members of local Land League Committees earned him the hatred of the Irish. He became the subject of perpetual questions by the Irish M Ps at Westminster. Lloyd was, as it happened, merely carrying out instructions from Dublin Castle, where the Viceroy and the Chief Secretary for Ireland were struggling to keep order in the country with very inadequate forces; but his narrow, literal mind and his insolent manner made him countless enemies, English as well as Irish. 'Few public men have been better abused than Clifford Lloyd by political opponents' [we read in a brief memoir published after his death] 'and, keenly as he felt the sting of unjust reproach, assuredly no man ever more calmly and courageously pursued the path of active duty, unmoved by the voice of calumny.' After eleven years in Ireland Lloyd was transferred in 1883 to the service of the Khedive of Egypt as Inspector-General of Reforms. Wilfrid Scawen Blunt, who had known and not liked Clifford Lloyd in Cairo, records in his diary for 1884 a conversation about him with George Trevelyan, then Chief Secretary for Ireland. Blunt had asked Trevelyan whose idea it had been to send Lloyd to Egypt (where he proved a signal failure and was withdrawn on Gladstone's instructions after eight months). 'It was ours,' [Trevelyan replied] 'we would have sent him anywhere to get rid of him.' Trevelyan added that Lloyd was self-sufficient and energetic, spoke as though he were 'a Clive or a Warren Hastings', and was entirely bent on self-advertisement. In 1885 Lloyd had returned to Ireland for eighteen months' further duty as a Resident Magistrate. In November 1885 he was gazetted Lieutenant-Governor and Colonial Secretary in Mauritius.

Sir Evelyn Baring (later Lord Cromer), who was Consul-General in Cairo when Lloyd was working for the Khedive, has written in his *Modern Egypt* that he had 'rarely come across any man, who, on first acquaintance, created such a favourable impression as Mr Clifford Lloyd'. He speaks of his clear blue eyes, courteous manner and mixture of decision and moderation; but he goes on to say that Lloyd, 'despite his high character and unquestionable ability . . . was not the right man in the right place. He was not fitted for the delicate work of Egyptian administration. As well might it be expected that a brawny navvy should be able to mend a Geneva watch with a pickaxe.' Another contemporary of Lloyd's in his short Cairo period likened him to a bull in a china shop.

An all-important factor in Clifford Lloyd's make-up was a curvature of the spine which had led one of the more offensive Irish priests to speak of him as a re-incarnation of Richard the Third. Lloyd suffered acutely from what was then diagnosed as rheumatism, but is more likely, given his physical malformation, to have been that agonising ailment, a slipped disc. While still a comparatively young man in Ireland he could not endure long days in the saddle without pain. He was in pain during the voyage to Mauritius. He landed at Port Louis a fairly sick man.

VII

Not only was Clifford Lloyd in poor physical shape when he reached Mauritius, he was also in a thoroughly discontented frame of mind. 'He deserves much consideration' [Sir Robert Herbert wrote] 'as he was practically forced to go to Mauritius under circumstances which I need not detail here.' These circumstances were concerned with his failure in Egypt, which Lloyd reckoned had left him £2,000 out of pocket and with the fact that he was not being given a pension for his long and arduous Irish services. In his first interview with Sir John Pope Hennessy, Clifford Lloyd informed him that he had been given to understand in Downing Street that he was to be Acting Governor of Mauritius with salary of £3,000 a year and a free, 'well-furnished' official house—all this on the supposition that Pope Hennessy himself was taking twelve months' leave of absence, or would at least be setting forth on a slow, extended tour of Rodrigues and the other Mauritian dependencies. The Governor replied that, while there were reasons which could have led the Colonial Office staff to assume that he might be going on leave he did not now intend to do so; as to the slow extended tour of the outlying dependencies he said that he had thought of asking Clifford Lloyd to undertake this journey in his place. Lloyd then declared that he was disappointed and that he had been deceived. He felt that he had been brought out to Mauritius under false pretences. It was, moreover, the first time that Lloyd had worked in a Crown Colony. He had no correct idea of the relative positions of a Governor and a Colonial Secretary, regarding himself as in some ways the constitutional equal of his superior. Taken in conjunction with the natural antipathy of these two Irishmen—the one a Roman Catholic and a Home Ruler, the other a Protestant and a 'coercionist'— Lloyd's frame of mind made an open breach between himself and the Governor inevitable.

This breach was delayed some weeks, largely owing to Sir John Pope Hennessy's diplomacy. Lloyd later admitted that for the first two months in the colony he had had nothing to complain of. The

Governor, he wrote, had received him in 'a cordial and friendly manner', and had placed at his disposal the Government House in Port Louis, 'an official residence unoccupied at that particular season of the year'. Whether this gesture was, in fact, a disingenuous one we cannot know; for on enquiry, Lloyd discovered that 'owing to the deadly nature of the fever that attacks Europeans venturing to stop in Port Louis at the season when I arrived', to settle in to the official residence there in February could have proved fatal. He was, however, persuaded by Pope Hennessy to sleep there his first three nights in Mauritius and got a severe bout of the fever from which he never fully recovered for the rest of his life. Declining the offer of Government House, Lloyd and his wife therefore rented St Cloud, a country villa with a tennis-court, in the uplands of the island. The Governor next suggested that Lloyd should be given a salary increase of five hundred pounds a year. This offer, which Clifford Lloyd afterwards asserted to have been made conditional on his acceptance of a Mauritian, Monsieur G. V. K/Vern, as his Assistant Colonial Secretary, was also declined. The only help which Clifford Lloyd would accept from the Governor was the loan of monogrammed crockery and glass from Le Réduit, to be used whilst he and Mrs Lloyd were awaiting the arrival of their own household goods from Ireland.

Although he had refused to live down in pestiferous Port Louis, Clifford Lloyd's illness continued. 'On his arrival he did not seem to be in good health' [the Governor wrote to Downing Street] 'and he was laid up for some weeks.' Pope Hennessy would visit him in his sick-room, where, seated by the bedside, he would try to assess just how ill Clifford Lloyd actually was. 'Towards the end of March' [the Governor continued] 'he was able to attend in the Colonial Secretary's office, but in little more than a month he practically ceased to do any work except to write letters of complaint to your Lordship.'

As soon as he was mobile again, Clifford Lloyd began to consort with Antelme, Coriolis and the other leading opponents of his chief's policies. To the Governor's warm admirer, Sir Virgile Naz, he had the tactlessness to say that 'the Colonial Office was sick of the Governor'. A repeated comment is always maddening and there is no doubt that this remark, and others like it, lost nothing in the telling at Réduit. Once aroused to combat, Pope Hennessy retaliated with speed. He withdrew the permission he had given Lloyd to re-organise the Colonial Secretary's office so that working-hours were shortened and chaos reduced. He began concealing from him the despatches of the Secretary of State in London. He 'abstained from transacting business with him personally'. He sent Lloyd a stream of 'bickering, fault-finding minutes' to which Lloyd would reply in an angry black-ink script. Finally, Sir John virtually ignored his Lieutenant-Governor and Colonial Secretary when they met on official public occasions. The main crisis in their relations occurred from mid-April to late May 1886.

The year 1885 had seen a slump in international trade which had affected both Great Britain and the Colonial Empire. In London and other cities in the United Kingdom there had been riots by unemployed working men. New taxation had been introduced. Mauritius had suffered with the rest of the Empire and its finances, despite Governor Pope Hennessy's assurances to the contrary, were not at all in a satisfactory state. His opponents blamed the Governor, who was alleged to have squandered the colony's capital assets in an effort to maintain a semblance of prosperity. Profiting by this situation, the Democratic Party, led by Antelme and Coriolis, threatened to attack the Governor's management of affairs at the first session of the new Council of Government, which he was to open formally on 19 April 1886. It was at this moment of anxiety that Clifford Lloyd reached the Colony: 'When I arrived in Mauritius' [he wrote] 'the excitement in the Island was bordering upon disturbance, and the fact that the Governor's acts were to be strongly assailed upon the opening of the Council by half the elected members was well-known to everyone.' The Governor himself expected riots and wished to confine the troops to barracks. He told Lloyd that at the first stone hurled he would order the immediate arrest of the Democratic Party leaders, and he wanted to set detectives to watch Antelme, Beaugeard and Coriolis; Lloyd dissuaded him from such a measure. In fact, the opening of the Council of Government passed off without public demonstrations, but it gave rise to a disagreeable dispute amongst the members on a paragraph laudatory to the Governor which Naz and Hennessy's other supporters wished to annex to the official address replying to the Speech from the Throne. At a subsequent session in May Mr Clifford Lloyd rose to his feet and five times asked the Governor in a markedly insulting manner a question about the Secretary of State and the choice of nominated members. The sessions were held in public, the atmosphere was explosive, and the Governor refused to reply. This unsavoury public exhibition of antagonism between the Queen's representative and his second-in-command gave the colonists and their newspapers scope for a good deal of comment.

Meanwhile, the four leaders of the Democratic Party—Coriolis and Beaugeard, who were elected Members for Port Louis, Antelme who was Member for Plaines Wilhems, and Planel who was Member for Pamplemousses—had submitted to Clifford Lloyd, to be passed on through the Governor to the Secretary of State in London a memorial requesting that a Royal Commission should be sent out to Mauritius to enquire into the Governor's administration. This memorial accused Sir John Pope Hennessy of an 'improvident policy' which had created discontent throughout the Colony; of reducing the finances to 'a disastrous condition'; of persecuting officials and others who did not agree with him; of creating enmity amongst the different classes and communities of the island; of intervening in ecclesiastical and judicial matters; of applying 'exaggerated ideas of philanthropy'; of 'complete disdain' of public opinion in the Colony; and of disregarding instructions from Downing Street. This document, prepared with the knowledge and almost certainly with the connivance, of Clifford Lloyd was sent by the Governor to London in the second week of May. By the same mail he wrote the Secretary of State a confidential despatch demanding the recall of Clifford Lloyd.

The rift in the political life of the Colony was now complete. Hitherto Antelme and the other opponents of Pope Hennessy had had to rely on their own resources. They now could count on the sympathy and positive aid of the Lieutenant-Governor, Clifford Lloyd himself. Sir Virgile Naz and the other 'Hennessyites' organised a monster petition signed by some seven thousand Mauritians, expressing their wholehearted approval of the Governor and his administration. The Democrats thereupon sent a further memorial to the Secretary of State asserting that the signatures to this petition had been obtained by force. Clifford Lloyd, whose tone had become increasingly excited as the weeks went by, now took a step which proved his own undoing. He secretly sent off to London via Durban a coded telegram to the Secretary of State. 'Governor's long continued attacks upon me productive of scandal' [he cabled] 'generally believed that he is suffering from mental derangement. . . .' He later defended his unusual action by saying that he had counsulted the Chief Medical Officer, Dr Lovell, on the question of the Governor's sanity, and on the 'numerous acts of Sir J. P. Hennessy quite inconsistent with a healthy mental condition'. Governor Pope Hennessy was likewise busy telegraphing to the Secretary of State: 'Clifford Lloyd's misconduct increases. . . . Government cannot be administered in the face of his opposition. . . . Shall I interdict him and frame charges? Shall I invite him to apply for leave of absence? Please reply by telegraph.'

The spate of telegrams, despatches, private letters, memorials and petitions from Mauritius in these summer weeks of 1886 confused the officials of the Eastern Department of the Colonial Office and left them at a loss. This was the period of Gladstone's short-lived second 'Home Rule' Administration, and he had put old Lord Granville back as Secretary of State for the Colonies, a post he had not held since 1870. Granville, who was famous for his gift for evading positive decision, was intermittently ill with gout, and Lord Kimberley, who was Foreign Secretary, now sometimes acted for him at the Colonial Office. Neither of these peers, nor their subordinates inside the Office, could decide exactly what to do about the volcanic state of affairs in Mauritius. Granville grumbled at the stupidity of the selection of Clifford Lloyd for a Colony governed by Pope Hennessy, while Lord Kimberley telegraphed to the Governor that he could not 'undertake to advise as to action to be taken with regard to Mr Lloyd. No objection to giving him leave if he likes to take it.'

All the same, the Colonial Office felt that they could hardly maintain in his position a Colonial Secretary who had accused his Governor of insanity. The problem was finally solved by appointing Clifford Lloyd as Civil Commissioner in the remote Mauritian dependency of the Seychelles, which lie far up in the Indian Ocean and remain difficult of access even today. Before entering upon this term of exile, Clifford Lloyd left Mauritius for sick leave in the United Kingdom in August 1886. In London a medical examination showed that his nervous system was 'shattered' and that the 'Mauritius fever' (or malaria) he had contracted during his first days in Port Louis had permanently impaired his health. He was once more wracked by rheumatic pains. Clifford Lloyd never went to the Seychelles. In the autumn of 1889 he was made British Consul in Kurdistan, and in 1891 he died at Erzeroum of an attack of pleuro-pneumonia. News of his death was welcomed in the Irish press, clippings from which on the subject are preserved amongst the papers of Sir John Pope Hennessy.

It had taken the Governor seven months, not three, to achieve the smashing of Clifford Lloyd. But, back in London and calling at Downing Street, this inveterate enemy could still do Pope Hennessy great harm. The troubles in Mauritius had exhausted the patience of even the most lenient of the Governor's critics. 'No man has ever had so much forbearance shown to him' [Sir Robert Herbert had written two years before] 'and he appears determined to commit official suicide.' Hennessy's satisfaction at getting rid of Clifford Lloyd was to prove astonishingly short-lived.

VIII

Just one month after the withdrawal of Clifford Lloyd from the Colony, Governor Pope Hennessy, his wife and their two boys sailed for the neighbouring island of Réunion-Bourbon on leave. Although less than 200 miles distant from Mauritius, the French island of La Réunion is of a dissimilar formation, with narrow pebbly beaches, high mountains and a live volcano. The fresh mountain air at Cilaos, a charming old resort with forest walks and alpine cataracts, had long been considered an antidote to the more torpid climate of Mauritius. The Hennessys had been there once before, on leave in 1884, and Sir John would speak nostalgically of the 'dear old haunts and woods' of Cilaos, where he would collect land-shells and pluck mosses which looked like miniature trees and with which, stuck on sheets of paper, he made delicate little tropical landscapes. They would climb the small mountain peaks and bathe in the ice-cold waters of the shady river ravines. They now looked forward to six weeks of complete rest and peace.

This peace was not to be. Two days before Sir John left Port Louis for St Denis, Réunion, an urgent telegram for him had been despatched from the Secretary of State in Downing Street. At that time telegrams from London for Mauritius went direct to Durban, and there awaited a boat to waft them on. This particular telegram did not reach Mauritius until the first week of October, when it was opened by Mr Nicolas Beyts, who was administering the Colony in the Governor's stead. It contained the fateful news that the Secretary of State—now, owing to another change in Government and another General Election, a Tory, Mr Edward Stanhope—and the Cabinet had 'advised the Queen to direct an enquiry as to the affairs in Mauritius. Sir Hercules Robinson has been appointed Commissioner' [the cable continued], 'and will probably arrive early in November'. It added that Clifford Lloyd had been instructed to return to the Colony to give evidence against the Governor, and that Pope Hennessy must leave Réunion for Mauritius at the beginning of November.

The decision to send out a Special Commissioner virtually to try a Governor in his own Colony was without precedent and was a graver threat to his career than Pope Hennessy seems at first to have realised. The original request for such a commission, in the memorial concocted by Antelme, Clifford Lloyd and their associates in April of this year, had been rejected by Lord Granville. '. . . We know by private information from almost every one who comes to England from Mauritius during Sir J. Hennessy's Governorship a very unhappy state of feeling has prevailed in the Colony—and this is generally attributed to his anti-English sentiments which seem to be almost a monomania', Mr Wingfield of the Colonial Office had minuted on this Memorial. But, despite these tales brought back by English officials on leave, there seemed to Lord Granville and his advisers to have been no sufficient grounds to justify either a commission of enquiry or a move to suspend the Governor from the exercise of his duties. During the summer of 1886, however, another memorial from the Antelme party had been received, as well as numerous letters from English officials complaining of unjust treatment at the Governor's hands. Less forbearing than any of his predecessors, the new Secretary of State for the Colonies, Mr Stanhope, determined to get to the root of the matter once and for all. When entrusting the conduct of the Enquiry to Sir Hercules Robinson, Governor of Cape Colony, he told him that personally he felt more interest in the welfare of the people of Mauritius than in that of either Sir John Pope Hennessy or Mr Clifford Lloyd. It was in the spirit of this remark, Sir Hercules later said, that he accepted what he himself described as the 'simply hateful' task of 'condemning a brother Governor'.

On 3 November 1886, His Excellency Sir Hercules Robinson, Governor of the Colony of the Cape of Good Hope and Griqualand West and Her Majesty's High Commissioner in South Africa, together with his secretary, his staff and his servants steamed into the harbour of Port Louis aboard a man-of-war—a mode of transport Robinson considered 'more convenient and seemly' than arriving by the mail-boat *Duart Castle* from the Cape. Landing next day, he was welcomed by the Governor of Mauritius on the quay, and inspected a guard of honour. Robinson had been urged by the Colonial Office 'not to sleep a night in Port Louis' and so he established himself and his attendants in a house called 'The Glen' at Vacoas below Curepipe. This house belonged to one of the Governor's 'enemies', the English planter Shand-Harvey, who had been an intimate of Clifford Lloyd and now lent 'The Glen' to Sir Hercules for nothing.

During their first interview Sir Hercules Robinson showed Governor Pope Hennessy his instructions and terms of reference. He stated, with perfect candour, that he could not be away from the Cape for more than a month. Hennessy replied sympathetically that he could not imagine that Robinson's enquiries could possibly take up even that short space of time. Within the week the Legislative Council had, at the Governor's instance, passed one Ordinance permitting the Royal Commission to function in Mauritius, and another voting £1,800 to cover its expenses. An interesting proviso, which Robinson does not then seem to have thought significant, specified that this sum would be paid only on the condition that the Commission did not last more than five weeks. It was also announced that, on the advice of his London doctors, Mr Clifford Lloyd had not been able to come to Mauritius to give evidence. The Commission of Enquiry thus opened in the absence of its principal instigator and, so to speak, witness for the prosecution; and with a time limit upon its duration.

By Naz, Newton and the Mauritian créoles the mistrust of Pope Hennessy implicit in the appointment of a Special Commissioner was interpreted as mistrust of themselves as well. '. . . It is important that we should prepare ourselves for the coming struggle' [William Newton, the coloured barrister, wrote to the Governor on hearing of the news] '. . . Alas! We are in the midst of a phase of ill-luck . . . I know I am going to be on my trial at the same time as you. I feel absolutely strong in the justice of our cause—if the Commissioner is only a man of honour, he will have only to look on the contending parties, and this will be sufficient to enlighten him'. 'On the whole' [Nicolas Beyts wrote to Pope Hennessy when he had seen Sir Hercules] 'he seems to me to be a *clear-sighted man*,—likely to see through the empty clamour of your adversaries—and to form a right estimate of the true position of the Colony.'

Sir Hercules Robinson was certainly a man of honour, and in many ways he was a clear-sighted man as well. But he lived to rue the day when he had accepted the 'distasteful and thankless task' of taking on the Mauritian enquiry: '. . . a task [he wrote subsequently] 'which was practically forced upon me, against my inclination . . . by Mr Stanhope'. The Special Commission formed, indeed, an unpleasant interlude in Robinson's distinguished career.

IX

Sir Hercules Robinson had been chosen to conduct the Mauritian enquiry because he was a Colonial official of long experience and good reputation and because, as Governor of the Cape he was within twelve days of Mauritius by sea. A tall man with a passion for racing, he came of an Anglo-Irish family in County Westmeath. He had started in life as an officer in the Royal Irish Fusiliers, made a reputation in famine relief during the Great Hunger of 1848 and had subsequently, by way of a minor Governorship in the West Indies, been successively promoted Governor of Hong Kong, of Ceylon, Administrator of Western Australia, Governor of New Zealand, and now, since 1880, Governor of the Cape Colony and High Commissioner in South Africa. He was in his sixty-second year.

Robinson's rule in Hong Kong had been made easy for him by the fact that that Colony was then going through a period of 'irrepressible prosperity'. He had paid much attention to financial measures, but had neglected sanitation and drainage, treated the colonials 'with a certain amount of contempt' and had introduced the Chinese Brothel Regulations which Sir John Pope Hennessy afterwards repealed as 'a revolting abuse'. Sir Hercules had also laid out the public gardens in Hong Kong and cut a path to the top of Victoria Peak. What he lacked in affability of manner was compensated for by the charm of Rose d'Amour Robinson, his wife.

It is clear that Sir Hercules Robinson began by treating Sir John Pope Hennessy with great courtesy in circumstances which were for both of them invidious. He suggested that the Governor should be present at the hearings of the Commission (which sat *in camera*) so that he could cross-examine witnesses himself; or that he should depute counsel for the same purpose. Sir John replied that he did not wish to take time off from his own administration of the Colony, and that he feared that his presence might intimidate and muzzle witnesses hostile to himself. Robinson thereupon arranged to have the day's evidence sent up at evening to Réduit, where Pope Hennessy could peruse it and draft comments for his defence. This worked well for the first three days, after which no word from the Governor was forthcoming at all. Day after day the 'parole evidence' was transcribed and sent by special messenger to Réduit, where the tables and chairs of the offices of the Governor and of Monsieur Gaud, his private secretary were soon covered with bundles of manuscript; after a week or two the files of evidence lay knee-deep on the floor as well. Sir John received private news of the commission's doings from such friends as Beyts and Newton; but between the Governor and the Royal Commissioner a curtain of silence fell. A straightforward man, Sir Hercules Robinson was baffled by the absence of response from Le Réduit. The Governor was almost behaving as if no Royal Commission were being conducted at all.

The Commission, passed under the Royal Sign Manual and Signet of Queen Victoria at Balmoral in September 1886, had empowered Sir Hercules Robinson to make a 'diligent and full enquiry' into the state of affairs in Mauritius, into the relations between the Governor of that Colony and his public officers and into 'other matters relating to the peace, order and good government of Our said Colony'. This general request had been amplified in a despatch to Robinson from the Secretary of State, in which nine subjects for special enquiry were specified. These subjects, into the detail of which we need not enter, included Sir John Pope Hennessy's relations with Clifford Lloyd, his alleged créole partisanship, his financial mal-administration, his 'persecution' of officials of English birth and his leniency to prisoners and criminals. Robinson had set about this enquiry by inserting into the seven Port Louis newspapers an advertisement, drafted with Pope Hennessy's approval, requesting anyone who wished to give evidence of any kind to submit their names to the secretary of the Royal Commission at once. The evidence was to be heard in the English language only, a tactical error with which Governor Pope Hennessy was able later on to make much play.

Robinson's task was a formidable one. He had not only to hear and cross-examine those who came forward to testify for or against the Governor, he had also to examine 'more than once' the voluminous official correspondence of the last two years dealing with Pope Hennessy's 'numerous quarrels' with those around him. There was, further, the written evidence of men such as Clifford Lloyd who were no longer in the Colony and could not appear in person. During the twenty-two sessions in which he took evidence on parole, the Commissioner interviewed eighty voluntary witnesses, thirty-six of whom proved favourable to the Governor, thirty-six were hostile and eight were loosely categorised as 'neutral'. His vanity at length satisfied, Monsieur Célicourt Antelme was much to the fore in these proceedings, as were Coriolis and Antelme's other henchmen. The English officials, headed by the neurotic Bishop Scarisbrick, likewise hastened to become prosecution witnesses. The actual bulk of the evidence, written up from the shorthand-writer's notes, was later destroyed after having been carefully sifted and assessed in Downing Street; but there remains a closely printed document of one hundred and ninety-five foolscap pages in which all the relative correspondence is preserved. This document is in itself a tribute to Robinson's fairness of mind; for while he found some of the more general accusations against Sir John Pope Hennessy amply proven, he was able to dismiss as baseless the suggestion that he had tampered with the Mauritian elections, had mismanaged the Colony's finances or had encouraged crime by shortening prison sentences or pardoning criminals. As regards the controversy with Clifford Lloyd, Sir Hercules allowed that, while the Governor may have been irritating and insulting once his suspicions were awakened, Lloyd had shown himself 'disrespectful, insubordinate and disloyal'.

In the single interview which Robinson seems to have had with Pope Hennessy during the hearings, he told Hennessy frankly that he thought Lloyd much to blame. Thus encouraged, the Governor sent the Commissioner a note suggesting that he could, if Robinson wished, 'run through the evidence with you, and put aside whatever you think needs no explanation. This would probably shorten my work considerably' [he added] ' . . . As you think our finances seem to be satisfactory, that point, like Mr. Lloyd's affairs, will not delay us. But I must not presume to suggest more than I have ventured already to hint at.' This strange proposal, which would have put Pope Hennessy in the position of sharing the Commissioner's powers and sitting in judgement on himself was curtly rejected by Sir Hercules.

This letter of the Governor's was dated 3 December; Robinson had now been in Mauritius a whole month. He had already indicated that he wished to leave for the Cape on 6 December, but, since there was no sign of Sir John Pope Hennessy's defence, he was compelled to postpone his departure. Antelme, Beaugeard and their colleagues now began to produce fresh evidence hostile to the Governor. Although he could give Pope Hennessy a clean bill so far as finances, prisons, and his treatment of Clifford Lloyd went, the Royal Commissioner became more and more convinced that there was 'no longer any hope of the chasm between [Pope Hennessy] and his opponents being spanned'. 'His policy of "Mauritius for the Mauritians" has, in the abstract, much to recommend it,' [Sir Hercules wrote in his final report] 'but it has, I think, been proclaimed in a needlessly ostentatious manner and carried out with a want of judgement which has, at all events, helped to revive race animosities, and led many to believe that he is influenced by antipathy to the English race and rule.' The hostile evidence of the British officials was, inevitably, more concise and better expressed than the kindly, meandering tributes to their Governor which Mauritians like Sir Virgile Naz gave the Commissioner in a flowery and indifferent English. Increasingly was Robinson swayed by the conviction that the situation in Mauritius was 'deplorable'. During these stuffy weeks in Port Louis, whither he would descend by railway from the heights of Vacoas, Sir Hercules Robinson made up his mind that the quarrel between Pope Hennessy and his official, political and religious opponents was irreconcileable: 'there seemed no chance what-ever of peace and good government so long as Sir John Pope Hennessy remained at the head of affairs'. But he was still without Pope Hennessy's defence, which was not yet ready, and he had not yet heard Pope Hennessy's chosen witnesses, for the list of these had not been sent down from Réduit. It slowly dawned upon Sir Hercules Robinson that the Governor was beginning to 'run cunning',—a fox-hunting phrase of which Robinson made use in a private letter to the Secretary of State.

Now, once he had recovered from the humiliation of having to receive a Royal Commissioner at all, Sir John Pope Hennessy's quiet aim had naturally been to stultify the course of the Enquiry. Robinson had made two initial mistakes: he had not insisted on the Governor being present at the Enquiry in person, and he had mentioned the fact that he himself must leave for the Cape not later than 6 December. The Governor was consequently able to retire mysteriously to Le Réduit, and to let the evidence sent to him accumulate, as we have seen, on tables, chairs and floors. When it had reached unmanageable propor-tions he said that he could not deal with it unless he had two counsel to help him; when this was permitted he supposed (in mid-December) that his preparation of his defence would take 'at least' another three weeks. He knew perfectly well that the Ministers at the Cape were anxiously awaiting Robinson's return, and that the Admiral who had loaned Sir Hercules HMS *Raleigh* for his journey to Mauritius needed the man-of-war back for a scheduled cruise up the West Coast of Africa. Further, the Legislative Council of Mauritius had, as we may remember, specified that the Colony would only pay for the Com-mission for five weeks. If Sir Hercules could be forced to leave the Colony without hearing Pope Hennessy's defence he could—according to Sir John Pope Hennessy's calculations—present no definite report. 'It appeared to me that as soon as the case began to go against him' [Robinson wrote later to the Secretary of State] 'his object was to pursue a Fabian policy, and thus to effect a change of *venue* from Mauritius to London, and secure the advantage of having there before you in person the last word. . . . It was obviously to Sir John Pope Hennessy's interest after a certain point that I should not be able to complete the enquiry in Mauritius. The means to his hand were the non-examination of witnesses, and the withholding of his defence. He and not I was in complete command of the position. . . .'

But Sir Hercules Robinson had not been sent out to Mauritius unarmed. After twenty years experience of Sir John Pope Hennessy's tactics, the Secretary of State's advisers had provided Sir Hercules with a deadly and secret weapon. On that crisp autumn morning at Balmoral when Queen Victoria's small, plump hand had affixed her flowing signature to the Commission requiring Sir Hercules Robinson to make 'a diligent enquiry' into the affairs of her Colony of Mauritius, the Queen had also signed a second Commission, to be kept secret unless used in case of need. This confidential document gave Sir Hercules discretion to suspend Governor Pope Hennessy from office, to take over the Government of the Colony himself, and to appoint a Deputy to administer the island when he should leave it for the Cape. Exasperated by Pope Hennessy's manoeuvres and by the recognition that he 'was being played with' Robinson now exercised this prerogative without warning. On 13 December 1886 he sent Mr Round, the Secretary of the Royal Commission, to Le Réduit with letters for Sir John Pope Hennessy informing him that he was no longer Governor and Commander-in-Chief of Mauritius and its Dependencies. Two days later Sir Hercules took the oaths of office in the Throne Room of Government House, Port Louis. He then sailed away from the Colony aboard HMS *Raleigh* leaving Hawley, the Commander of the Troops and now a Major-General, to act as Governor in his place.

With his suspension, Sir John Pope Hennessy's salary and allowances automatically ceased. He found himself in the position in which he had, at various times in various colonies, placed his subordinate officials. General Hawley gave him permission to stay on at Le Réduit, but as a private Irish gentleman with a wife and two children, with no status, no power, no work, no income and no prospects. The triumph of old Antelme and the English party was delirious, and complete.

CHAPTER THREE

—————

NEWS OF Sir John Pope Hennessy's suspension without salary reached the Colonial Office, via the Durban telegraph, just after the Christmas holiday of 1886. It caused, in all its aspects, anxiety rather than relief. 'It is, politically, very important that Sir J. Pope Hennessy's friends should not be able to say that he has been prematurely or unfairly deprived of salary', Sir Robert Herbert emphasised. Herbert's initial reaction had been equally apprehensive: 'The first enquiry that strikes me on reading this telegram is that Sir J. Pope Hennessy must be brought away. His presence in the Island may produce much mischief. . . . Whatever the Report may contain it will be necessary to afford Sir J. P. H. an opportunity of saying anything that he may desire to say upon it.'

Before he left Mauritius, Sir Hercules Robinson had asked Pope Hennessy to complete his defence and send it to him at the Cape. The ex-Governor understandably refused to have anything more to do with Robinson, wrote to him that he had pre-judged the case without hearing the defence and that he was appealing direct to the Secretary of State in London. 'I have every hope that Mr. Stanhope will reverse Sir H. Robinson's suspension of me, and I am awaiting the result here with the entire confidence in the justice of my cause', he said in a letter to Lord Carnarvon, one of a number of influential friends and acquaintances to whom he sent printed extracts from his own correspondence with Sir Hercules, on the grounds that they could not 'fail to take some interest in such an unusual event as the suspension from office and salary of one Governor by another'.

Sir John's continued presence in Mauritius very soon became an acute embarrassment to the Acting Governor, General Hawley, and so to the Colonial Office itself. On the day that the suspension was announced friends and admirers began thronging up to Le Réduit to present their 'homage'. More than six hundred visitors went to see the Hennessys in the first three days, those who could not go personally sent their cards, a committee of sympathy was formed, and deputations of the young Mauritians, of *Les Dames de Maurice* and of other local

bodies appeared upon the Réduit verandahs. When Lady Pope
Hennessy went to mass at the church of St-Pierre-ès-liens at Moka the
congregation spontaneously formed up to make a human aisle down
which she passed, and as she stepped into her carriage at the end of the
service all the gentlemen waved their hats. *The Cape Times* reported
great unrest among the coloured population, and described the streets
of Port Louis as plastered with home-made posters bearing slogans:
'Vive Sir John! A bas Sir Hercule!' and, more sinisterly, 'Mort aux
Anglais!' At a public concert at Curepipe the *Marseillaise* was played
instead of *God Save the Queen* and when some British officers in the
audience demanded the National Anthem there were screams of 'Non!
Non!' Protest meetings were held and a great petition for Hennessy's
re-instatement sent to the Queen. It really seemed as though, deposed,
Sir John Pope Hennessy might prove even more difficult to handle
than when he had been in power. Sir Hercules Robinson had most
meticulously noted the evidence of eighty literate witnesses in twenty-
two days; he had not even attempted to gauge the strength of that
intangible factor, the real feeling of the people of the country. The
ex-Governor had soared to popularity on the wings of his 'Mauritius
for the Mauritians' convictions; that he had been shot down by an
emissary of the Colonial Office was taken, all over the island, as an
attack upon the national cause. Hitherto, Pope Hennessy had seemed
the symbol of restless Mauritian aspirations. He had become their
martyr, now.

It seems likely that Sir John rather enjoyed the three months which
he spent at Le Réduit after his suspension. There were many devious
means of harrying General Hawley (whom he detested) and most of
these he used. Six of the Mauritian newspapers were now, in Hawley's
words, 'openly and defiantly hostile to Her Majesty's Government',
and with these the ex-Governor was thought to be in collusion. He
gained pleasure, too, from sending back to the Colonial Office cuttings
from these local journals or (as he called them) 'these various and
independent organs of public opinion', which concurred in stating that
'Sir Hercules Robinson's proceedings have done more to alienate the
Mauritian population from England than anything that has occurred
since the conquest of the island. I say nothing now' [he concluded,
to the Secretary of State], 'as to how Her Majesty's Government should
face that unhappy result and remedy it'. In private letters to English
friends his tone was less lofty and, as often before, he indulged in many
irrelevant and extravagant charges, saying that Sir Hercules Robinson

'has long had the reputation of being a creature of Downing Street ready to carry out any orders', that his own abolition in Hong Kong of the Inspectorship of Brothels originally set up by Robinson had influenced the latter against him, and, even, that there should be a Parliamentary enquiry into the conduct of Sir Robert Herbert—the Permanent Under-Secretary of the Colonial Office who, as we have repeatedly seen, was the one man in that building who had consistently supported and striven to condone Pope Hennessy's proceedings all over the globe. Immediately after his suspension, Sir John had informed the Secretary of State by telegram that he would come back to London to defend himself as soon as he was re-instated in his Government. As the weeks went by, the Secretary of State's advisers veered towards considering the acceptance of this ultimatum. When Robinson's *Report* reached London it caused concern in Downing Street, since the Commissioner's reasons for the suspension seemed to be legally 'not good'. 'He did right in interdicting Sir J. but his grounds were not the right ones', Sir Robert Herbert wrote in a specially obscure minute. '. . . It might be desirable to reinstate him before final decision on Report' [wrote the Secretary of State Sir Henry Holland, who had just succeeded the intransigent Stanhope as head of the Colonial Office]. 'This postponement of consideration till his arrival here may bring him out of Mauritius, which is what is desired.' Various forms of pressure to get Hennessy to leave Mauritius were considered in Downing Street, including that of threatening him with a loss of his future pension if he remained there longer. In the end the simple and obvious course prevailed: the Secretary of State ordered him by telegram to return. Sir John and Lady Hennessy left Mauritius in the second week of March, after holding packed receptions at Réduit, at the Hôtel de Ville (lent them by the municipality of Port Louis, since they no longer had the right to use the old Government House in the town) and at a house in the Rue Bourbon belonging to a friend of my grandmother's, Madame Veuve Langlois.

To his enemies, Sir John Pope Hennessy's departure by the mail boat on the evening of 9 March 1887 looked pretty final and pretty like total defeat. Sir John, however, was perfectly determined to return.

II

Sir John Pope Hennessy and his family reached London in early April 1887. It was the year of Queen Victoria's Golden Jubilee, and

the Queen had recently taken the unaccustomed step of staying at
Buckingham Palace for ten consecutive days in March, and was
proposing to return to the capital for the Jubilee celebrations that
June. In this atmosphere of Empress-worship and distracting gaiety
the little ex-Governor began to prepare his defence. In this he was
aided by William Newton, who had been sent from Mauritius in
January, his journey paid from a popular fund raised for that purpose.
Besides the Jubilee, the year 1887 was notable for the sessions of the
first Colonial Conference. These were already in progress when Pope
Hennessy arrived. The Secretary of State, Sir Henry Holland, who
presided over the daily meetings of this Conference, explained to the
ex-Governor that for this reason he could not fix 'an early day' to
begin hearing his defence. He suggested that Pope Hennessy should
answer certain specific charges on paper, and also get ready his verbal
defence.

Inside the Colonial Office there reigned the awkward conviction
that Sir Hercules Robinson had blundered. Herbert believed that
there was 'no case for the removal of Sir J. Pope Hennessy, and he
will be re-instated in Mauritius'; and that even if the ex-Governor
failed 'to put any single point in the Report in a more favourable light
as regards his conduct than it stands in at present, the Report does not
justify the refusal to him of further employment, either in his present
post, or in one of not less value, for the unexpired portion of his
present 6-year term'. Herbert would have liked the Government to
tell Hennessy that, although Sir Hercules Robinson's arguments did
not necessitate his removal, it would be impossible to advise the Queen
'to retain in Mauritius a Governor whom a large portion of the Civil
Service and of the people distrust and fear'. He admitted that he was
not sanguine enough to suppose that the Cabinet would ever come
to this conclusion, but that they should at least consider it. Since the
whole matter would, in the end, have to be laid before Parliament it
seemed to the Colonial Office full of traps; there were a number of
confidential despatches which it was judged unwise to release publicly.
The Prime Minister, Lord Salisbury, was himself somewhat disturbed
about the case. When it was all over he told Sir Henry Holland that
he had been 'much pleased' with the arrangements and that 'no other
man [than Holland] could have met with the same confidence on the
part of the House of Commons'.

Once the Colonial Conference had risen Sir Henry Holland heard
my grandfather and William Newton 'at length'. In mid-July he

embodied his conclusions in a thick despatch to the Officer Administering the Government of Mauritius. Copies of this were sent to Sir
John Pope Hennessy at the house he had taken in Curzon Street and
to Sir Hercules Robinson at the Cape. It was a judicious but ambiguous
document, conveying the crucial fact that the Secretary of State had
decided 'though not without considerable hesitation, that sufficient
cause has not been shown to justify the removal of Sir John Pope
Hennessy from the office of Governor of Mauritius'. Holland paid a
tribute to Sir Hercules Robinson for the 'ability and impartiality' with
which he had conducted the enquiry, whilst censuring him for not
having insisted on the presence of Pope Hennessy during the hearings.
He grudgingly acquitted the former Governor of most of the accusations against him, and drew attention to the hearsay nature of much
of the hostile evidence, adding that 'in justice to Sir John Pope
Hennessy, it must be borne in mind that a large portion of the community support his policy, and contend that it is in accord with the
feelings and wishes of the population'. 'I shall enforce upon him' [the
Secretary of State wrote in the penultimate paragraph of this despatch,
which he ordered to be published in Mauritius directly it arrived] 'the
necessity of working cordially with those who hold office under him,
and of subordinating his own personal views, religious or political, to
the general good of the Colony.' When this despatch was published in
Mauritius it caused 'a hot discussion' in the Legislative Council, and an
even hotter scene in the Throne Room at the close of the session, when
Gustave de Coriolis slapped one of Pope Hennessy's supporters in
the face, and attacked another with his fists in the yard of Government
House. A challenge to a duel was issued, but was not taken up.

It was arranged for Sir John Pope Hennessy, now once more
Governor of Mauritius, to return to his Colony in the autumn of the
year. 'We return by the French mail leaving Marseilles on the 19th
October' [he wrote to Sir Virgile Naz]. 'This has already been telegraphed by Sir Henry Holland to Mr Fleming, but I cannot resist the
pleasure of telling you the fact myself. To that fact I will only add that for
the sake of your dignity and that of your countrymen and for my own,
I would not yield to any compromise or temptation from the beginning to the end. To go back to Mauritius and to go back for the whole
of the remainder of my term of office was all I asked for and I would
accept no modification of that just demand. Lady Hennessy sends her
best love to Lady Naz and your daughters. With what pleasure we
shall all meet in November!'

They did not all meet in November, nor in the year 1887 at all. The Secretary of State, who used all his earnest eloquence to get Sir John to retire on the grounds of ill-health (by which pretext, although not yet sixty, he could have begun to draw his pension) was anxious, once it was clear that the Governor was adamant about returning to Mauritius that he should go back there as soon as practicable. But Pope Hennessy had issued a writ for libel against *The Times* for a report from their correspondent in Mauritius implying that he had falsified the transcripts of a Legislative Council meeting of May 1886 and had sent these back to Downing Street as true records. This was an old charge trumped up by Clifford Lloyd. A man less tenacious than Sir John might, in his hour of triumph, have let it slide—more particularly as the Secretary of State had declared himself quite positively out of sympathy with the libel action. Even without the law's delays the case could hardly have come on for trial in 1887; but, to gather evidence for their defence, *The Times* proprietors had arranged to send out a fact-finding mission of their own to Mauritius. It would not have been at all appropriate for Governor Hennessy to arrive in the island whilst this mission was still ferreting around in Port Louis. This consideration, together with his own purchase of the Queenstown estate, Rostellan Castle which he had coveted from boyhood, detained Sir John in the United Kingdom. When the case ultimately came up for trial, in November 1888, the defendants' counsel submitted that their enquiries had proved there had been no tampering with the transcripts, and that there need be no trial. An agreement was reached by which *The Times* paid the full costs incurred by the prosecution which, added to their own, amounted to a tidy sum. All imputations were withdrawn and deep regret for the unfounded charge was formally expressed. The counsel for Governor Pope Hennessy stated on his behalf that in bringing the case his client had had 'no desire to put money in his pocket' and readily agreed to nominal damages of forty shillings.

This second victory—one over the most powerful organ of public opinion in Great Britain—achieved, Sir John, Lady Hennessy and their youngest son prepared to set out for Mauritius. A crowd of friends and well-wishers came to Charing Cross Station to bid them farewell—for Sir John's ordeal had aroused much sympathy, and his vindication was variously interpreted as a victory for liberalism over bureaucracy, for humanity over imperialism, for the Irish over the English and, more than anything else, as a brave and successful personal challenge to the powers that were. In Paris a concourse of French Mauritians met them at the Gare du Nord to bear them off to their hotel. They landed in the Seychelles on the seventeenth of December, transhipped to *l'Amazone* and, with a brief pause at the island of Réunion-Bourbon, arrived outside the harbour of Port Louis on Saturday the twenty-second of December 1888, at dawn.

III

Before he left London, Sir John Pope Hennessy had been requested—had been, indeed, virtually implored—by the Secretary of State to ensure that there should be no public demonstration on his return to Mauritius. Encouraged by the equivocal tone of the despatch by which Lord Knutsford (Sir Henry Holland, newly raised to the peerage, had selected this interesting name as his title) re-instated Pope Hennessy in the Governorship, old Célicourt Antelme and his friends had written to the Colonial Office predicting riots and probable bloodshed when the Governor should land. Sir John had promised to do his best to prevent too showy a welcome; but neither he, nor the Secretary of State, could curb or control the exuberant excitement of the Mauritian people. At the time, the reception of Sir John and Lady Pope Hennessy in Port Louis was said to have been without parallel in Mauritian history. Persons still living, who can recall the welcome when, as schoolboys, they were almost crushed to death by the crowds, confirm this view.

Once a firm date for the Governor's arrival had been fixed, a reception committee got to work. On a part of the quayside known as the *Chien de Plomb* a gay marquee, decorated with flowers and evergreens had been erected. The Royal Standard, surrounded by other flags and banners, floated above the roof in the brilliant, warm December air. The statue of Labourdonnais in front of Government House was strewn with flowers, and above it another Royal Standard waved. The road from the quay to the Place d'Armes was lined by Venetian masts bearing pennants. On the Place d'Armes itself and on the Chaussée *arcs de triomphes* had been set up. Over the central arch of that in the Place d'Armes, beneath an achievement of the Royal Arms, ran the words: *Welcome to our good Governor Sir John Pope Hennessy*, while over one of the two subsidiary arches was *God Save the Queen—Vi vivo et Armis* and over the other *Maurice aux Mauri-*

ciens—Vi vivo et Armis. The Latin motto,* not altogether inappropriate to so combative a personage as my grandfather, was that from his own coat-of-arms. Private houses, go-downs and shops were also bright with bunting and flags.

From seven o'clock in the morning onward, what the French-language newspapers described as 'an extraordinary animation' was visible throughout the city. Many people, aware of the Governor's imminent arrival, had stayed down in Port Louis all night. The rest poured into the city that morning by rail (extra trains were run), by carriage, pony-cart, bullock-cart, on horse-back and on foot. Labourers from distant sugar estates had asked for, and been granted, the day off to attend. At its peak the crowd squashed on the quay, in the Place d'Armes and along the route from Government House to the Cathedral, was estimated at thirty thousand—the largest number of people ever to have assembled together in Mauritian history. Windows, balconies and verandahs were filled with ladies ready to throw roses or to wave lace handkerchiefs. The rooftops round the port were chequered with human beings, there were boys up in the trees and other people perched on bales and packing-cases. Beflagged boats scudded to and fro in the harbour, laden with Mauritians who sang and blew trumpets.

Just before eleven the notabilities and officials took up their stand in the reception tent. A hundred troops with their officers and a military band were stationed on the quay. A few minutes past the hour the Governor's barge, which had been brought into the *rade* by tug and there released to be solemnly rowed inshore, was sighted. As the little Governor, in gold-braided uniform, stepped ashore, cheer after cheer went up—a roar which drowned not only the band playing '*Le God Save*' but the very thunder of the twenty-one gun salute from Fort Adelaide as well. After a formal reception in the marquee, the Governor elected to set out on foot through the Place d'Armes to the Hôtel du Gouvernement where a formal address was to be presented. He and Lady Hennessy, who was on the arm of the Mayor of Port Louis, Monsieur K/Vern, could hardly fight their way through the dense enthusiastic crowd, the outstretched hands, the brandished hats. The ladies on the balconies fluttered handkerchiefs and swelled the uproar with their high-pitched voices. The ceremony in the stifling Throne Room over, the Governor and his wife entered an open carriage and drove slowly down the street which now bears his name to the

* 'I live by force and arms.'

Cathedral of St. Louis, where Archbishop Meurin received them at the open doors and conducted them to seats in the choir while the organ pealed out a triumphal march. At the end of the *Te Deum* they returned to Government House. The Governor changed from his uniform into civilian clothes, and they set off, again in an open carriage, on their progress to Réduit. As the carriage passed beneath the triumphal arch on the Chaussée it was greeted with a rain of flowers.

The spontaneity and unanimity of this popular reception surprised and pained the Colonial Office staff when they learned of it from Sir John Pope Hennessy. The Secretary of State directed that despatches describing it were on no account to be published. On Pope Hennessy's former opponents in the Colony it had an altogether extinguishing effect. The demagogue Gustave de Coriolis resigned his seat on the Council of Government within the week. In a letter to the Governor, published in the local press, he wrote that ´. . . the manner in which you have been received by the population, the enthusiasm shown on your landing, proves beyond all doubt that the Secretary of State's judgement has not been ratified by this country, that you have been welcomed without reservation and that you have been given a blank signature by the people of this colony'. Coriolis later applied for the post of Government Surveyor, which Governor Pope Hennessy granted him. The Governor also asked the Secretary of State to grant a pension to his old enemy, Dr Beaugeard, reduced to penury by the defection of almost all his patients, who wished thus to mark their disapproval of his behaviour to Sir John. Célicourt Antelme remained inimical, but politically impotent, to the end.

Sir John Pope Hennessy's term of office was slightly extended by Lord Knutsford, who made it clear, however, that no further Governorship would be offered to him. He remained in Mauritius until December 1889. This was a peaceful, sunset period at Réduit, although Sir John was already planning his return to Parliament and his future life at Rostellan on cold Queenstown Harbour, while his wife busied herself with sewing-rooms and other charities, counted the linen and arranged flowers on the verandah. The chief event of the week was now their Wednesday dinner-party, followed by a musical reception. 'It was a beautiful moonlight night and was a great success', Sir John wrote to his eldest son, then at school in England, of one of these entertainments. 'The music of the Mauritians was unrivalled, both instrumental and vocal. Lady Louisa Hall said to Mrs. Fraser and a group of the

British born, "We English are completely thrown into the shade by the Créoles". She spoke with sincerity. Madame Paul Langlois and Madame Gambeau astonished everyone with their exquisite voices . . . But I must not tantalise you by describing scenes you will have no chance of ever enjoying here again.'

And so, as the refrain of some old Mauritian song echoes through the great drawing-room at Le Réduit, and the guests stray in groups along the verandahs, looking at the moon through the gauzy tropical night, we, too, must prepare to leave Mauritius—remembering only that evenings such as these were rewards for the lonely and thankless task of Colonial Governorship, and formed, if not the most memorable, at any rate the most agreeable episodes of life in the Crown Colonies those many years ago.

EPILOGUE

ALTHOUGH, IN FORM and content, this book has been conceived as a panorama of colonial life more than as a biography of my grandfather, the picture would be incomplete without some mention of his subsequent career. This was sadly and singularly brief.

When he left Mauritius for the last time, John Pope Hennessy was a man of fifty-five, already suffering from tropical anaemia. Determined to return to Parliament as an Irish Home Ruler, he was accepted by Parnell as his candidate for a bye-election in North Kilkenny in November 1890. Between this choice and the opening of the electoral campaign in December the fatal split between Parnell and his followers over the O'Shea divorce case occurred. Sir John Pope Hennessy was thereupon adopted as the anti-Parnellite candidate for the same constituency, strongly supported by the priests. After a campaign notable for its acrimony and its freezing weather, during which the former Governor drove about in his carriage with a hot water bottle at his feet and a fur rug over his knees, Pope Hennessy was returned to the House of Commons by a two-thirds majority. He was planning a career there—and later, as he hoped, in the House of Lords to which it was thought Gladstone might promote him—as an expert on imperial affairs. He had always planned adroitly, and usually with ultimate success. But there was now one factor which he had not taken into account—his own approaching death. In October 1891, less than one year after his election, he died of heart failure at Rostellan Castle at the age of fifty-seven. He was buried in the chilly cemetery above Cork City which we examined at the beginning of this book.

Obituary notices attributed John Pope Hennessy's death to the biting winter weather of the Kilkenny Election, but it is more likely that he was simply worn out—worn out by the torrid climates in which he had battled for the rights of what were then termed 'the subject races', worn out by the nervous and emotional strain of these battles themselves. That his tactics and his judgement were often faulty seems, in retrospect, to matter less than the fact that he acted always from passionate convictions, and from a belief in racial equality which was shared by a mere minority of the British people in his own day, but is accepted as obvious, and indeed as axiomatic, in ours. As a Colonial Governor he did, at the least, some good. As an individual he had the supreme merit of being unlike others, and of being, for so long as he was so, very much alive.

THE END

INDEX

GEORGE ALLEN & UNWIN LTD

London: 40 Museum Street, WC1

Auckland: 24 Wyndham Street
Bombay: 15 Graham Road, Ballard Estate, Bombay 1
Bridgetown: P.O. Box 222
Buenos Aires: Escritorio 454–459, Florida 165
Calcutta: 17 Chittaranjan Avenue, Calcutta 13
Cape Town: 109 Long Street
Hong Kong: 44, Mody Road, Kowloon
Ibadan: P.O. Box 62
Karachi: Karachi Chambers, McLeod Road
Madras: Mohan Mansions, 38c Mount Road, Madras 6
Mexico: Villalongin 32–10, Piso, Mexico 5, D.F.
Nairobi: P.O. Box 4536
New Delhi: 13–14 Asaf Aℓ Road, New Delhi 1
São Paulo: Avenida 9 De Julho 1138–Ap. 51
Singapore: 36c Prinsep Street, Singapore 7
Sydney: N.S.W.: Bradbury House, 55 York Street
Tokyo: 10 Kanda-Ogawamachi, 3-chome, Chiyoda-Ku
Toronto: 91 Wellington Street West, Toronto 1